Black's Myth

ERIC PALICKI

WENDELL CAVALCANTI

ROB STEEN

AHOY COMICS

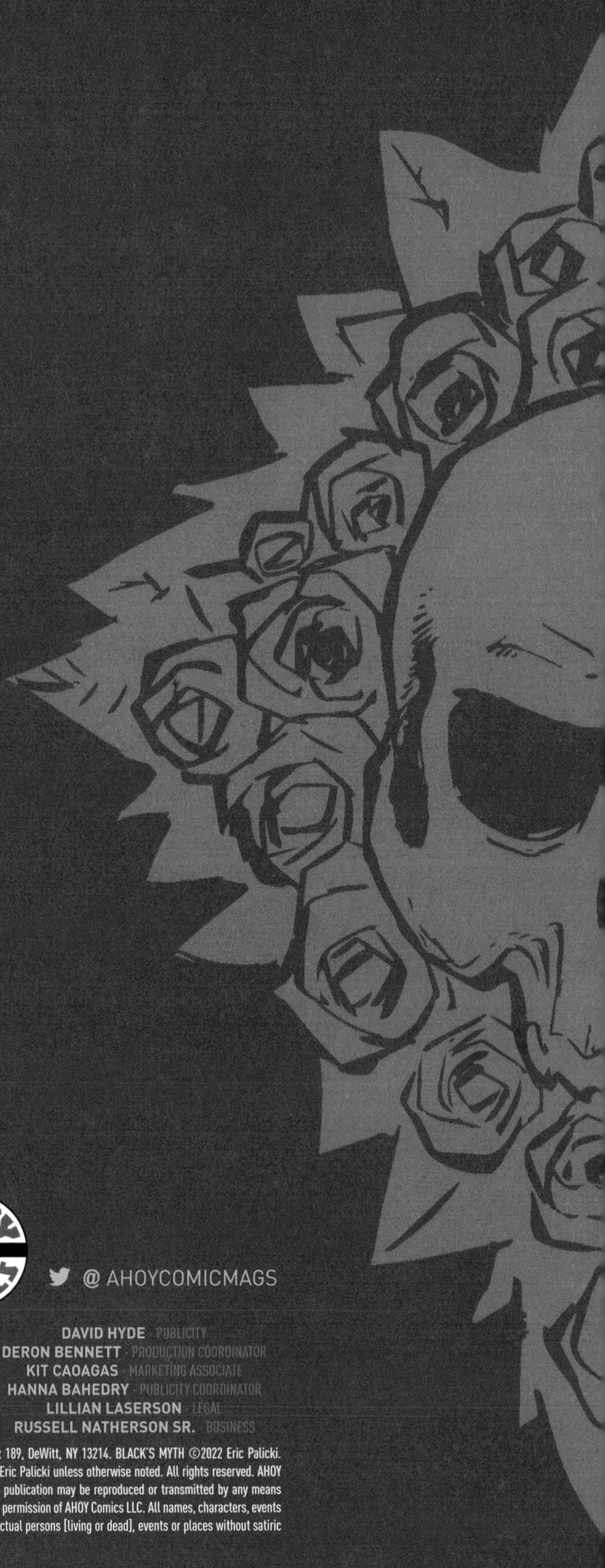

COMICSAHOY.COM @ AHOYCOMICMAGS

HART SEELY - PUBLISHER
TOM PEYER - EDITOR-IN-CHIEF
FRANK CAMMUSO - CHIEF CREATIVE OFFICER
STUART MOORE - OPS
SARAH LITT - EDITOR-AT-LARGE
CORY SEDLMEIER - COLLECTIONS EDITOR

DAVID HYDE - PUBLICITY
DERON BENNETT - PRODUCTION COORDINATOR
KIT CAOAGAS - MARKETING ASSOCIATE
HANNA BAHEDRY - PUBLICITY COORDINATOR
LILLIAN LASERSON - LEGAL
RUSSELL NATHERSON SR. - BUSINESS

BLACK'S MYTH VOL. 1 - Published AHOY Comics LLC, PO Box 189, DeWitt, NY 13214.

PRINTED IN THE U.S.A. - FIRST PRINTING - FEBRUARY 2022 - ISBN: 978-1-952090-17-2

BLACK'S MYTH

ERIC PALICKI | WRITER
WENDELL CAVALCANTI | ARTIST
ROB STEEN | LETTERS

LIANA KANGAS | COVER ARTIST & LOGO
JOHN J. HILL | DESIGN
SARAH LITT | EDITOR
CORY SEDLMEIER | COLLECTION EDITOR

CREATED BY **ERIC PALICKI** AND **WENDELL CAVALCANTI**

CONTENTS

BLACK'S MYTH

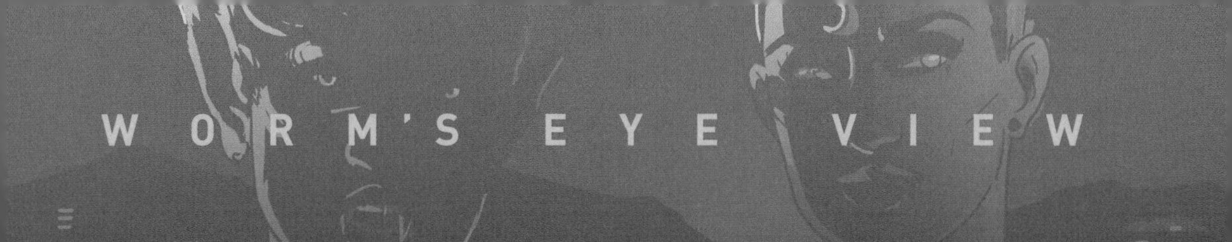

W O R M ' S   E Y E   V I E W

I guess the jig is up. No more hiding, no more secrets. And I owe it all to *BLACK'S MYTH*. Y'see, I'm not actually John Layman, half-assed comic writer, sometimes letterer, and TPB introduction hack. I'm actually *Olghoi-khorkhoi*, the Mongolian death worm from all those legends and tales of yore that terrified you as a child; the ones that kept you up at night screaming for mommy and left you with yellow puddles soaking your bedsheets. (Not AN *Olghoi-khorkhoi*, by the way, THE *Olghoi-khorkhoi*.) I burrow underground, spit lethal venom, have an electric discharge, and live in a swank subterranean lair that houses both Genghis Khan's tomb and his priceless collection of plundered treasure and artifacts. My mortal enemy is Húxiān, the nine-tailed (worm-eating) fox-spirit, and ours is a hatred that spans the eternities. You only *think* you know me from all my little bullshit comics—but *BLACK'S MYTH* has inspired me to tell the truth!

That's the thing about *BLACK'S MYTH*, and the world inhabited by private investigator Janie Jones "Strummer" Mercado. It's only *ostensibly* our world, a world inhabited by normies, Muggles, and "mundanes." Deceptively normal on the surface, though, in truth, around every corner is somebody with a secret, a strange secret, a *weird* secret. And for a P.I. who we are told deals primarily in "mundanes" (a code word for boring normal folk like you!) our dear Ms. Mercado sure has a knack for sniffing out the weirdness.

Of course, Strummer's ability to sniff things out is part of *her* unique weirdness. No ordinary P.I. is she, but I'll let you discover *that* for yourself as you venture further into these pages. No ordinary partner, or contacts, or even cases. Or pets, for that matter! The whole world of *BLACK'S MYTH* is weird. Now, I don't want to say writer Eric Palicki throws the Weird World everything-but-the-kitchen-sink into this book, because that may sound like a bad thing, and it absolutely isn't. So I'll rephrase: Around every twist and turn of this book is some strange and bizarre surprise, and that's what makes *BLACK'S MYTH* such a goddamn delight.

A P.I. with a supernatural secret might be high-concept enough to carry some books, but Palicki doesn't stop there, populating the story with creatures of the night, creatures of legend, characters from myth, monsters, gods and... and...what the hell was that fish dude, anyway? Rich, lush world-building here, and I'm surprised how much world was introduced in only five issues, without ever seeming overdone or overwhelming. At the same time, Palicki keeps things grounded but with some familiar noir procedural trappings, while a hearty dose of sly humor keeps things light and fun even as blood is spilled and bodies drop. This book is many things, but one thing above all else: Entertaining as hell!

It's a good-looking book, too. Credit to Wendell Cavalcanti for bringing this story to life, being equally adept at acting and action, quiet moments and ultraviolence. Fine storytelling, and Rob Steen's lettering ain't too shabby either. (As a letterer in my former life as a mundane human and closeted Mongolian death worm, lettering is something I tend to be overly critical about, and Steen, alas, gives me nothing to complain about.)

The truest test of a book like this, and all the magnificent world-building that went into it, is whether the reader wants to return to this world. I absolutely do, and am eager to read more tales of Strummer Mercado, and see even more weirdness from Paliciki and Cavalcanti. This isn't just a world I want to return to, this is a world I want to *live* in. That's what's given me the courage to reveal *my* true, weird self, my Mongolian death worm self. The world of *BLACK'S MYTH* seems like a place where a Mongolian death worm can be perfectly at home, where I can fit in, where I can not just survive, but thrive. As long as I stay out of trouble, that is.

Or, at least, don't get on Strummer Mercado's bad side.

John Layman
Somewhere in underground Mongolia
Living his best Mongolian death worm life
December 2021

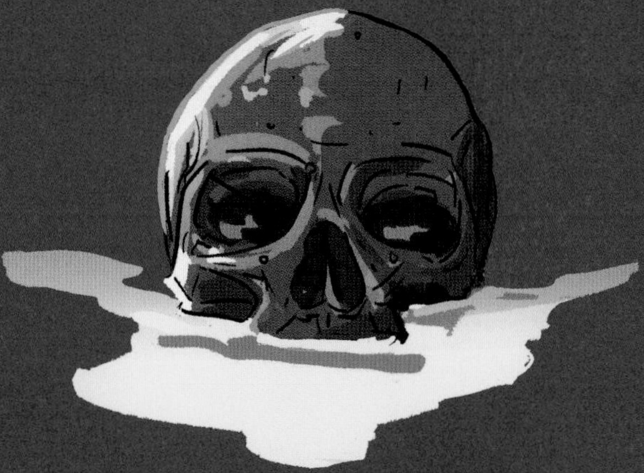

John Layman is the writer and letterer of various comics, including Chew, Chu, Bermuda, The Man Who F#%&ed Up Time, Mars Attacks, Godzilla, *and various bullshit corporate superhero books. He also, along with AHOY editor-in-chief Tom Peyer, wrote* Stephen Colbert's Tek Jansen. *None of this matters. Layman is, in fact, the dreaded Mongolian death worm of legend,* Olghoi-khorkhoi. *He is sick to death of humans. You disgust him, and he has grown weary of your antics. RUN FOR YOUR LIVES!*

1

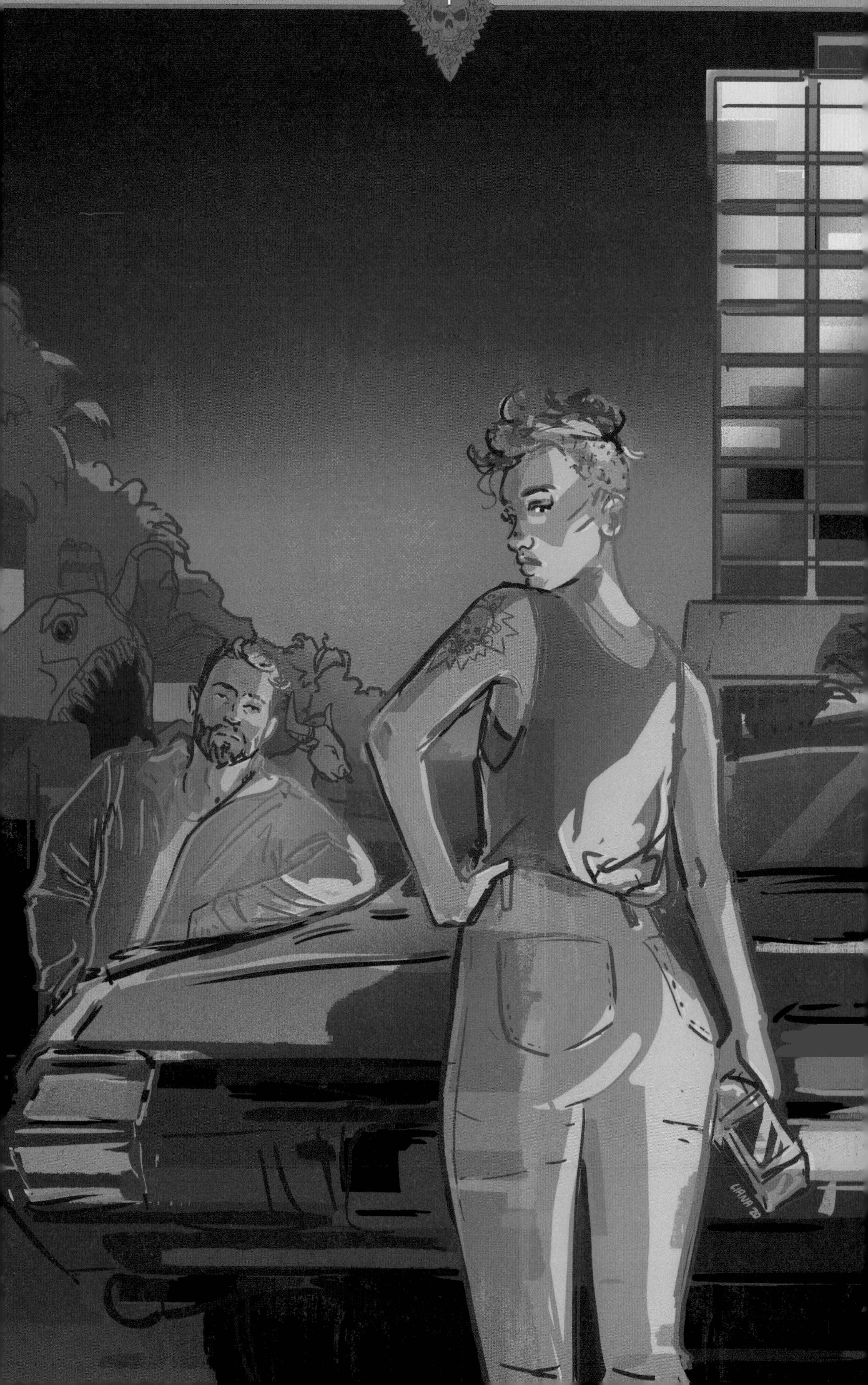

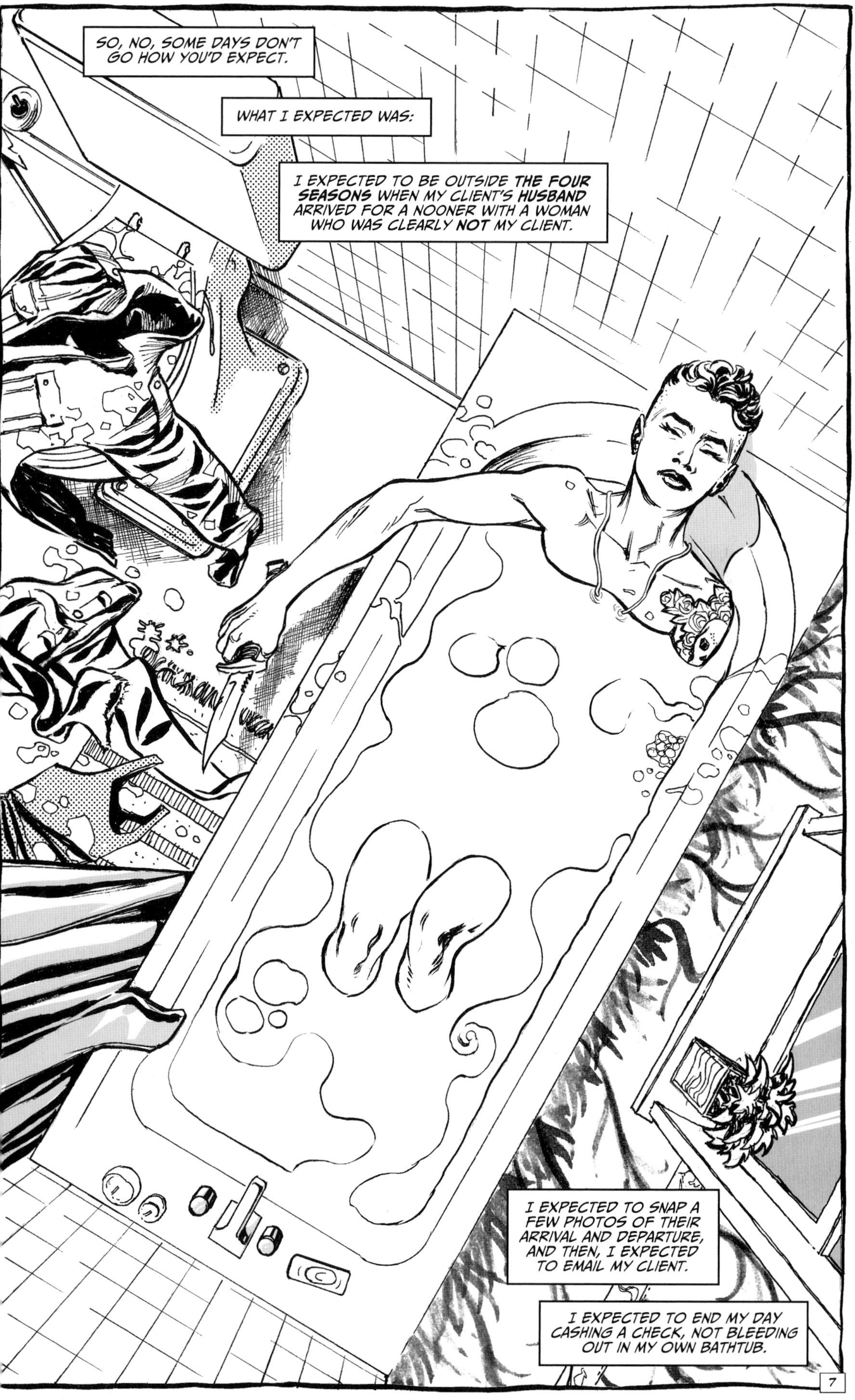

SO, NO, SOME DAYS DON'T GO HOW YOU'D EXPECT.
WHAT I EXPECTED WAS:
I EXPECTED TO BE OUTSIDE **THE FOUR SEASONS** WHEN MY CLIENT'S **HUSBAND** ARRIVED FOR A NOONER WITH A WOMAN WHO WAS CLEARLY **NOT** MY CLIENT.
I EXPECTED TO SNAP A FEW PHOTOS OF THEIR ARRIVAL AND DEPARTURE, AND THEN, I EXPECTED TO EMAIL MY CLIENT.
I EXPECTED TO END MY DAY CASHING A CHECK, NOT BLEEDING OUT IN MY OWN BATHTUB.

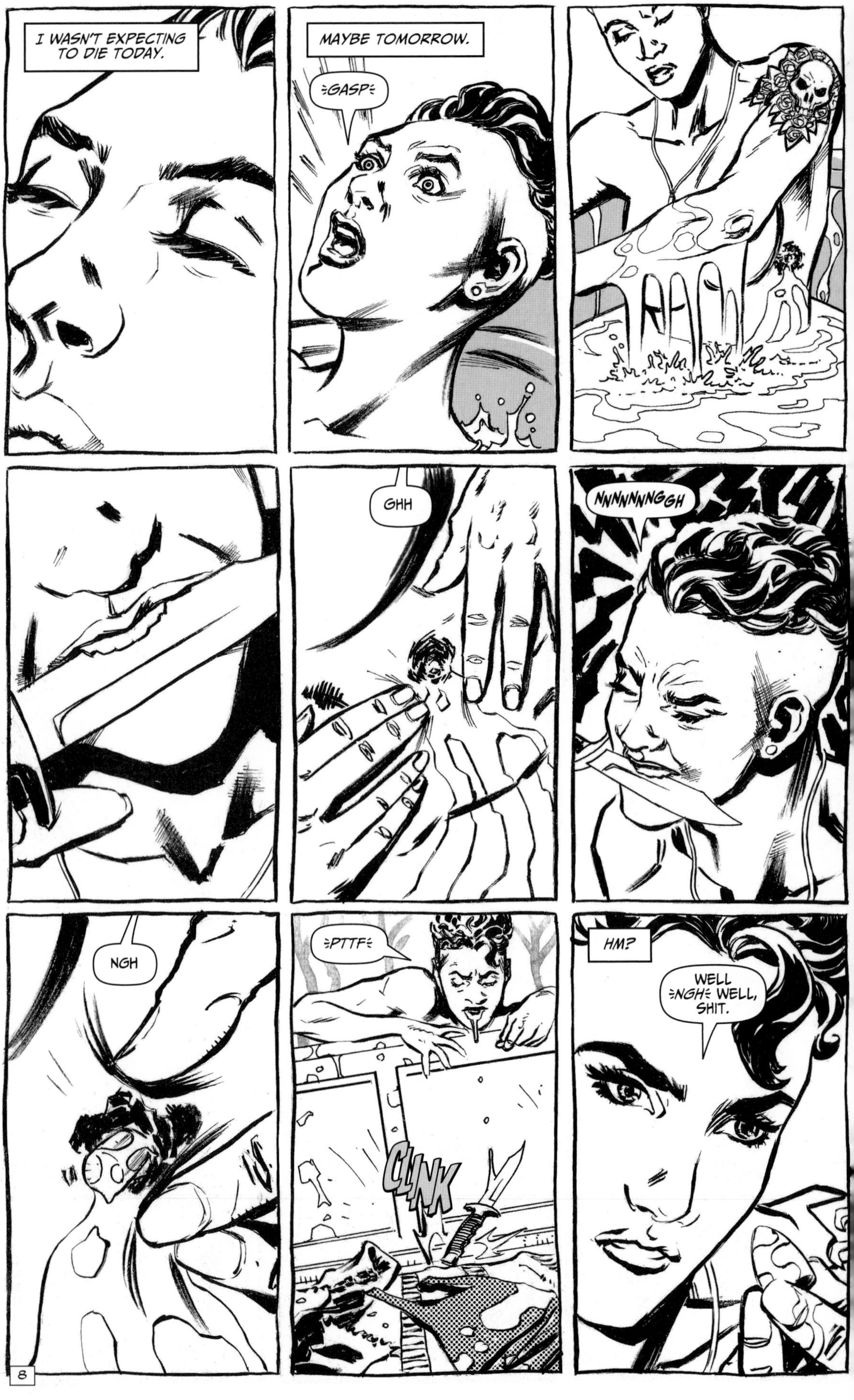
I WASN'T EXPECTING TO DIE TODAY.
MAYBE TOMORROW.
GASP
GHH
NNNNNNNGGH
NGH
PTTF
CLINK
HM?
WELL NGH WELL, SHIT.

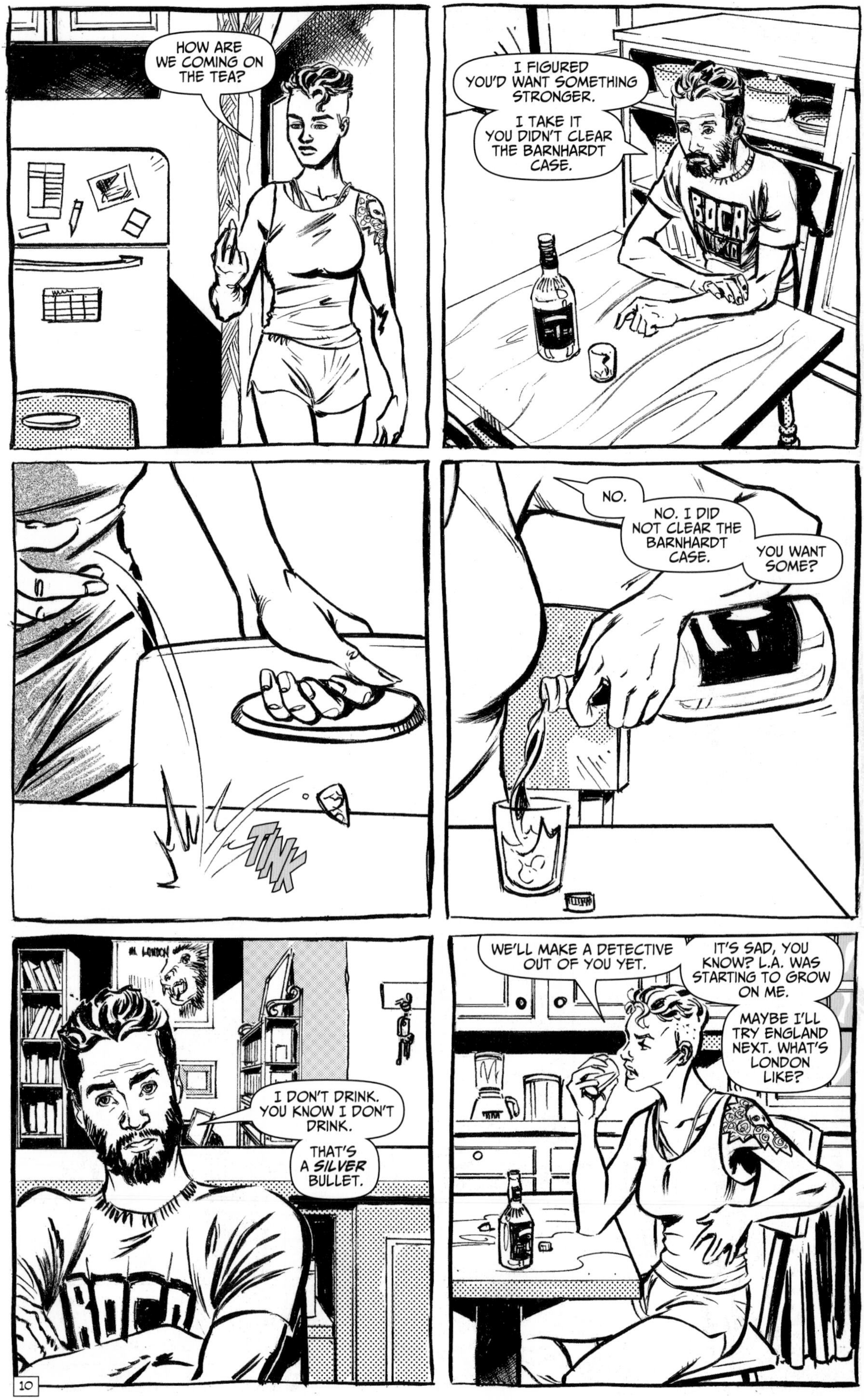
HOW ARE WE COMING ON THE TEA?
I FIGURED YOU'D WANT SOMETHING STRONGER.
I TAKE IT YOU DIDN'T CLEAR THE BARNHARDT CASE.
TINK
NO.
NO. I DID NOT CLEAR THE BARNHARDT CASE.
YOU WANT SOME?
I DON'T DRINK. YOU KNOW I DON'T DRINK.
THAT'S A *SILVER* BULLET.
WE'LL MAKE A DETECTIVE OUT OF YOU YET.
IT'S SAD, YOU KNOW? L.A. WAS STARTING TO GROW ON ME.
MAYBE I'LL TRY ENGLAND NEXT. WHAT'S LONDON LIKE?

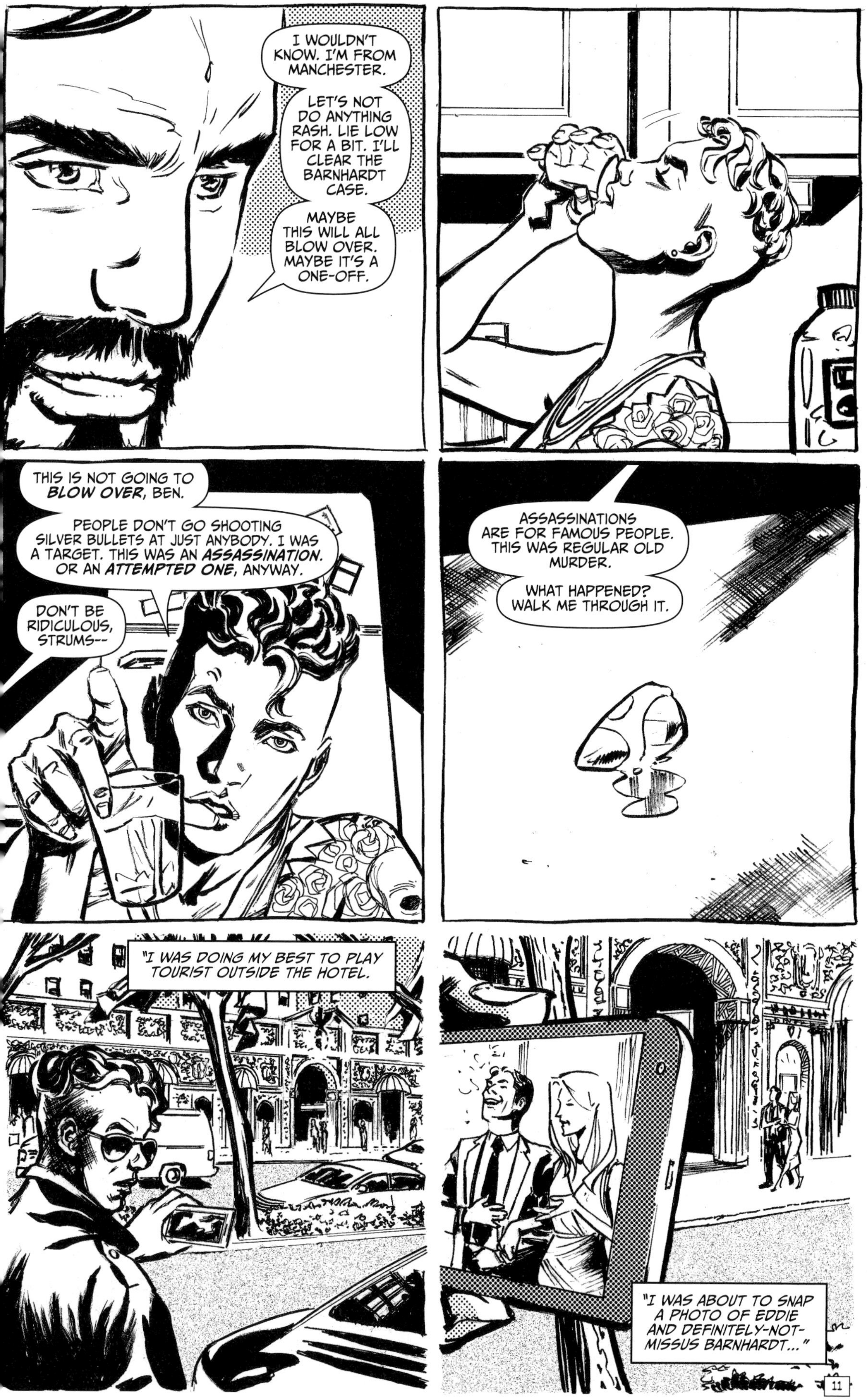
I WOULDN'T KNOW. I'M FROM MANCHESTER.
LET'S NOT DO ANYTHING RASH. LIE LOW FOR A BIT. I'LL CLEAR THE BARNHARDT CASE.
MAYBE THIS WILL ALL BLOW OVER. MAYBE IT'S A ONE-OFF.
THIS IS NOT GOING TO *BLOW OVER*, BEN.
PEOPLE DON'T GO SHOOTING SILVER BULLETS AT JUST ANYBODY. I WAS A TARGET. THIS WAS AN *ASSASSINATION.* OR AN *ATTEMPTED ONE*, ANYWAY.
DON'T BE RIDICULOUS, STRUMS--
ASSASSINATIONS ARE FOR FAMOUS PEOPLE. THIS WAS REGULAR OLD MURDER.
WHAT HAPPENED? WALK ME THROUGH IT.
"I WAS DOING MY BEST TO PLAY TOURIST OUTSIDE THE HOTEL.
"I WAS ABOUT TO SNAP A PHOTO OF EDDIE AND DEFINITELY-NOT-MISSUS BARNHARDT..."

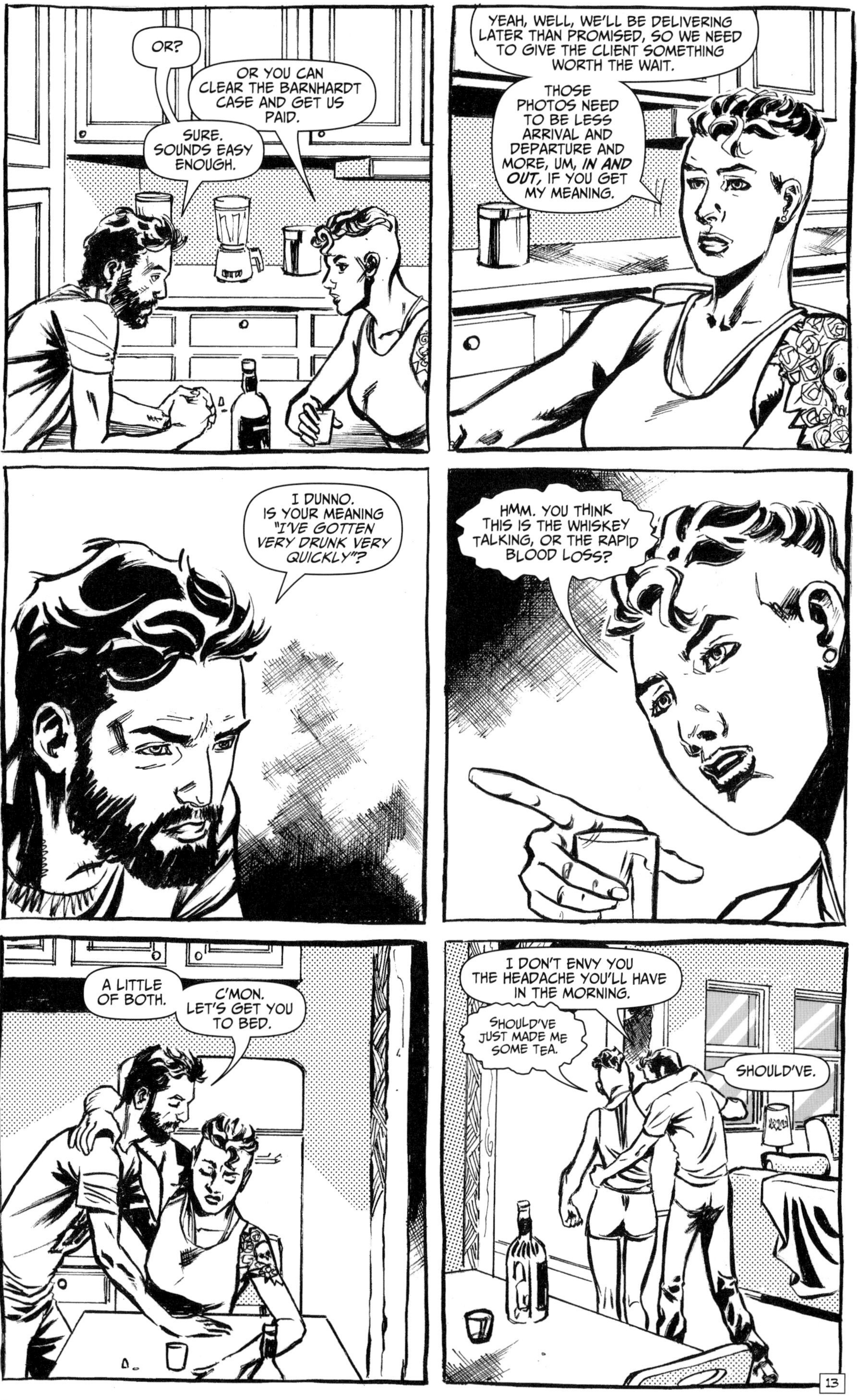
OR?
OR YOU CAN CLEAR THE BARNHARDT CASE AND GET US PAID.
SURE. SOUNDS EASY ENOUGH.
YEAH, WELL, WE'LL BE DELIVERING LATER THAN PROMISED, SO WE NEED TO GIVE THE CLIENT SOMETHING WORTH THE WAIT.
THOSE PHOTOS NEED TO BE LESS ARRIVAL AND DEPARTURE AND MORE, UM, IN AND OUT, IF YOU GET MY MEANING.
I DUNNO. IS YOUR MEANING "I'VE GOTTEN VERY DRUNK VERY QUICKLY"?
HMM. YOU THINK THIS IS THE WHISKEY TALKING, OR THE RAPID BLOOD LOSS?
A LITTLE OF BOTH.
C'MON. LET'S GET YOU TO BED.
I DON'T ENVY YOU THE HEADACHE YOU'LL HAVE IN THE MORNING.
SHOULD'VE JUST MADE ME SOME TEA.
SHOULD'VE.

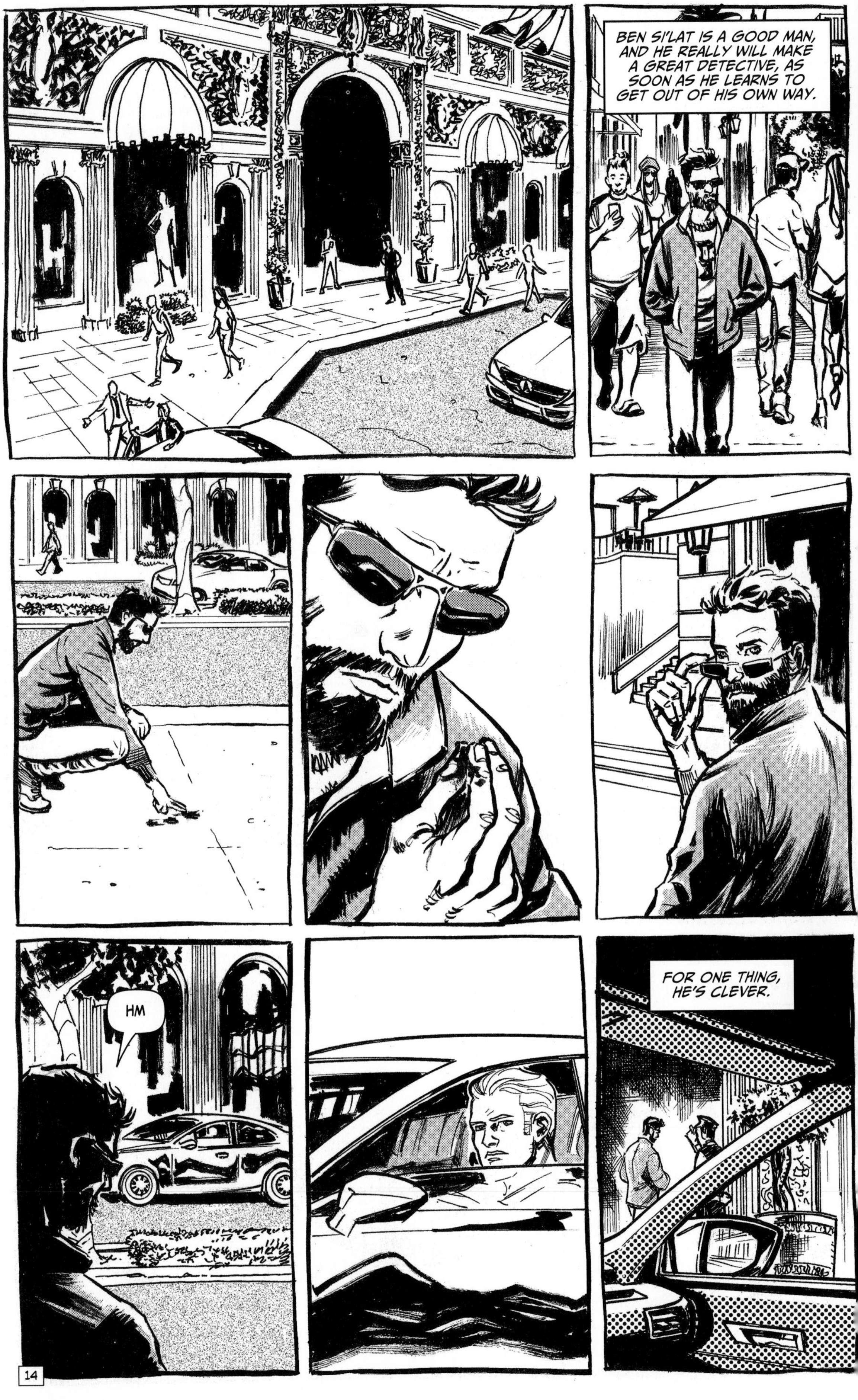
BEN SI'LAT IS A GOOD MAN, AND HE REALLY WILL MAKE A GREAT DETECTIVE, AS SOON AS HE LEARNS TO GET OUT OF HIS OWN WAY.
HM
FOR ONE THING, HE'S CLEVER.

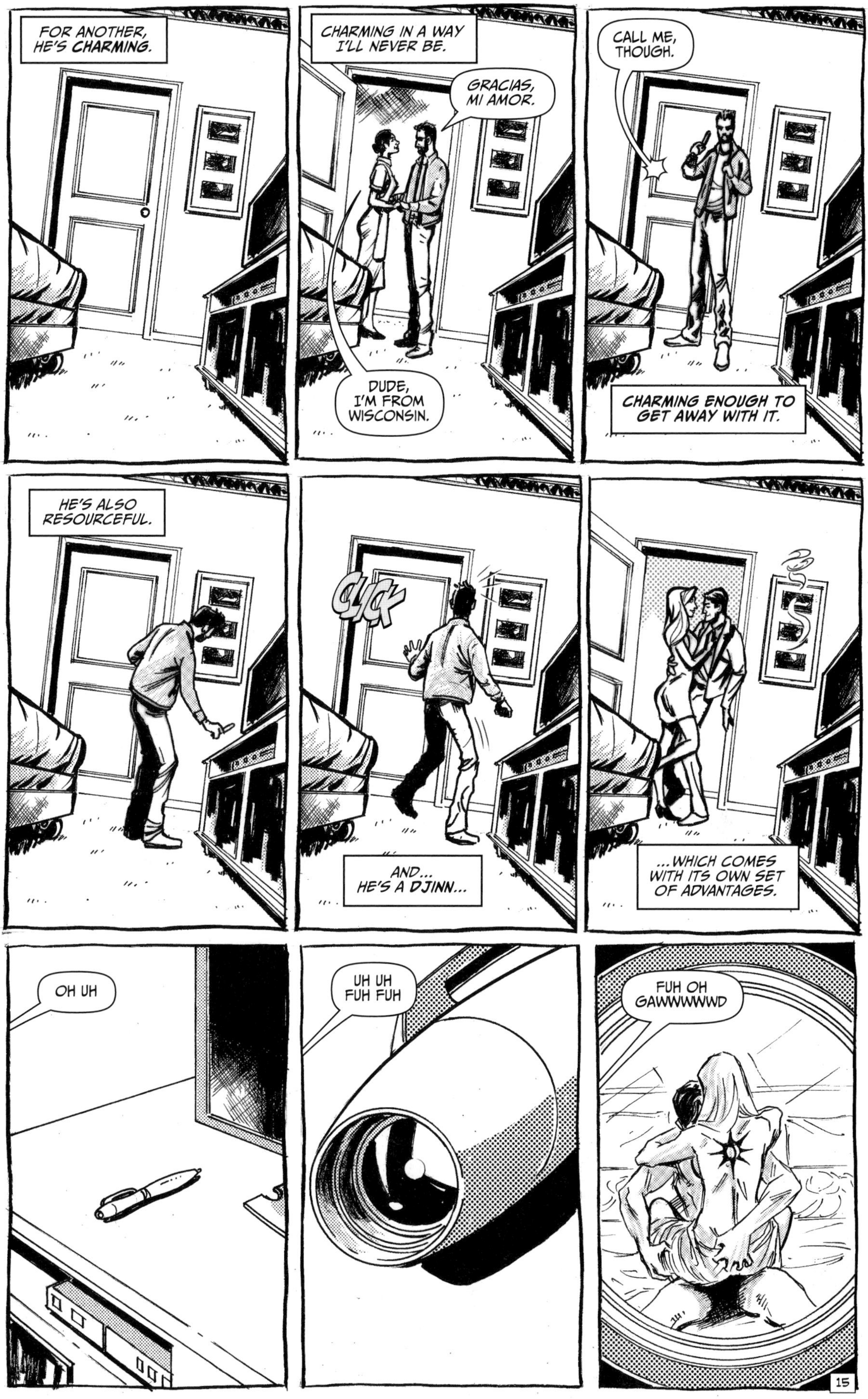
FOR ANOTHER, HE'S CHARMING.
CHARMING IN A WAY I'LL NEVER BE.
GRACIAS, MI AMOR.
DUDE, I'M FROM WISCONSIN.
CALL ME, THOUGH.
CHARMING ENOUGH TO GET AWAY WITH IT.
HE'S ALSO RESOURCEFUL.
CLICK
AND... HE'S A DJINN...
...WHICH COMES WITH ITS OWN SET OF ADVANTAGES.
OH UH
UH UH FUH FUH
FUH OH GAWWWWWD

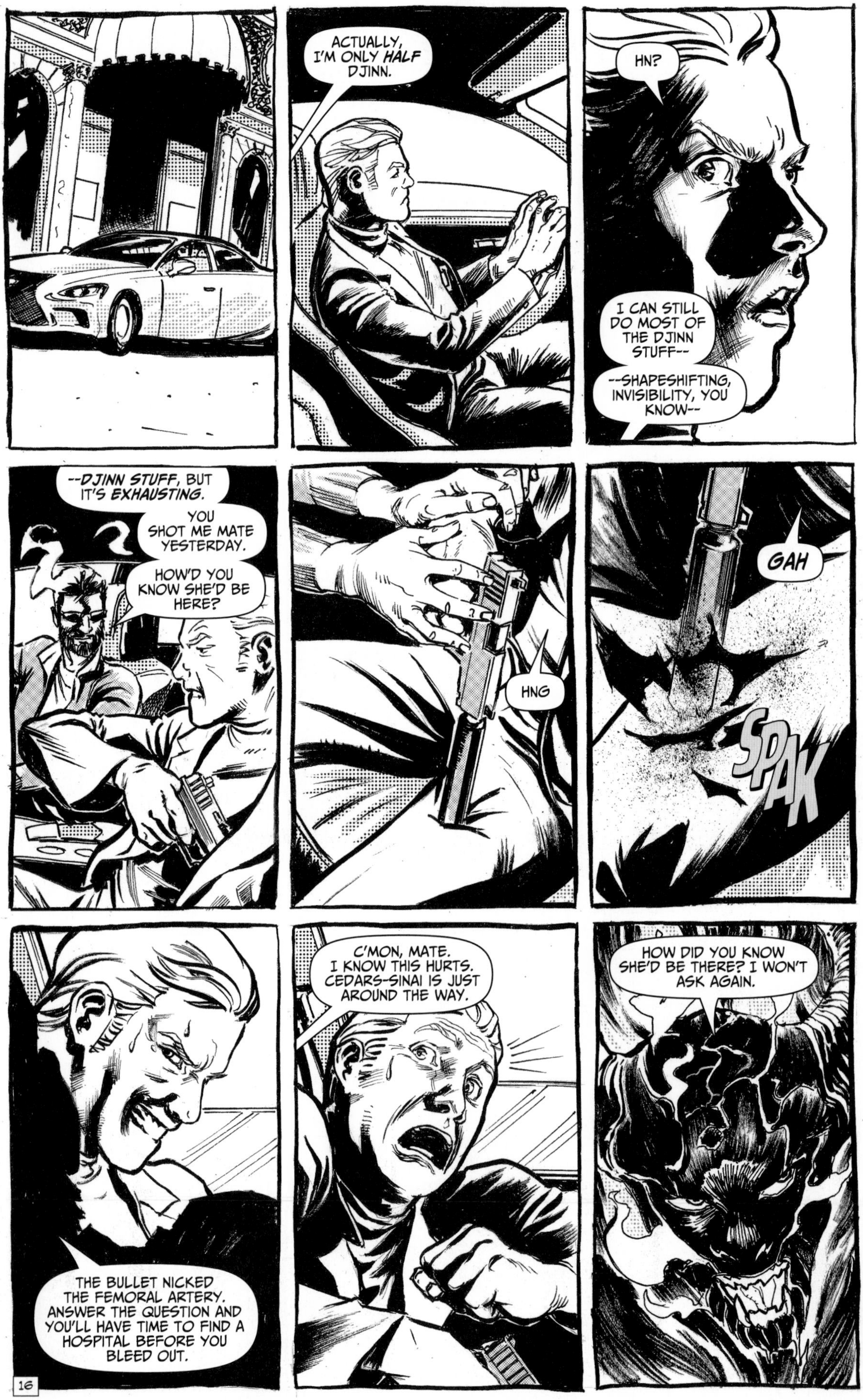
ACTUALLY, I'M ONLY *HALF* DJINN.
HN?
I CAN STILL DO MOST OF THE DJINN STUFF--
--SHAPESHIFTING, INVISIBILITY, YOU KNOW--
--*DJINN STUFF*, BUT IT'S *EXHAUSTING*.
YOU SHOT ME MATE YESTERDAY.
HOW'D YOU KNOW SHE'D BE HERE?
HNG
GAH
SPAK
THE BULLET NICKED THE FEMORAL ARTERY. ANSWER THE QUESTION AND YOU'LL HAVE TIME TO FIND A HOSPITAL BEFORE YOU BLEED OUT.
C'MON, MATE. I KNOW THIS HURTS. CEDARS-SINAI IS JUST AROUND THE WAY.
HOW DID YOU KNOW SHE'D BE THERE? I WON'T ASK AGAIN.

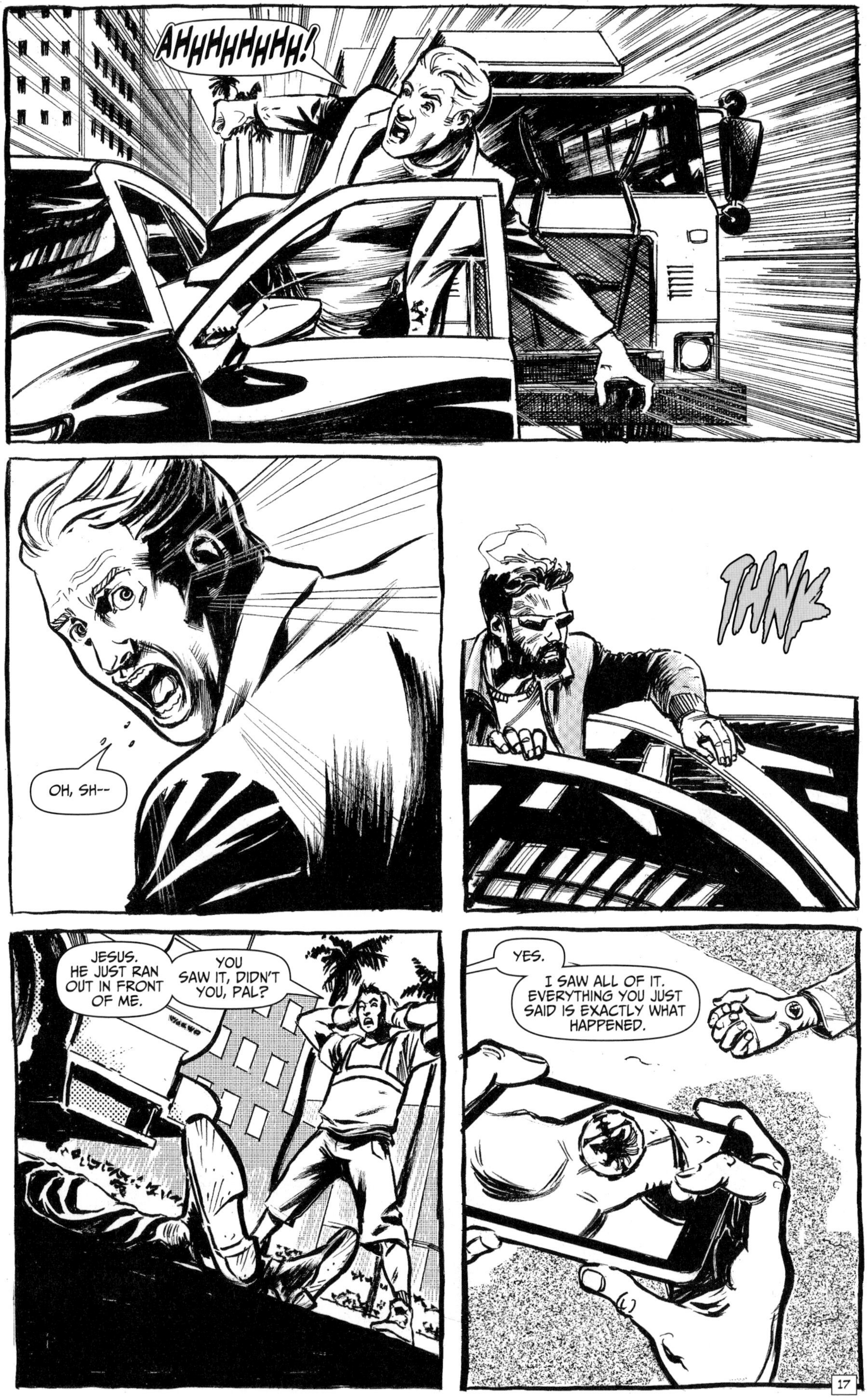

AHHHHHHHH!
OH, SH--
THNK
JESUS. HE JUST RAN OUT IN FRONT OF ME.
YOU SAW IT, DIDN'T YOU, PAL?
YES.
I SAW ALL OF IT. EVERYTHING YOU JUST SAID IS EXACTLY WHAT HAPPENED.

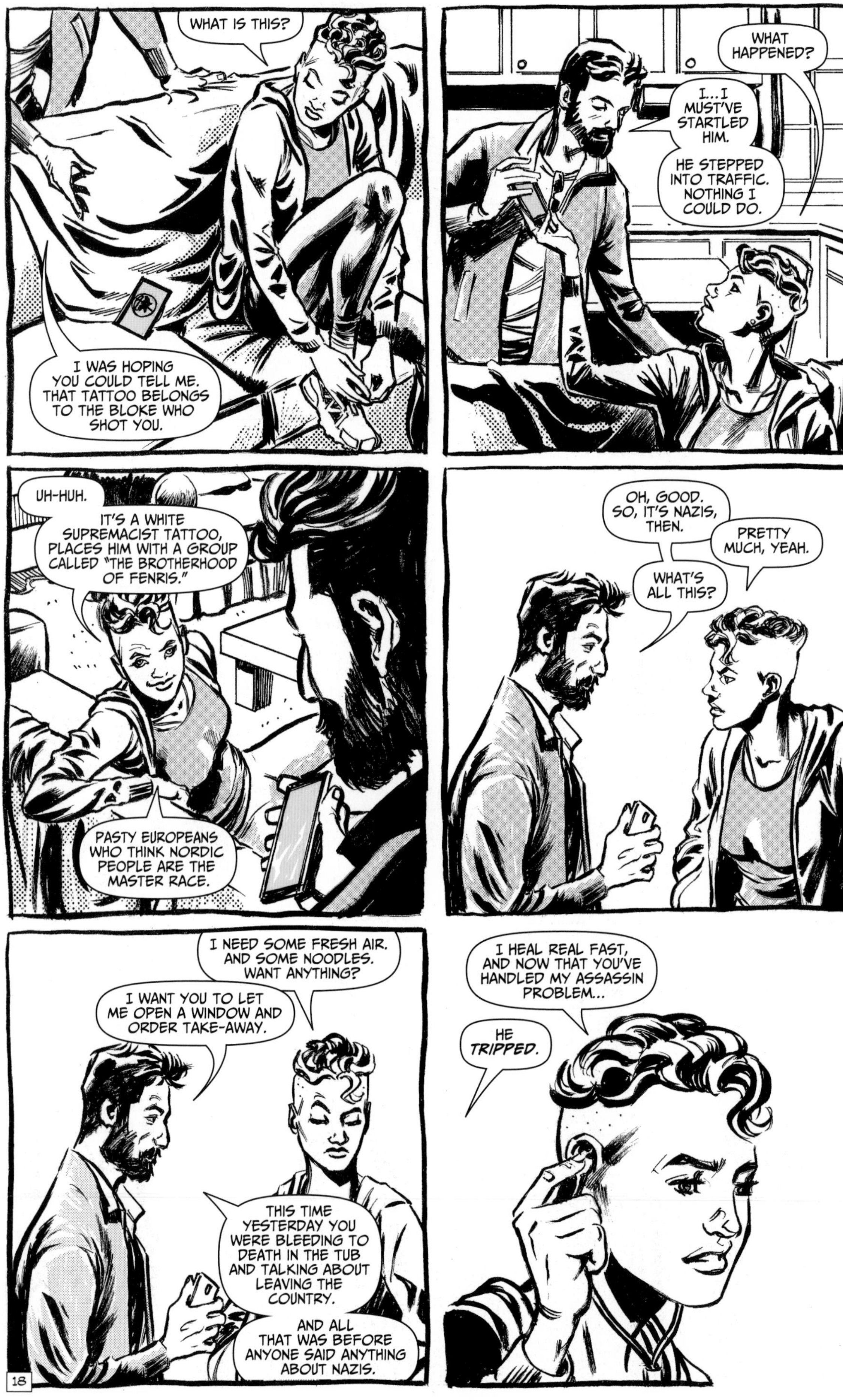

WHAT IS THIS?
I WAS HOPING YOU COULD TELL ME. THAT TATTOO BELONGS TO THE BLOKE WHO SHOT YOU.
WHAT HAPPENED?
I...I MUST'VE STARTLED HIM.
HE STEPPED INTO TRAFFIC. NOTHING I COULD DO.
UH-HUH.
IT'S A WHITE SUPREMACIST TATTOO, PLACES HIM WITH A GROUP CALLED "THE BROTHERHOOD OF FENRIS."
PASTY EUROPEANS WHO THINK NORDIC PEOPLE ARE THE MASTER RACE.
OH, GOOD. SO, IT'S NAZIS, THEN.
PRETTY MUCH, YEAH.
WHAT'S ALL THIS?
I NEED SOME FRESH AIR. AND SOME NOODLES. WANT ANYTHING?
I WANT YOU TO LET ME OPEN A WINDOW AND ORDER TAKE-AWAY.
THIS TIME YESTERDAY YOU WERE BLEEDING TO DEATH IN THE TUB AND TALKING ABOUT LEAVING THE COUNTRY.
AND ALL THAT WAS BEFORE ANYONE SAID ANYTHING ABOUT NAZIS.
I HEAL REAL FAST, AND NOW THAT YOU'VE HANDLED MY ASSASSIN PROBLEM...
HE *TRIPPED*.

STRUMMER...

BEN--

DON'T.

THE ATTACK WAS PREMEDITATED. WE AGREE ON THAT.

HOW'D HE KNOW TO CAMP IN FRONT OF THE FOUR SEASONS?

LIKE I SAID, HE'S CLEVER.

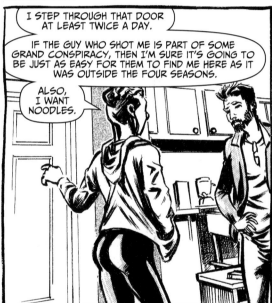

I STEP THROUGH THAT DOOR AT LEAST TWICE A DAY.

IF THE GUY WHO SHOT ME IS PART OF SOME GRAND CONSPIRACY, THEN I'M SURE IT'S GOING TO BE JUST AS EASY FOR THEM TO FIND ME HERE AS IT WAS OUTSIDE THE FOUR SEASONS.

ALSO, I WANT NOODLES.

FINE. AT LEAST TAKE GRIM WITH YOU.

ALWAYS.

19

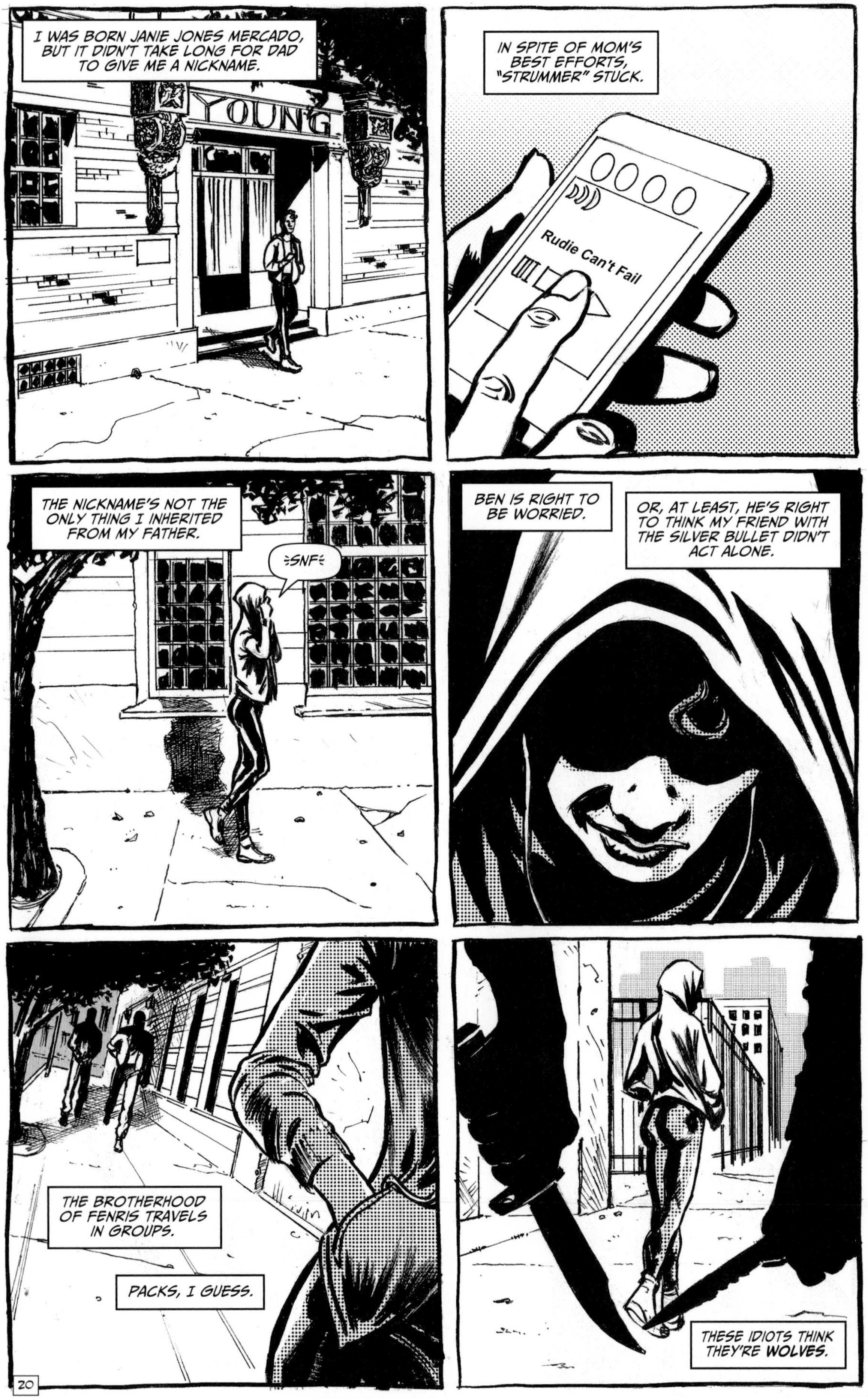
I WAS BORN JANIE JONES MERCADO, BUT IT DIDN'T TAKE LONG FOR DAD TO GIVE ME A NICKNAME.
YOUNG
IN SPITE OF MOM'S BEST EFFORTS, "STRUMMER" STUCK.
Rudie Can't Fail
THE NICKNAME'S NOT THE ONLY THING I INHERITED FROM MY FATHER.
SNF
BEN IS RIGHT TO BE WORRIED.
OR, AT LEAST, HE'S RIGHT TO THINK MY FRIEND WITH THE SILVER BULLET DIDN'T ACT ALONE.
THE BROTHERHOOD OF FENRIS TRAVELS IN GROUPS.
PACKS, I GUESS.
THESE IDIOTS THINK THEY'RE **WOLVES.**

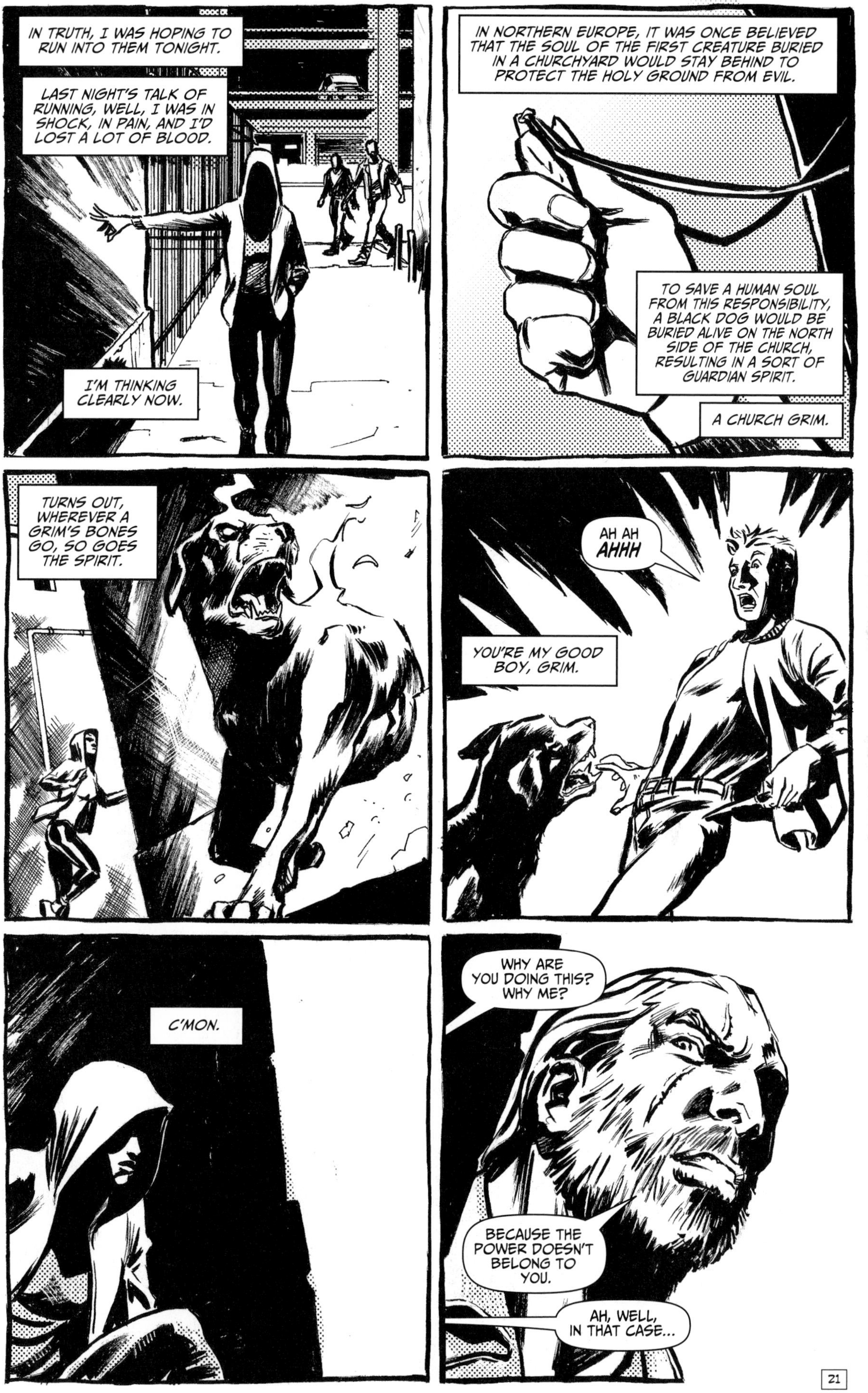
IN TRUTH, I WAS HOPING TO RUN INTO THEM TONIGHT.
LAST NIGHT'S TALK OF RUNNING, WELL, I WAS IN SHOCK, IN PAIN, AND I'D LOST A LOT OF BLOOD.
I'M THINKING CLEARLY NOW.
IN NORTHERN EUROPE, IT WAS ONCE BELIEVED THAT THE SOUL OF THE FIRST CREATURE BURIED IN A CHURCHYARD WOULD STAY BEHIND TO PROTECT THE HOLY GROUND FROM EVIL.
TO SAVE A HUMAN SOUL FROM THIS RESPONSIBILITY, A BLACK DOG WOULD BE BURIED ALIVE ON THE NORTH SIDE OF THE CHURCH, RESULTING IN A SORT OF GUARDIAN SPIRIT.
A CHURCH GRIM.
TURNS OUT, WHEREVER A GRIM'S BONES GO, SO GOES THE SPIRIT.
AH AH AHHH
YOU'RE MY GOOD BOY, GRIM.
C'MON.
WHY ARE YOU DOING THIS? WHY ME?
BECAUSE THE POWER DOESN'T BELONG TO YOU.
AH, WELL, IN THAT CASE...

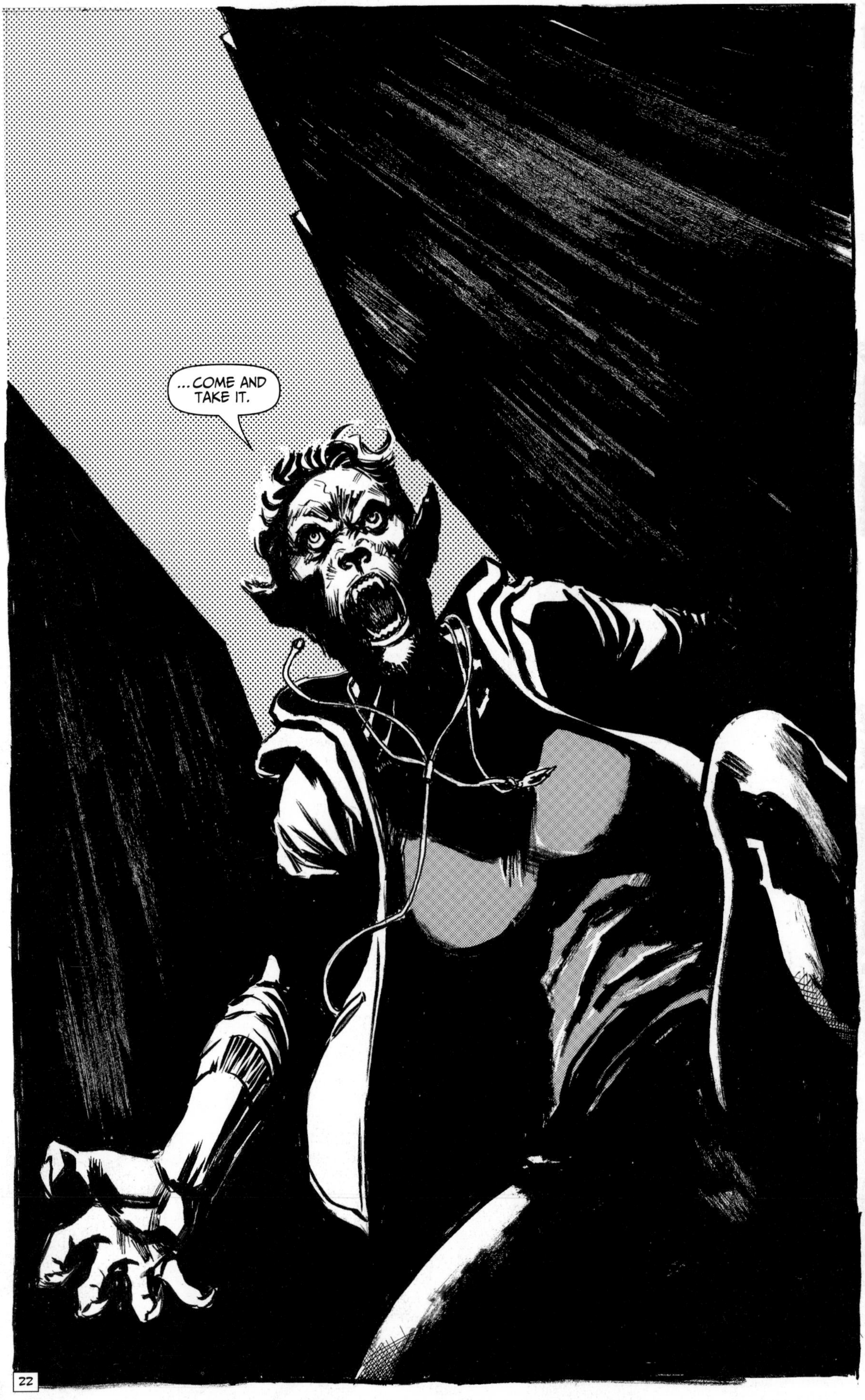
...COME AND TAKE IT.

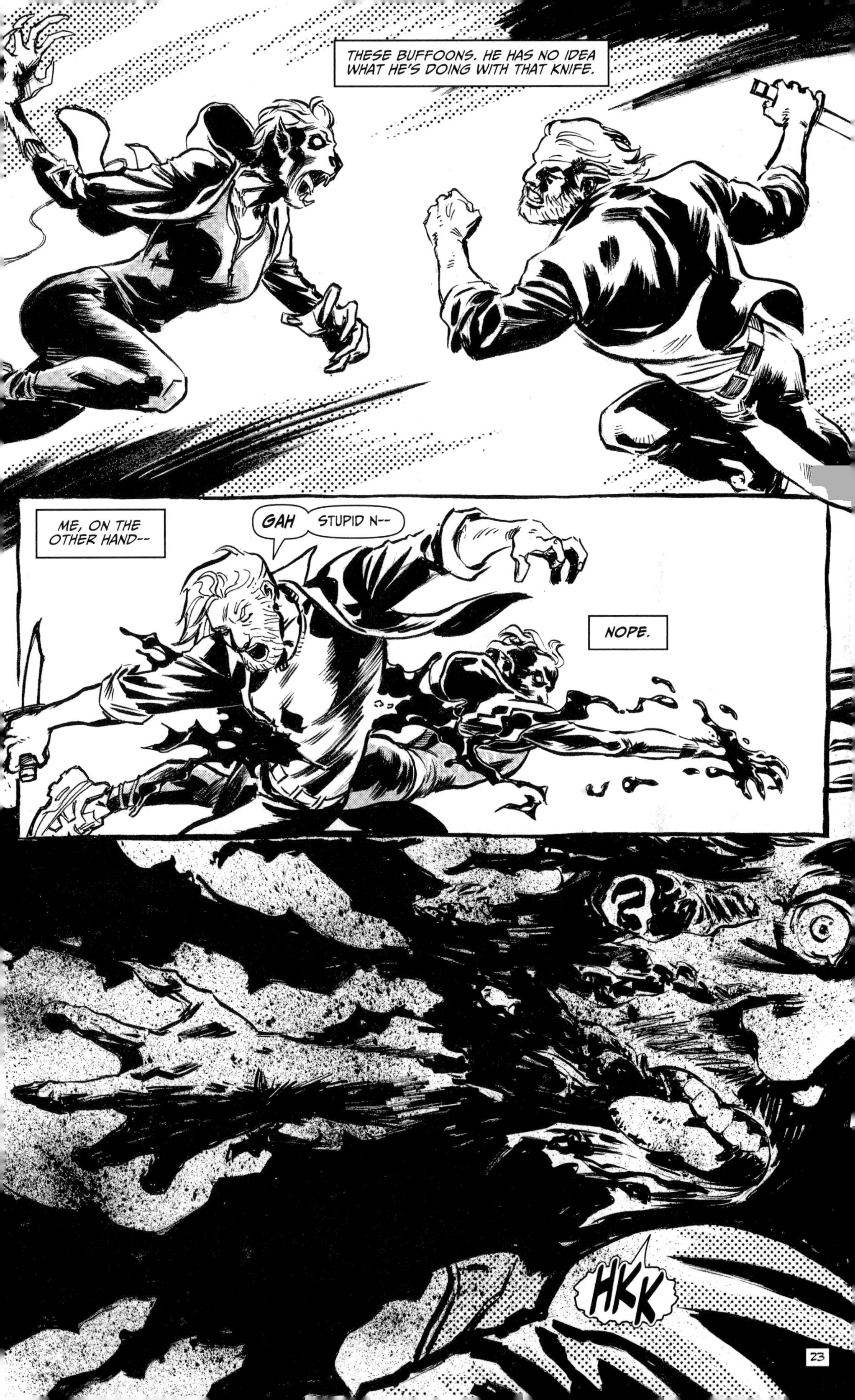
THESE BUFFOONS. HE HAS NO IDEA WHAT HE'S DOING WITH THAT KNIFE.
ME, ON THE OTHER HAND--
GAH
STUPID N--
NOPE.
HKK

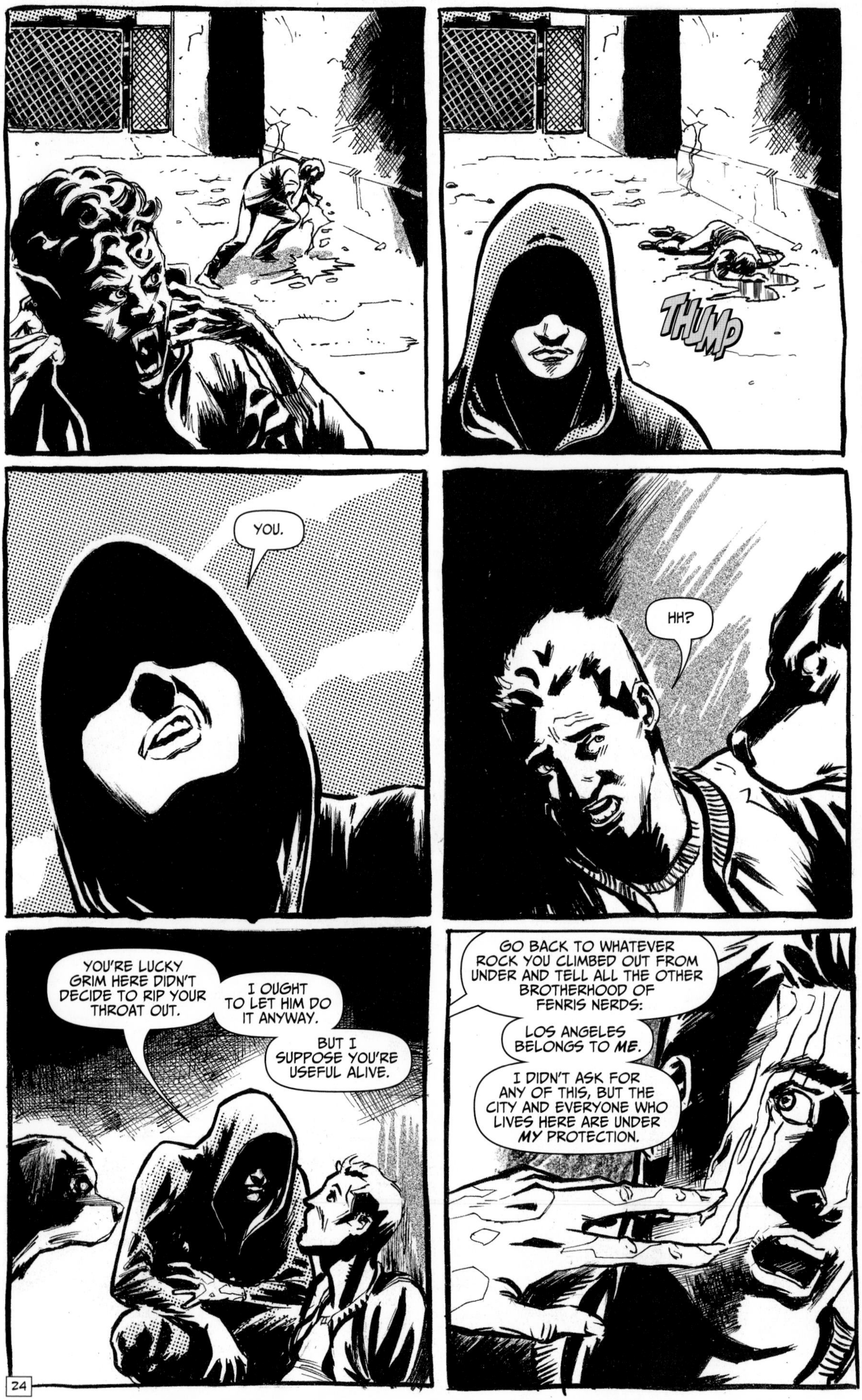
THUMP
YOU.
HH?
YOU'RE LUCKY GRIM HERE DIDN'T DECIDE TO RIP YOUR THROAT OUT.
I OUGHT TO LET HIM DO IT ANYWAY.
BUT I SUPPOSE YOU'RE USEFUL ALIVE.
GO BACK TO WHATEVER ROCK YOU CLIMBED OUT FROM UNDER AND TELL ALL THE OTHER BROTHERHOOD OF FENRIS NERDS:
LOS ANGELES BELONGS TO *ME*.
I DIDN'T ASK FOR ANY OF THIS, BUT THE CITY AND EVERYONE WHO LIVES HERE ARE UNDER *MY* PROTECTION.

STRUMMER?

THIS...

...IS NOT NOODLES.

YEAH. NO. I GUESS IT ISN'T.

I GUESS WE'LL HAVE TO GET SOMETHING DELIVERED.

WONDERFUL, THEN LET'S GO DO THAT ELSEWHERE--ELSEWHERE BEING *HOME*, I GUESS-- BEFORE THE COPS SHOW UP.

AND WHAT'S TO KEEP THIS ONE FROM TELLING THE AUTHORITIES YOU KILLED HIS FRIEND?

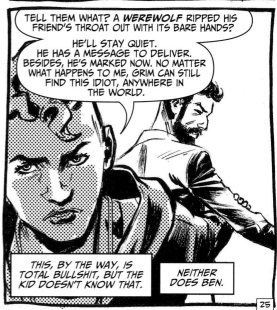

TELL THEM WHAT? A *WEREWOLF* RIPPED HIS FRIEND'S THROAT OUT WITH ITS BARE HANDS?

HE'LL STAY QUIET. HE HAS A MESSAGE TO DELIVER. BESIDES, HE'S MARKED NOW. NO MATTER WHAT HAPPENS TO ME, GRIM CAN STILL FIND THIS IDIOT, ANYWHERE IN THE WORLD.

THIS, BY THE WAY, IS TOTAL BULLSHIT, BUT THE KID DOESN'T KNOW THAT.

NEITHER DOES BEN.

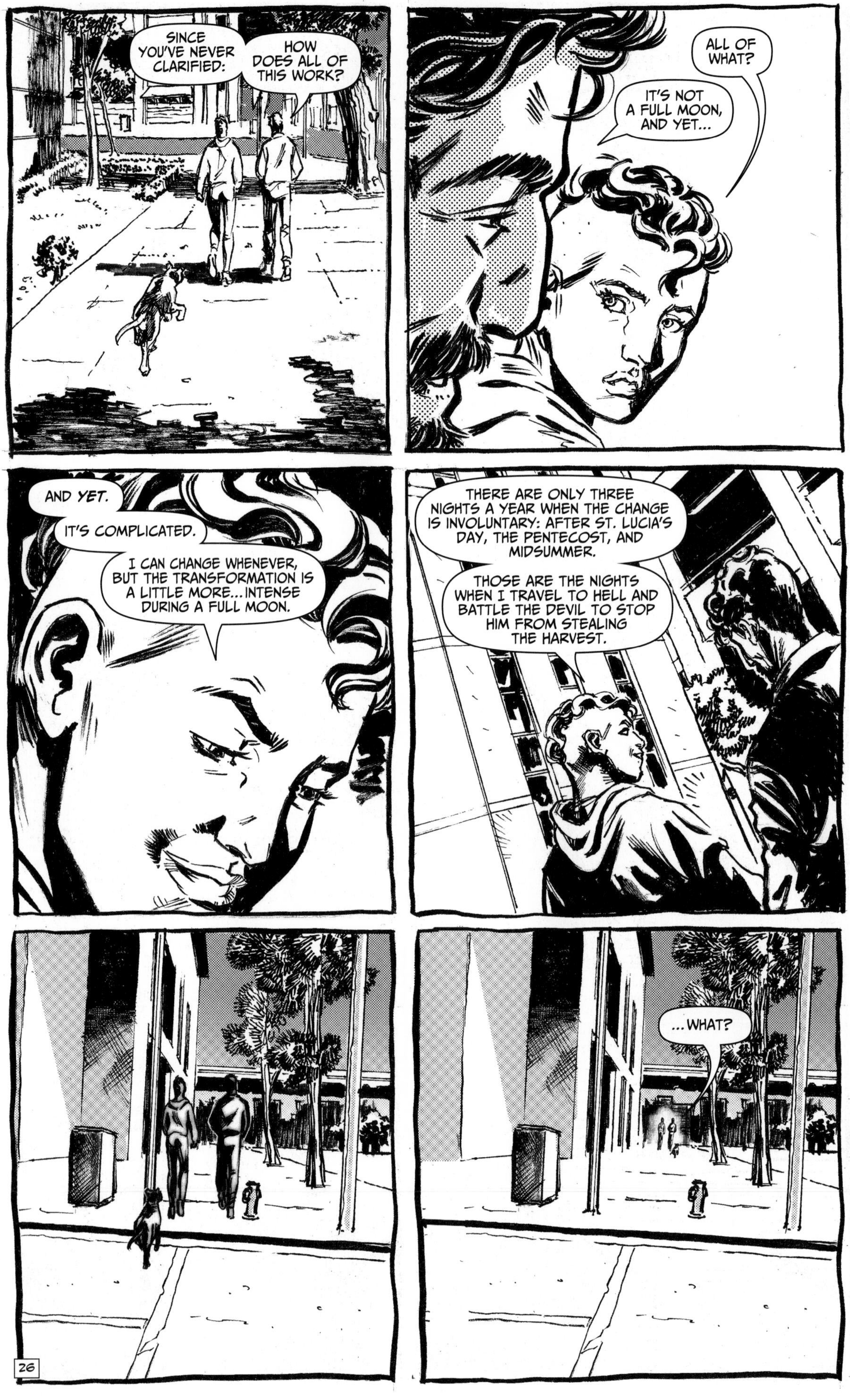
SINCE YOU'VE NEVER CLARIFIED:
HOW DOES ALL OF THIS WORK?
IT'S NOT A FULL MOON, AND YET...
ALL OF WHAT?
AND YET.
IT'S COMPLICATED.
I CAN CHANGE WHENEVER, BUT THE TRANSFORMATION IS A LITTLE MORE...INTENSE DURING A FULL MOON.
THERE ARE ONLY THREE NIGHTS A YEAR WHEN THE CHANGE IS INVOLUNTARY: AFTER ST. LUCIA'S DAY, THE PENTECOST, AND MIDSUMMER.
THOSE ARE THE NIGHTS WHEN I TRAVEL TO HELL AND BATTLE THE DEVIL TO STOP HIM FROM STEALING THE HARVEST.
...WHAT?

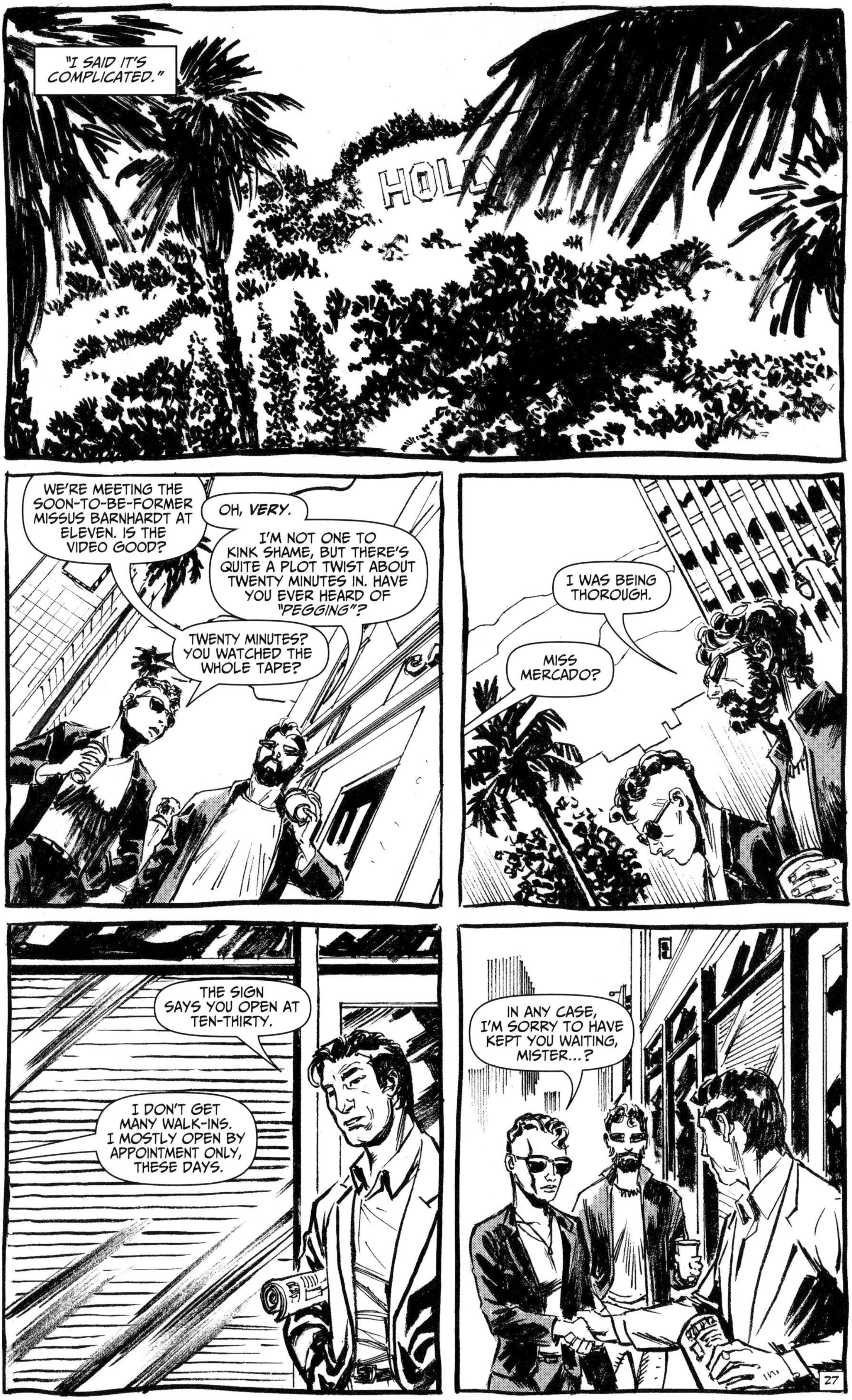
"I SAID IT'S COMPLICATED."
HOLL
WE'RE MEETING THE SOON-TO-BE-FORMER MISSUS BARNHARDT AT ELEVEN. IS THE VIDEO GOOD?
OH, VERY.
I'M NOT ONE TO KINK SHAME, BUT THERE'S QUITE A PLOT TWIST ABOUT TWENTY MINUTES IN. HAVE YOU EVER HEARD OF "PEGGING"?
TWENTY MINUTES? YOU WATCHED THE WHOLE TAPE?
I WAS BEING THOROUGH.
MISS MERCADO?
THE SIGN SAYS YOU OPEN AT TEN-THIRTY.
I DON'T GET MANY WALK-INS. I MOSTLY OPEN BY APPOINTMENT ONLY, THESE DAYS.
IN ANY CASE, I'M SORRY TO HAVE KEPT YOU WAITING, MISTER...?

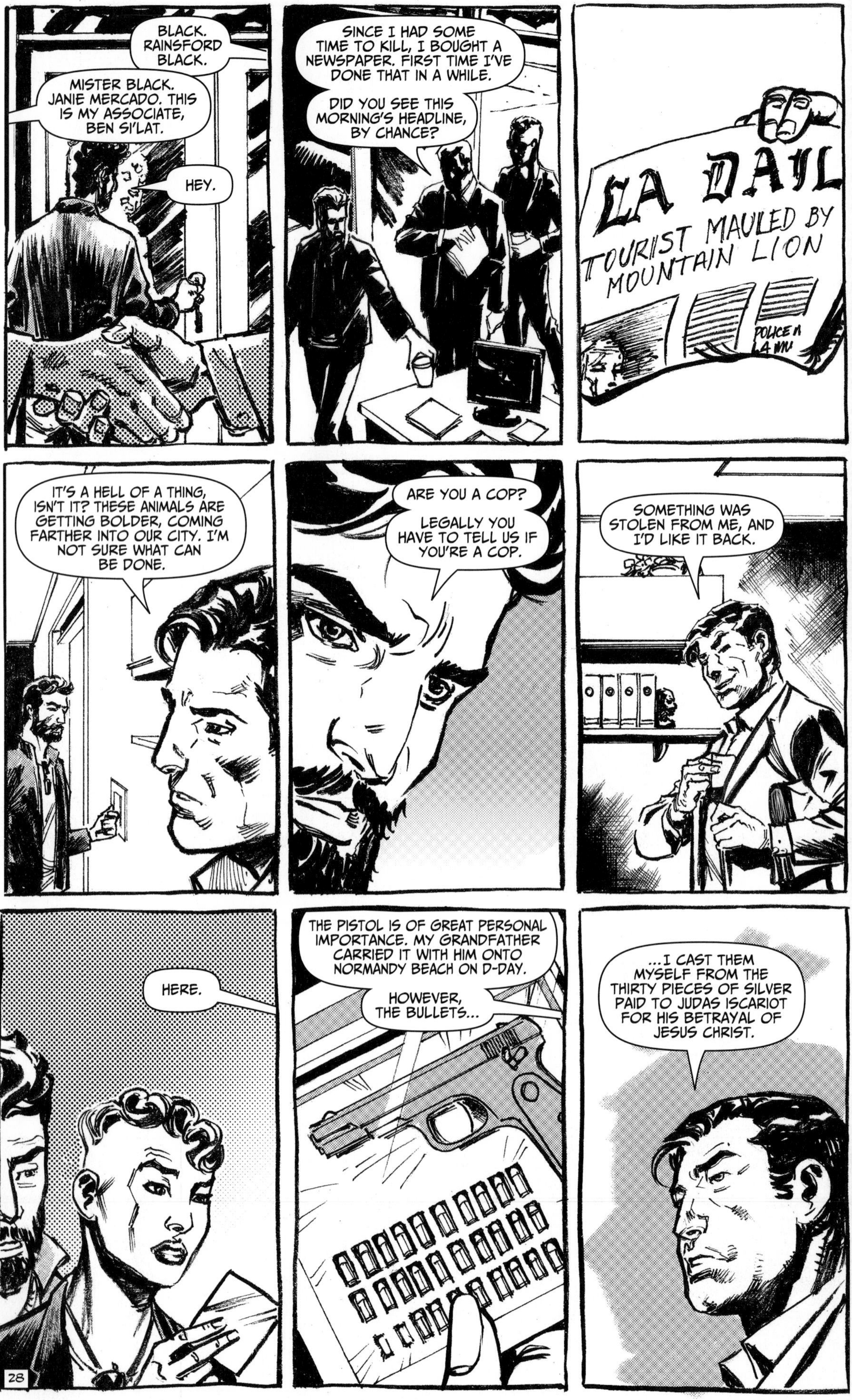
BLACK. RAINSFORD BLACK.
MISTER BLACK. JANIE MERCADO. THIS IS MY ASSOCIATE, BEN SI'LAT.
HEY.
SINCE I HAD SOME TIME TO KILL, I BOUGHT A NEWSPAPER. FIRST TIME I'VE DONE THAT IN A WHILE.
DID YOU SEE THIS MORNING'S HEADLINE, BY CHANCE?
LA DAIL
TOURIST MAULED BY MOUNTAIN LION
IT'S A HELL OF A THING, ISN'T IT? THESE ANIMALS ARE GETTING BOLDER, COMING FARTHER INTO OUR CITY. I'M NOT SURE WHAT CAN BE DONE.
ARE YOU A COP?
LEGALLY YOU HAVE TO TELL US IF YOU'RE A COP.
SOMETHING WAS STOLEN FROM ME, AND I'D LIKE IT BACK.
HERE.
THE PISTOL IS OF GREAT PERSONAL IMPORTANCE. MY GRANDFATHER CARRIED IT WITH HIM ONTO NORMANDY BEACH ON D-DAY.
HOWEVER, THE BULLETS...
...I CAST THEM MYSELF FROM THE THIRTY PIECES OF SILVER PAID TO JUDAS ISCARIOT FOR HIS BETRAYAL OF JESUS CHRIST.

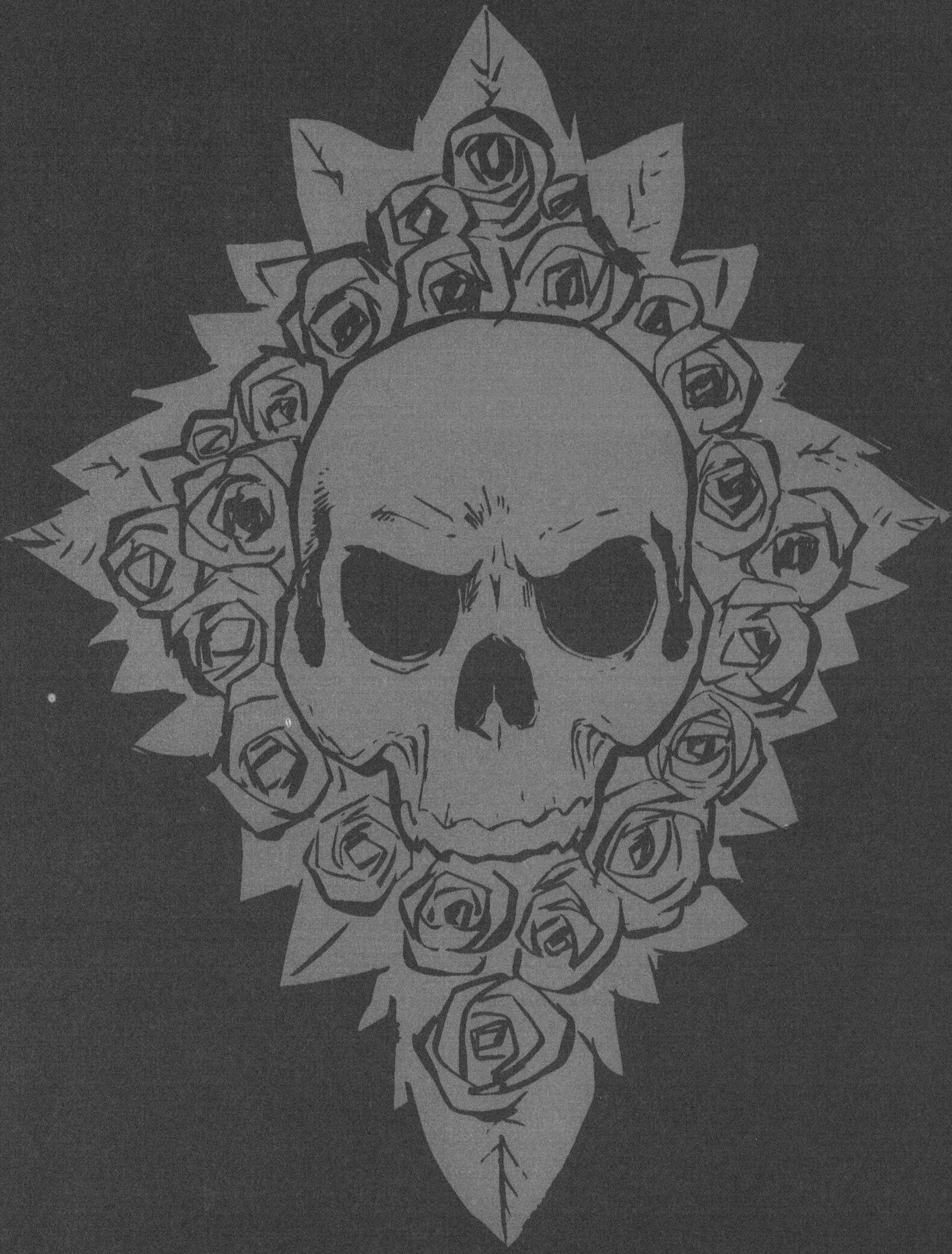

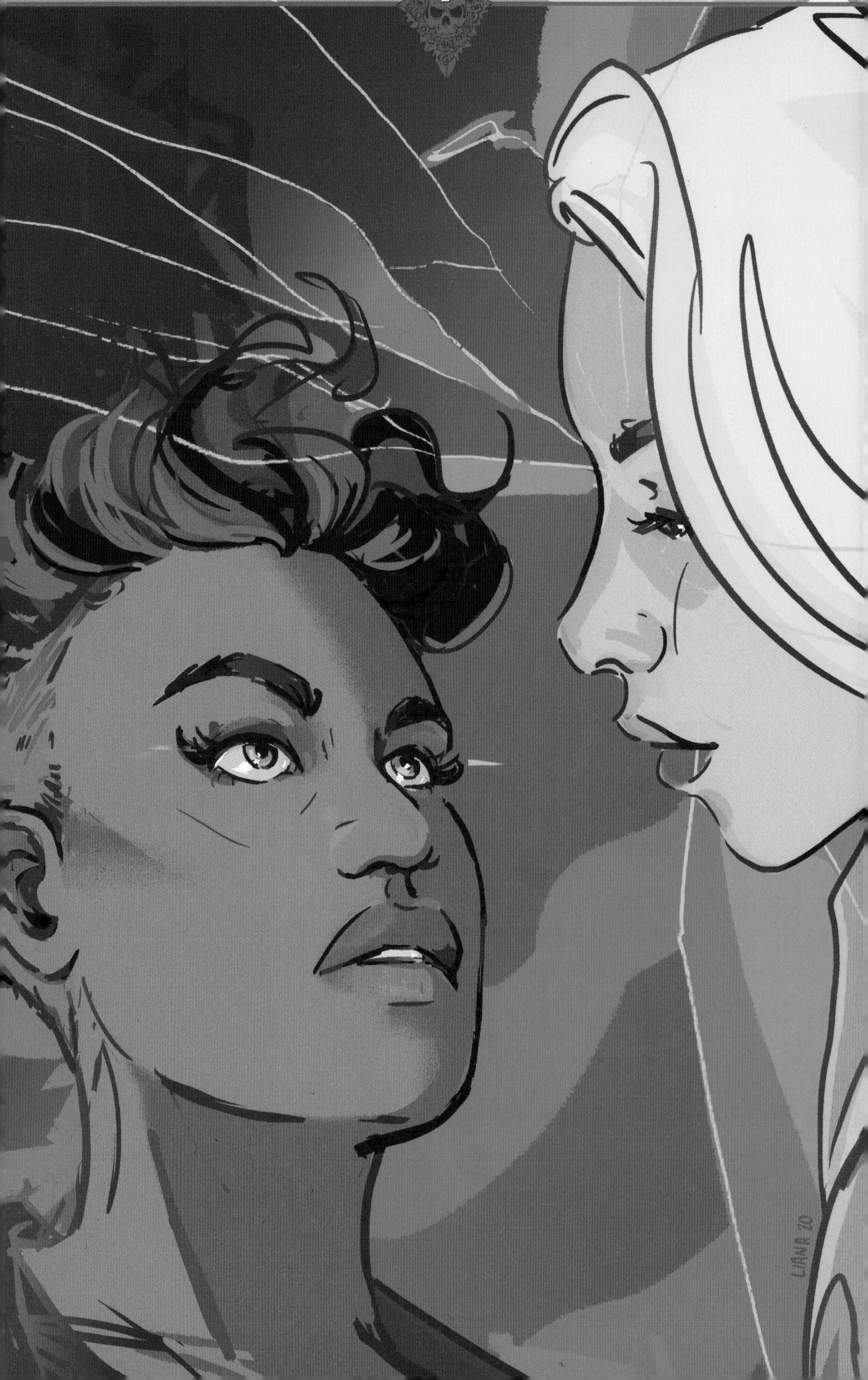
LIANA 20

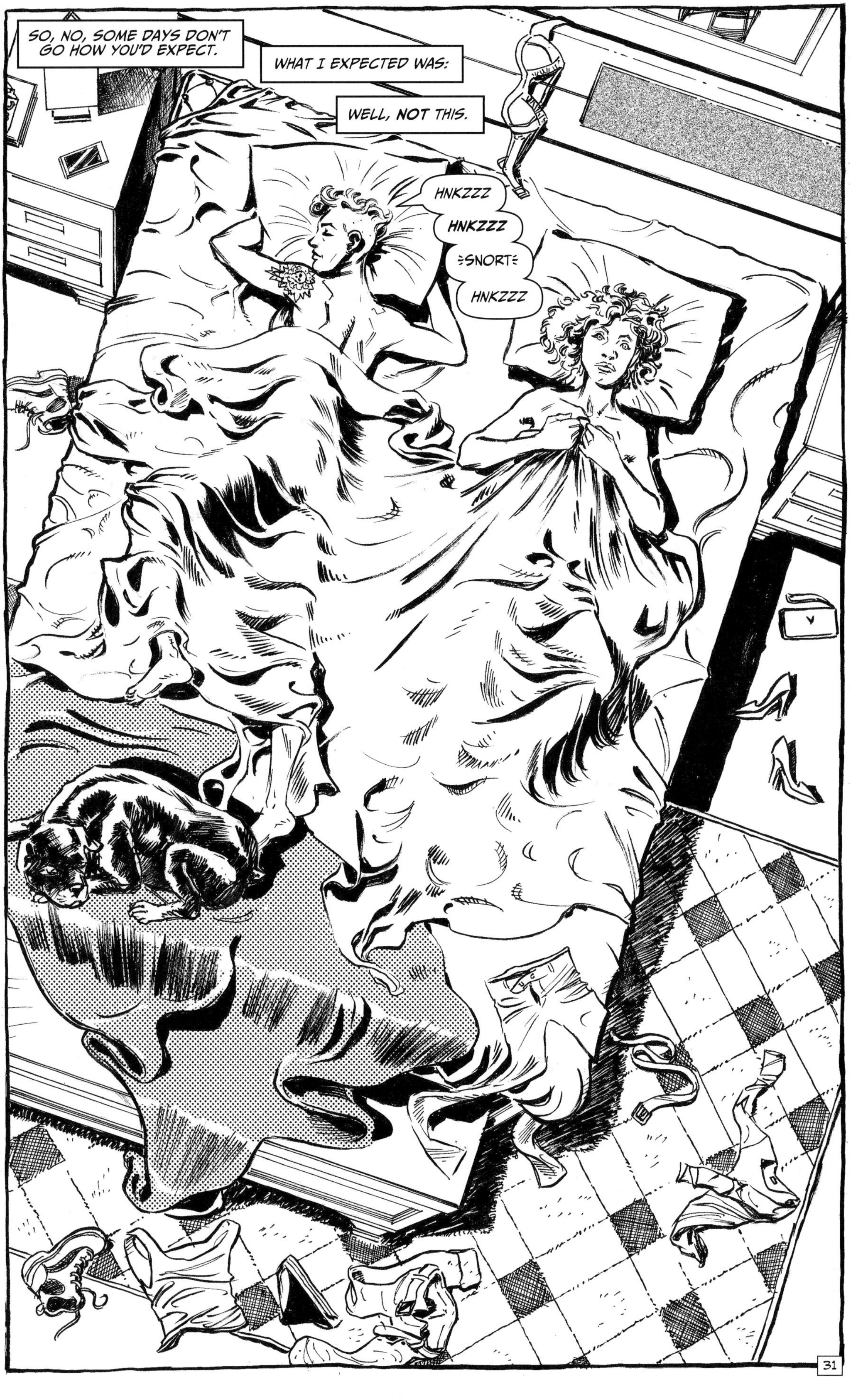
SO, NO, SOME DAYS DON'T GO HOW YOU'D EXPECT.
WHAT I EXPECTED WAS:
WELL, **NOT** THIS.
HNKZZZ
HNKZZZ
SNORT
HNKZZZ

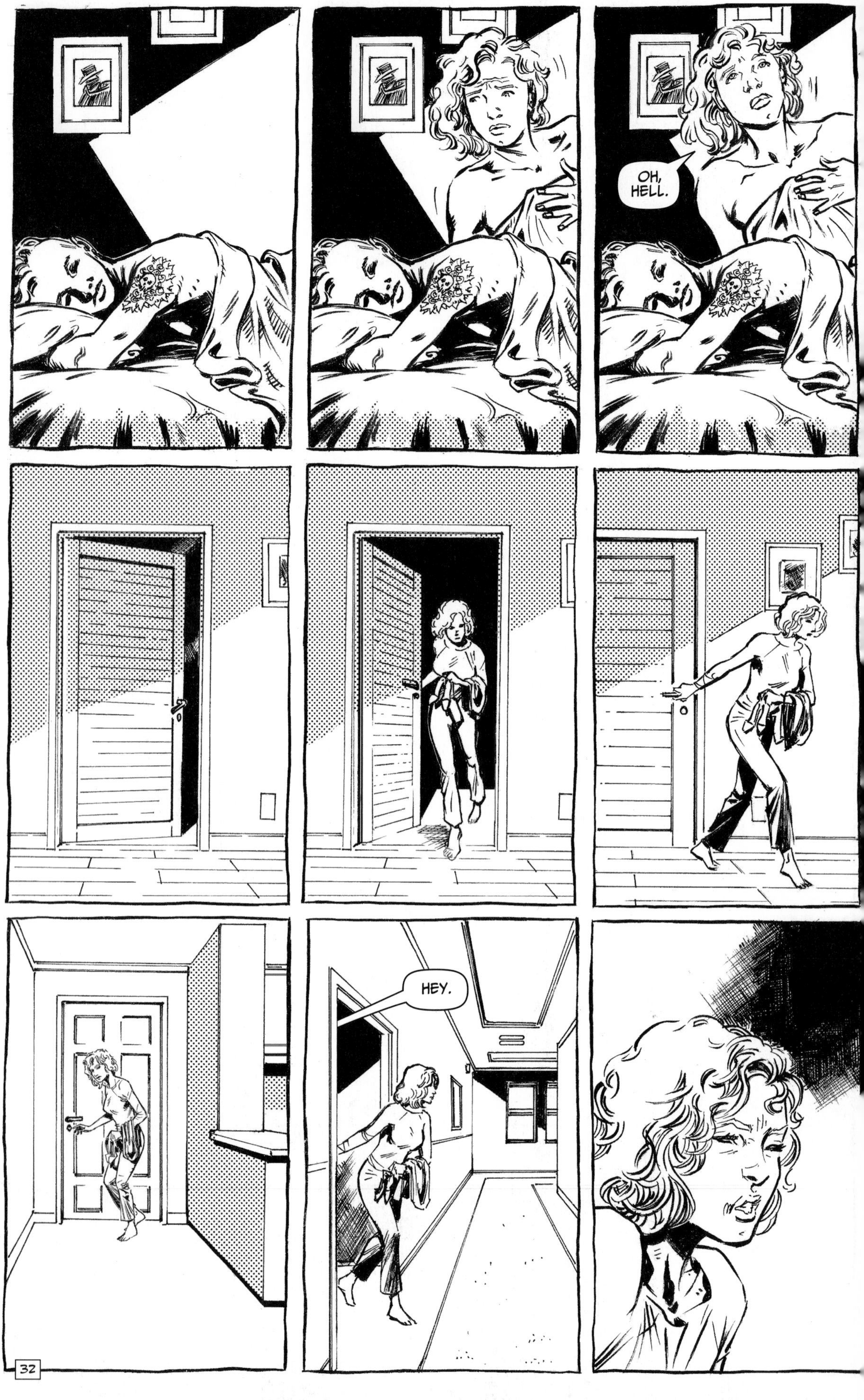
OH, HELL.
HEY.

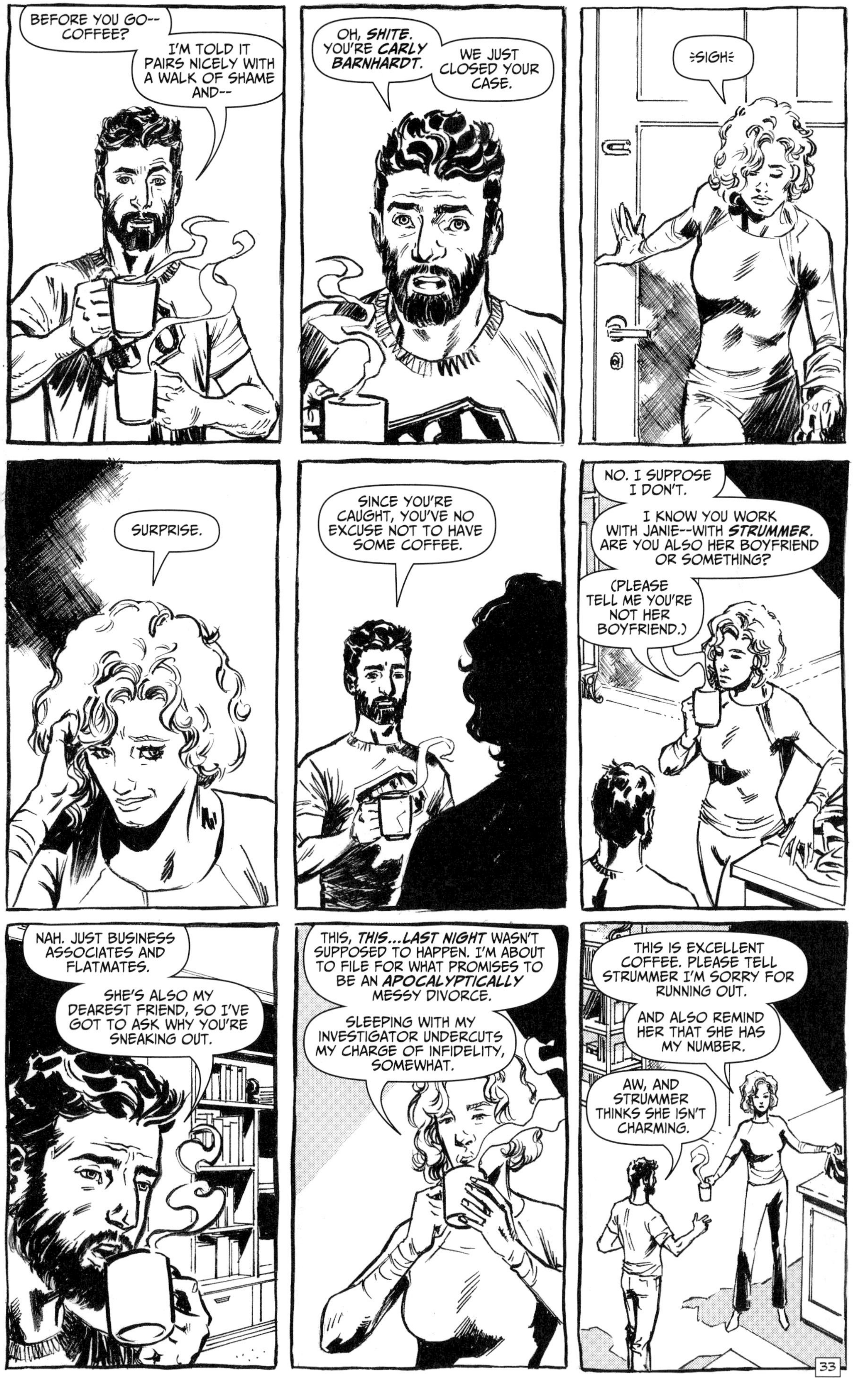
BEFORE YOU GO--
COFFEE?
I'M TOLD IT PAIRS NICELY WITH A WALK OF SHAME AND--
OH, SHITE. YOU'RE CARLY BARNHARDT.
WE JUST CLOSED YOUR CASE.
SIGH
SURPRISE.
SINCE YOU'RE CAUGHT, YOU'VE NO EXCUSE NOT TO HAVE SOME COFFEE.
NO. I SUPPOSE I DON'T.
I KNOW YOU WORK WITH JANIE--WITH STRUMMER. ARE YOU ALSO HER BOYFRIEND OR SOMETHING?
(PLEASE TELL ME YOU'RE NOT HER BOYFRIEND.)
NAH. JUST BUSINESS ASSOCIATES AND FLATMATES.
SHE'S ALSO MY DEAREST FRIEND, SO I'VE GOT TO ASK WHY YOU'RE SNEAKING OUT.
THIS, THIS...LAST NIGHT WASN'T SUPPOSED TO HAPPEN. I'M ABOUT TO FILE FOR WHAT PROMISES TO BE AN APOCALYPTICALLY MESSY DIVORCE.
SLEEPING WITH MY INVESTIGATOR UNDERCUTS MY CHARGE OF INFIDELITY, SOMEWHAT.
THIS IS EXCELLENT COFFEE. PLEASE TELL STRUMMER I'M SORRY FOR RUNNING OUT.
AND ALSO REMIND HER THAT SHE HAS MY NUMBER.
AW, AND STRUMMER THINKS SHE ISN'T CHARMING.

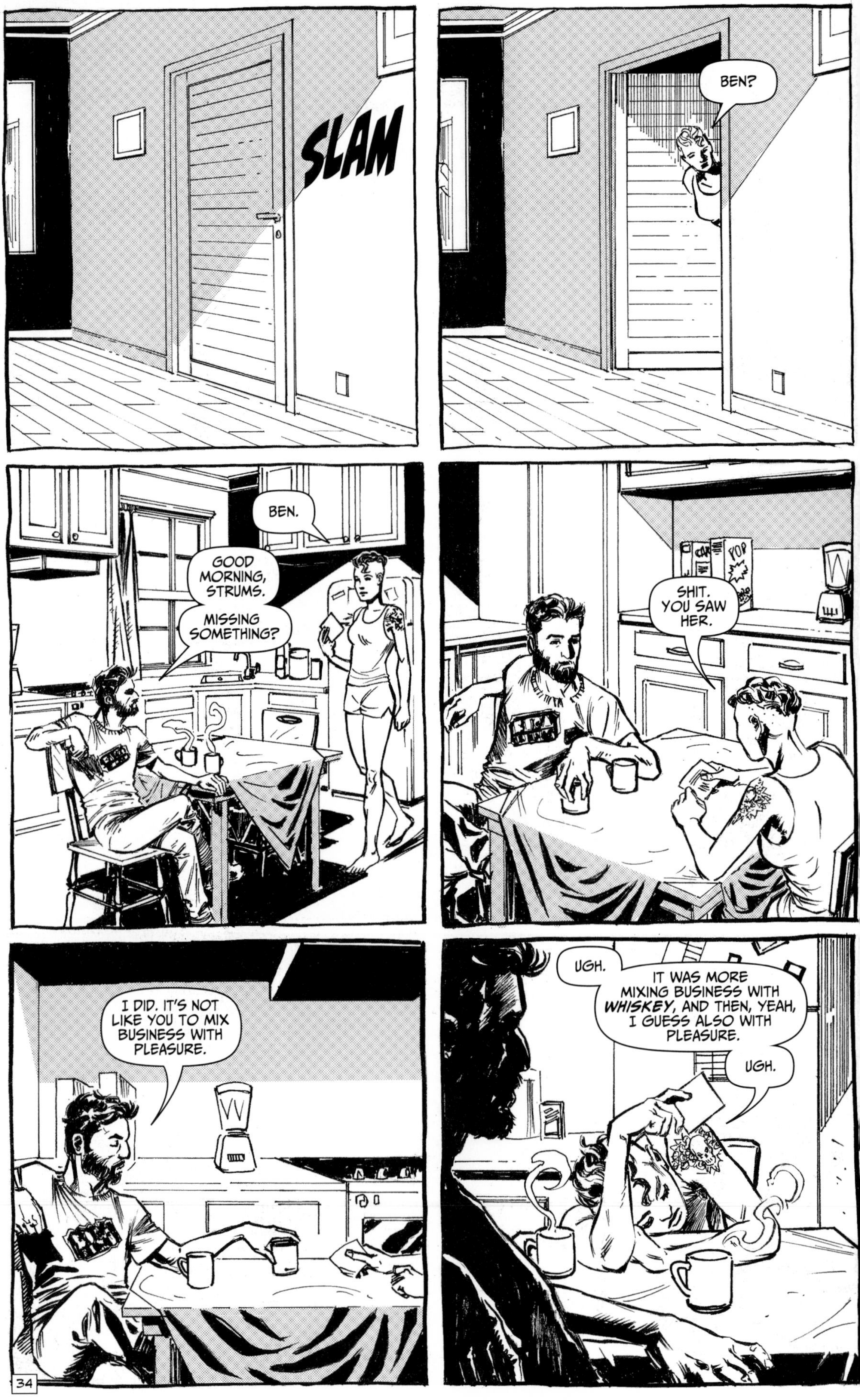
SLAM
BEN?
BEN.
GOOD MORNING, STRUMS.
MISSING SOMETHING?
SHIT. YOU SAW HER.
I DID. IT'S NOT LIKE YOU TO MIX BUSINESS WITH PLEASURE.
UGH.
IT WAS MORE MIXING BUSINESS WITH *WHISKEY*, AND THEN, YEAH, I GUESS ALSO WITH PLEASURE.
UGH.

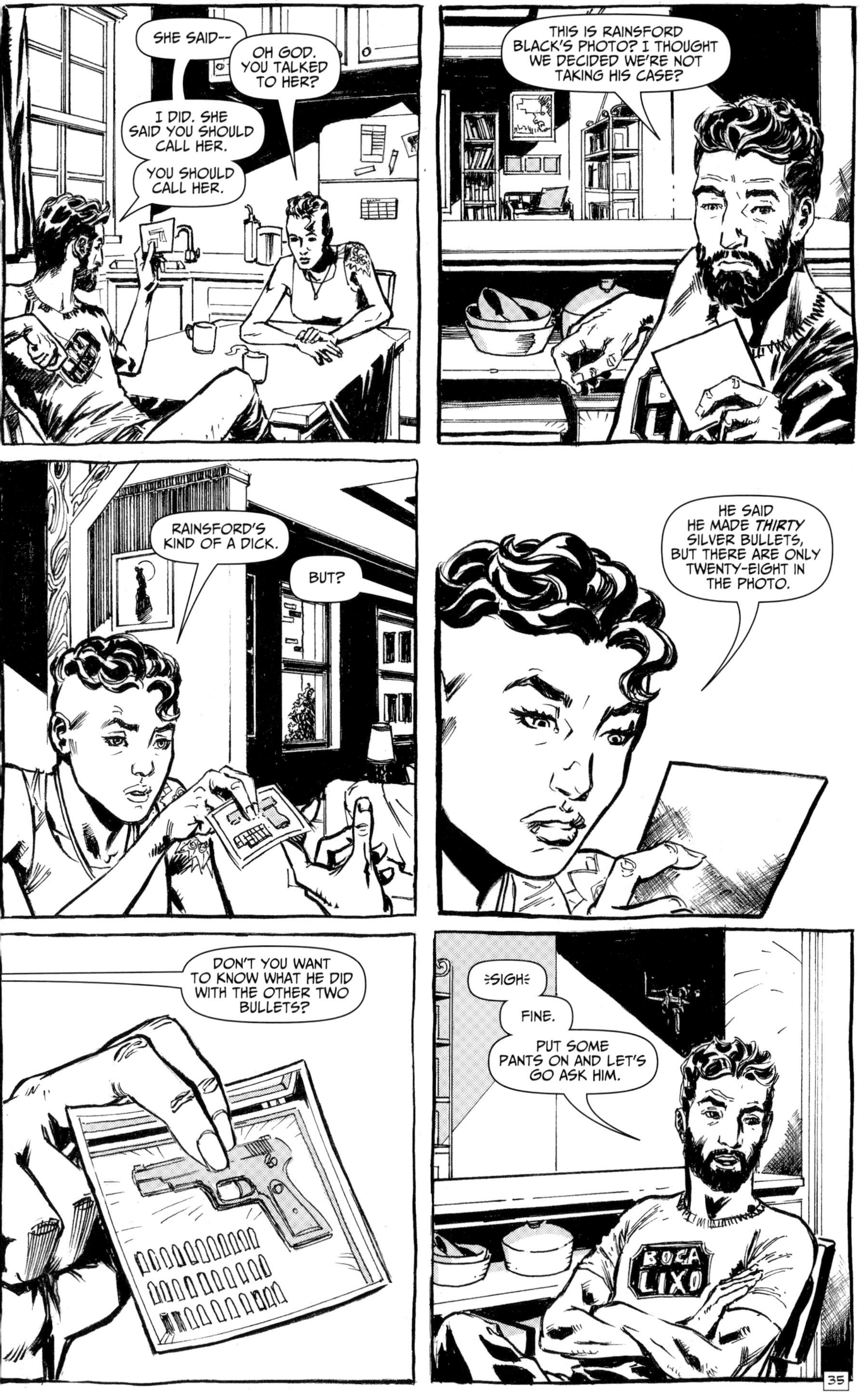
SHE SAID--
OH GOD. YOU TALKED TO HER?
I DID. SHE SAID YOU SHOULD CALL HER.
YOU SHOULD CALL HER.
THIS IS RAINSFORD BLACK'S PHOTO? I THOUGHT WE DECIDED WE'RE NOT TAKING HIS CASE?
RAINSFORD'S KIND OF A DICK.
BUT?
HE SAID HE MADE *THIRTY* SILVER BULLETS, BUT THERE ARE ONLY TWENTY-EIGHT IN THE PHOTO.
DON'T YOU WANT TO KNOW WHAT HE DID WITH THE OTHER TWO BULLETS?
SIGH
FINE.
PUT SOME PANTS ON AND LET'S GO ASK HIM.
BOCA LIXO

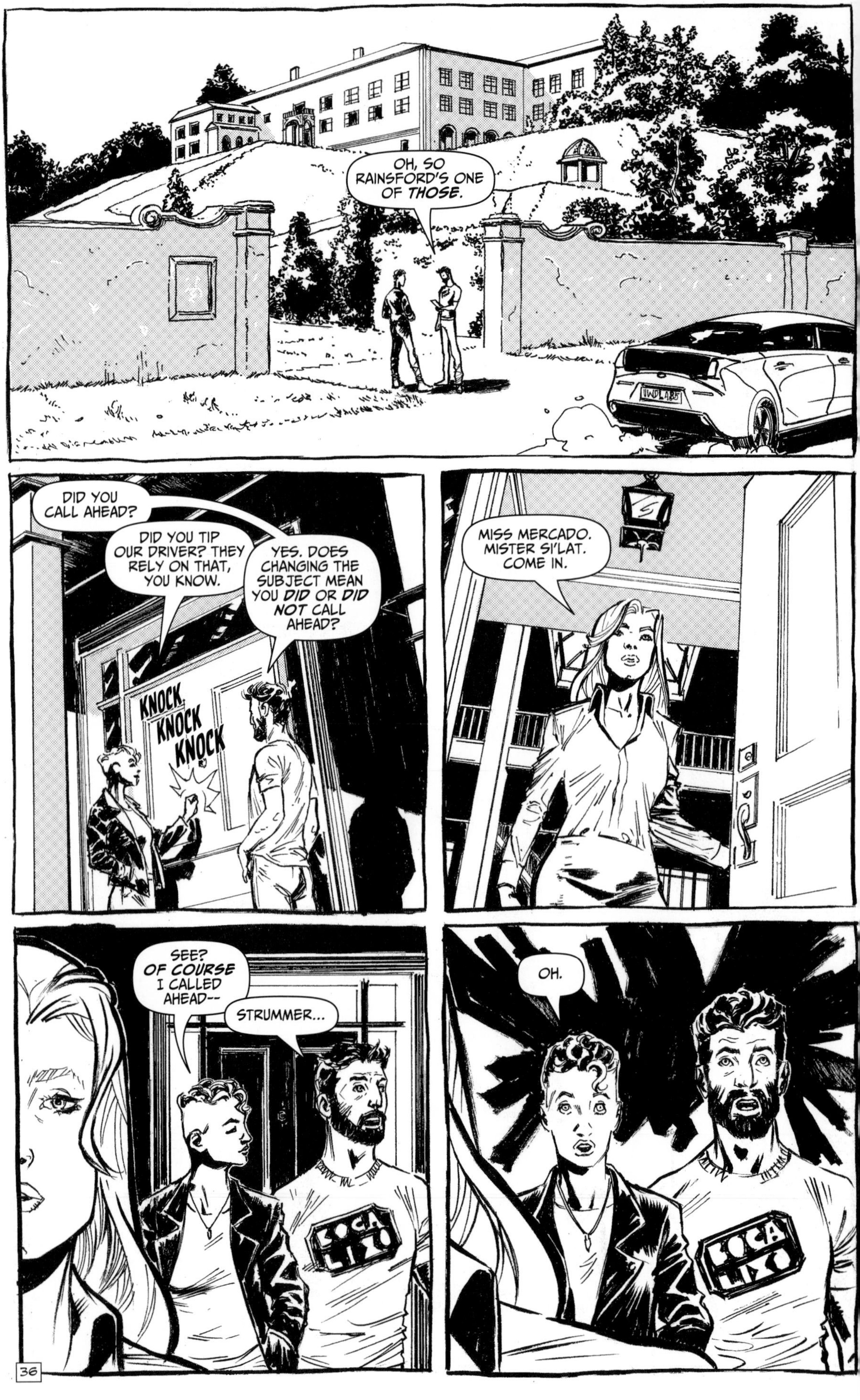
OH, SO RAINSFORD'S ONE OF *THOSE.*
DID YOU CALL AHEAD?
DID YOU TIP OUR DRIVER? THEY RELY ON THAT, YOU KNOW.
YES. DOES CHANGING THE SUBJECT MEAN YOU *DID* OR *DID NOT* CALL AHEAD?
KNOCK KNOCK KNOCK
MISS MERCADO. MISTER SI'LAT. COME IN.
SEE? *OF COURSE* I CALLED AHEAD--
STRUMMER...
OH.

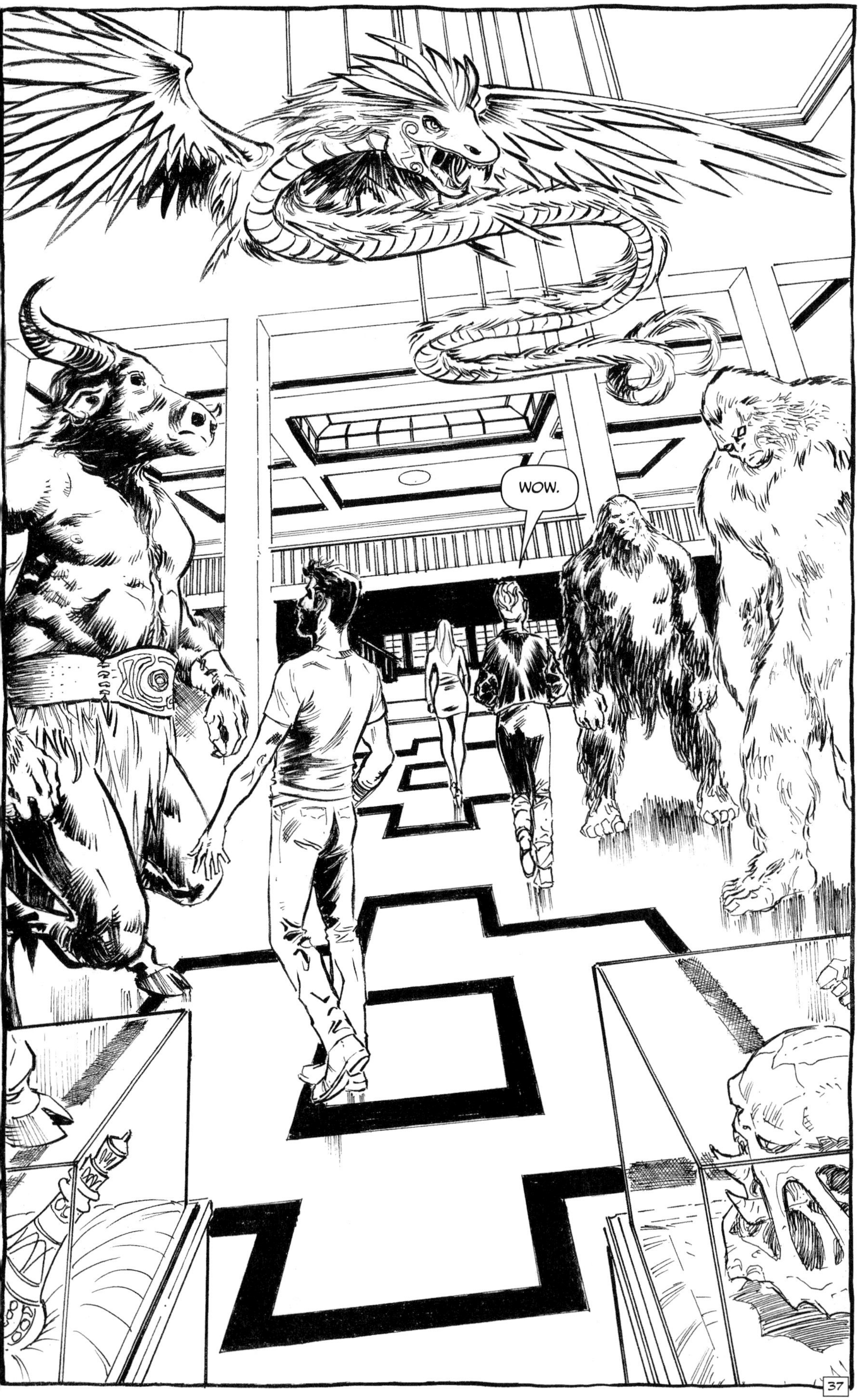
WOW.

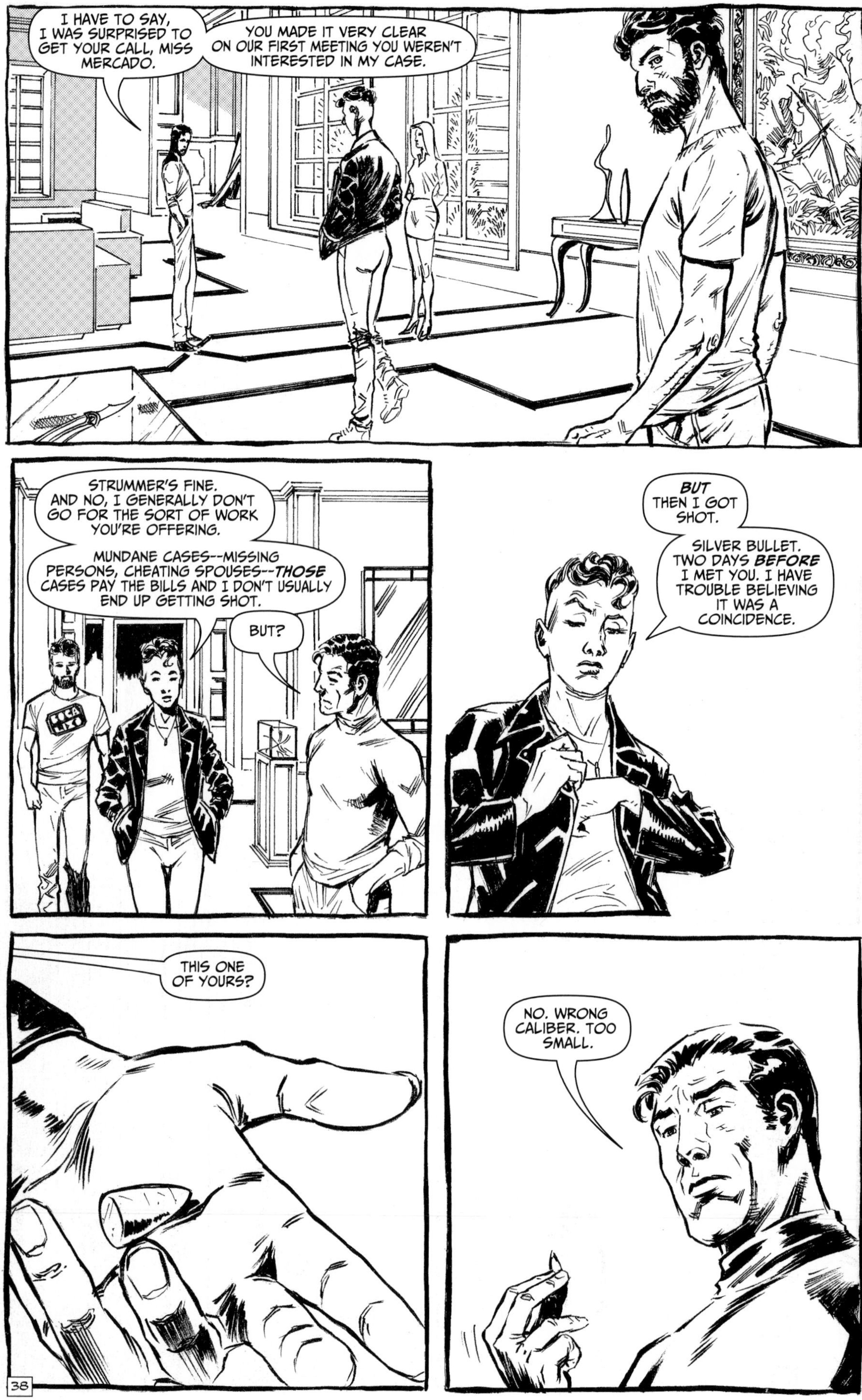
I HAVE TO SAY, I WAS SURPRISED TO GET YOUR CALL, MISS MERCADO.
YOU MADE IT VERY CLEAR ON OUR FIRST MEETING YOU WEREN'T INTERESTED IN MY CASE.
STRUMMER'S FINE. AND NO, I GENERALLY DON'T GO FOR THE SORT OF WORK YOU'RE OFFERING.
MUNDANE CASES--MISSING PERSONS, CHEATING SPOUSES--*THOSE* CASES PAY THE BILLS AND I DON'T USUALLY END UP GETTING SHOT.
BUT?
BUT THEN I GOT SHOT.
SILVER BULLET. TWO DAYS *BEFORE* I MET YOU. I HAVE TROUBLE BELIEVING IT WAS A COINCIDENCE.
THIS ONE OF YOURS?
NO. WRONG CALIBER. TOO SMALL.

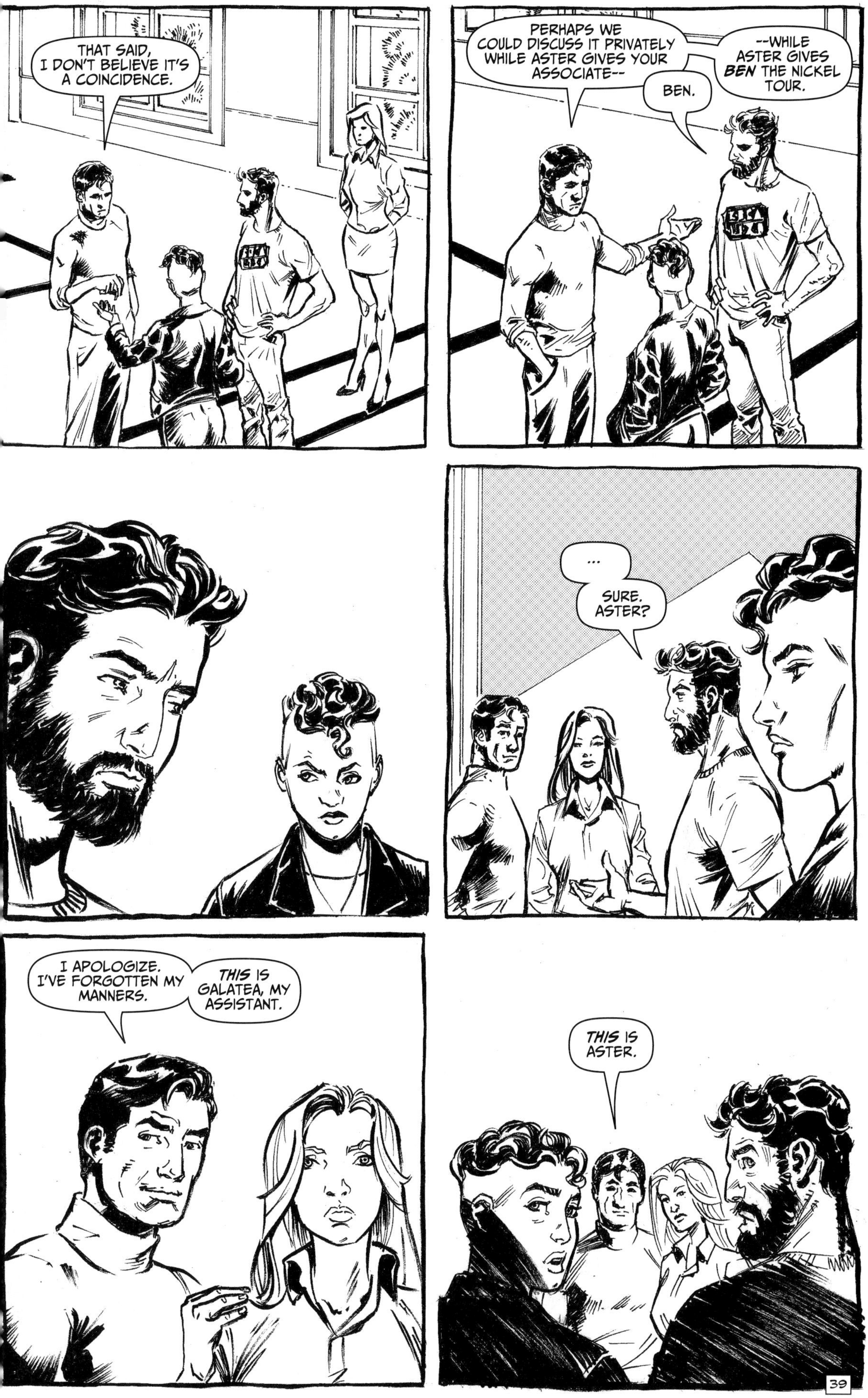
THAT SAID, I DON'T BELIEVE IT'S A COINCIDENCE.
PERHAPS WE COULD DISCUSS IT PRIVATELY WHILE ASTER GIVES YOUR ASSOCIATE--
BEN.
--WHILE ASTER GIVES BEN THE NICKEL TOUR.
...
SURE. ASTER?
I APOLOGIZE. I'VE FORGOTTEN MY MANNERS.
THIS IS GALATEA, MY ASSISTANT.
THIS IS ASTER.

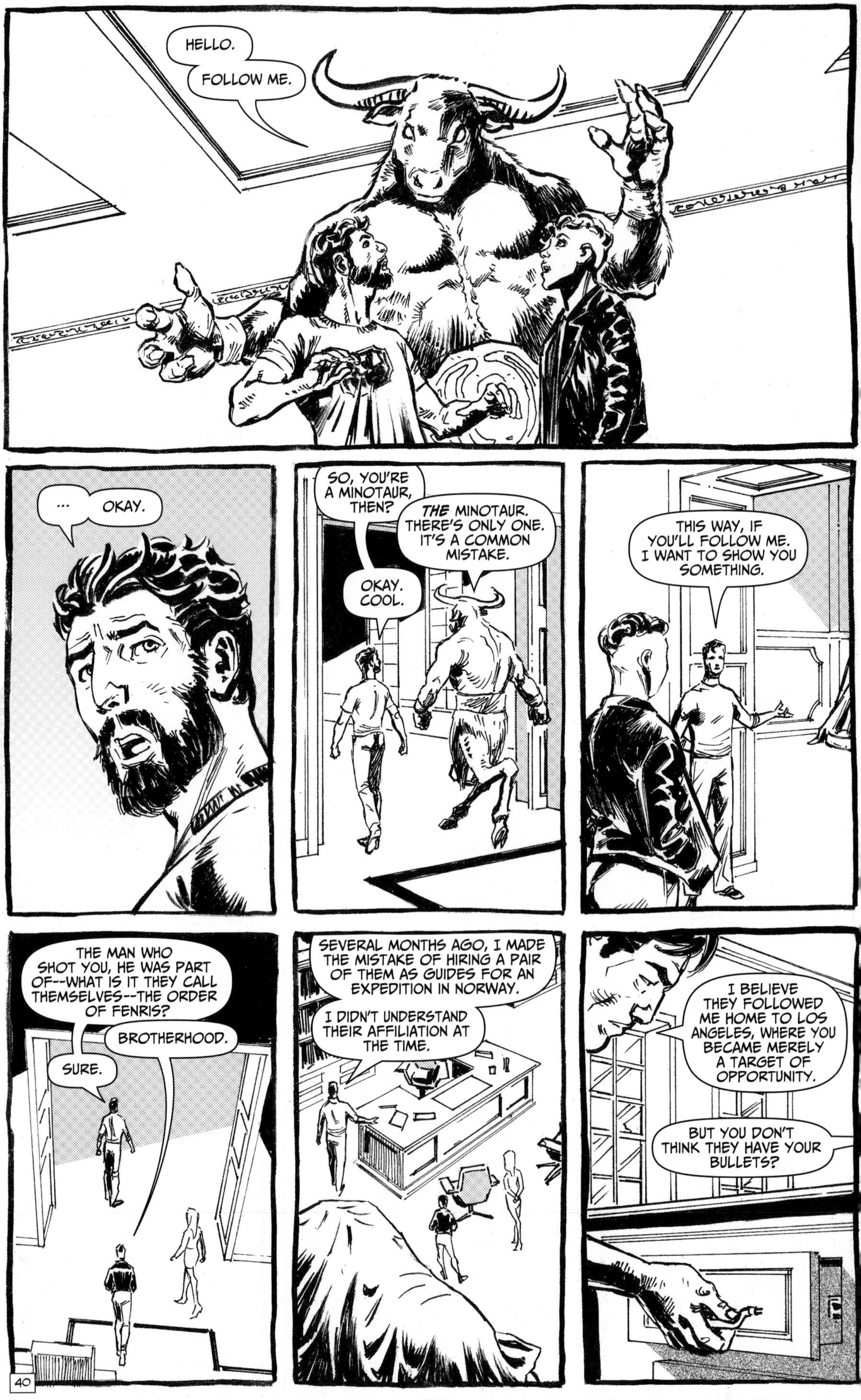
HELLO.
FOLLOW ME.
... OKAY.
SO, YOU'RE A MINOTAUR, THEN?
THE MINOTAUR. THERE'S ONLY ONE. IT'S A COMMON MISTAKE.
OKAY. COOL.
THIS WAY, IF YOU'LL FOLLOW ME. I WANT TO SHOW YOU SOMETHING.
THE MAN WHO SHOT YOU, HE WAS PART OF--WHAT IS IT THEY CALL THEMSELVES--THE ORDER OF FENRIS?
BROTHERHOOD.
SURE.
SEVERAL MONTHS AGO, I MADE THE MISTAKE OF HIRING A PAIR OF THEM AS GUIDES FOR AN EXPEDITION IN NORWAY.
I DIDN'T UNDERSTAND THEIR AFFILIATION AT THE TIME.
I BELIEVE THEY FOLLOWED ME HOME TO LOS ANGELES, WHERE YOU BECAME MERELY A TARGET OF OPPORTUNITY.
BUT YOU DON'T THINK THEY HAVE YOUR BULLETS?

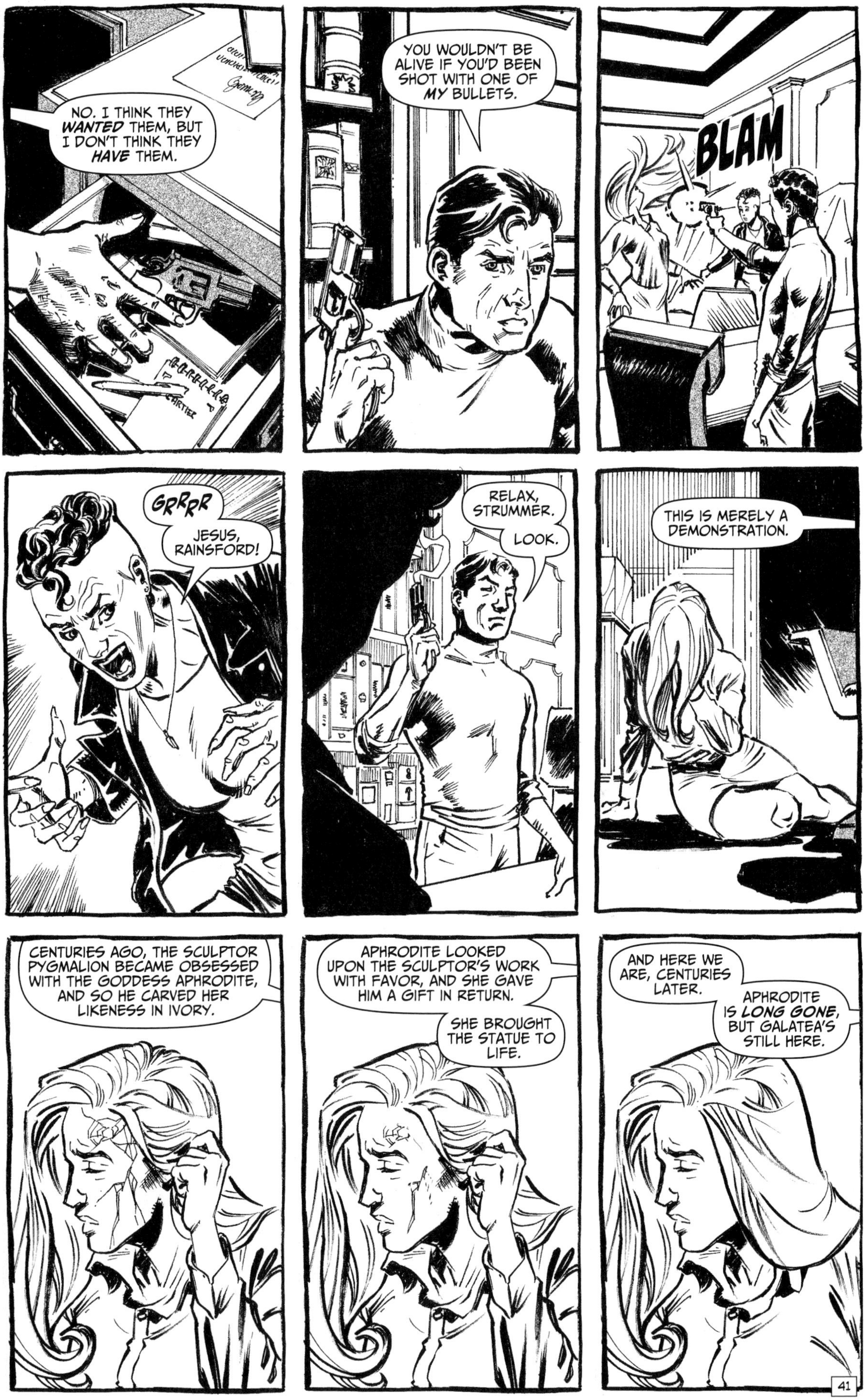
NO. I THINK THEY WANTED THEM, BUT I DON'T THINK THEY HAVE THEM.
YOU WOULDN'T BE ALIVE IF YOU'D BEEN SHOT WITH ONE OF MY BULLETS.
BLAM
GRRRR
JESUS, RAINSFORD!
RELAX, STRUMMER.
LOOK.
THIS IS MERELY A DEMONSTRATION.
CENTURIES AGO, THE SCULPTOR PYGMALION BECAME OBSESSED WITH THE GODDESS APHRODITE, AND SO HE CARVED HER LIKENESS IN IVORY.
APHRODITE LOOKED UPON THE SCULPTOR'S WORK WITH FAVOR, AND SHE GAVE HIM A GIFT IN RETURN.
SHE BROUGHT THE STATUE TO LIFE.
AND HERE WE ARE, CENTURIES LATER.
APHRODITE IS LONG GONE, BUT GALATEA'S STILL HERE.

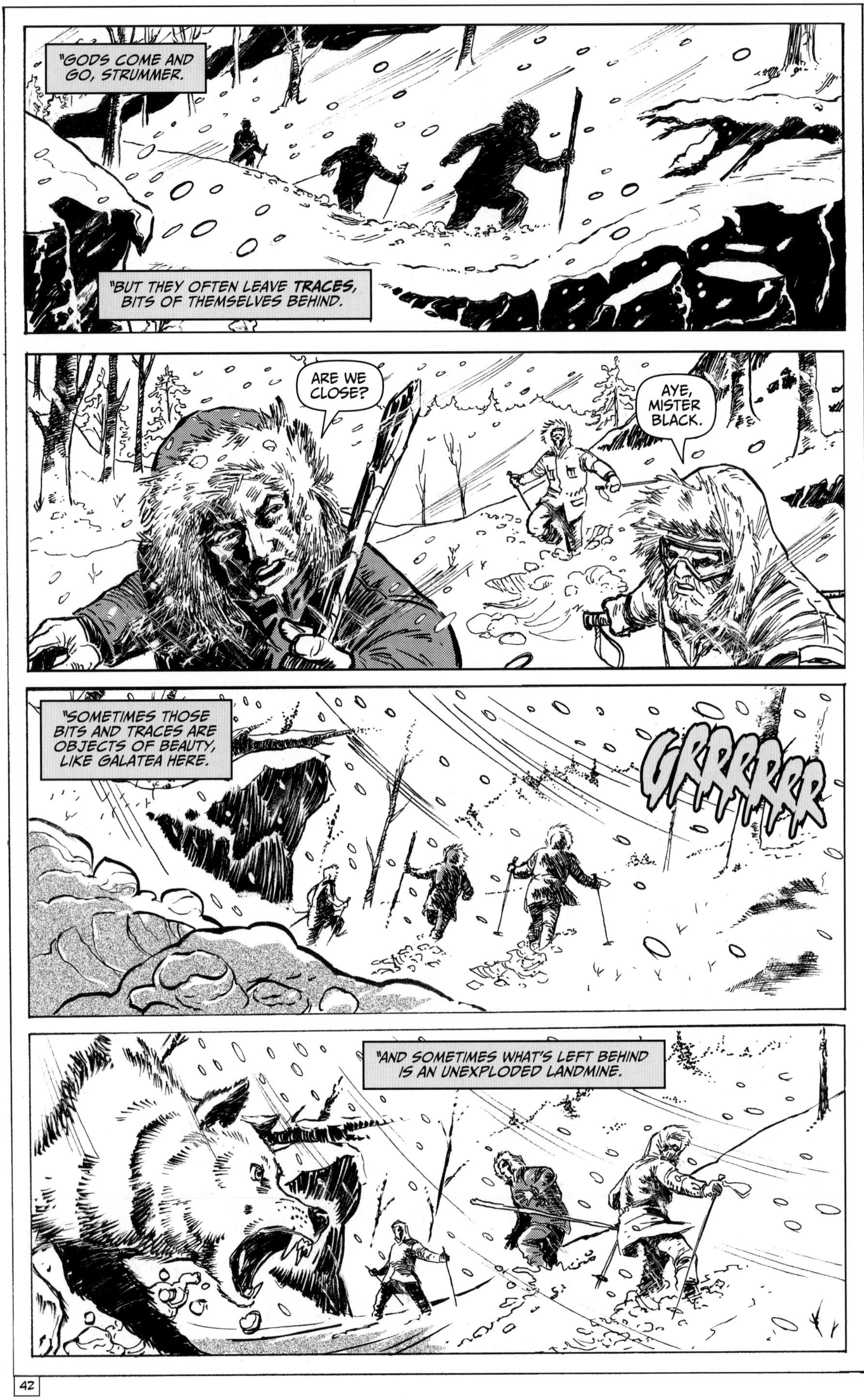
"GODS COME AND GO, STRUMMER.
"BUT THEY OFTEN LEAVE TRACES, BITS OF THEMSELVES BEHIND.
ARE WE CLOSE?
AYE, MISTER BLACK.
"SOMETIMES THOSE BITS AND TRACES ARE OBJECTS OF BEAUTY, LIKE GALATEA HERE.
GRRRRRR
"AND SOMETIMES WHAT'S LEFT BEHIND IS AN UNEXPLODED LANDMINE.

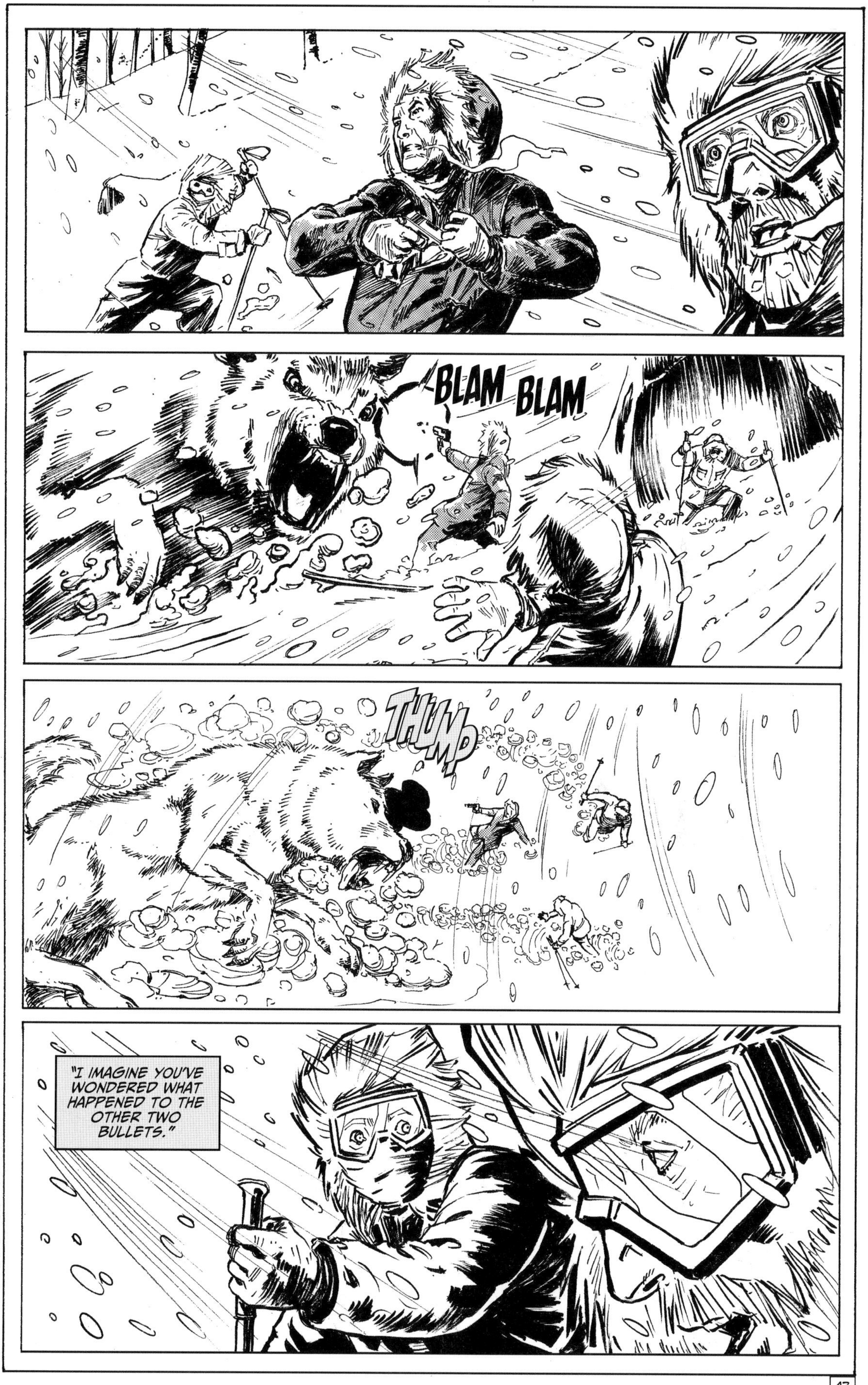
BLAM BLAM
THUMP
"I IMAGINE YOU'VE WONDERED WHAT HAPPENED TO THE OTHER TWO BULLETS."

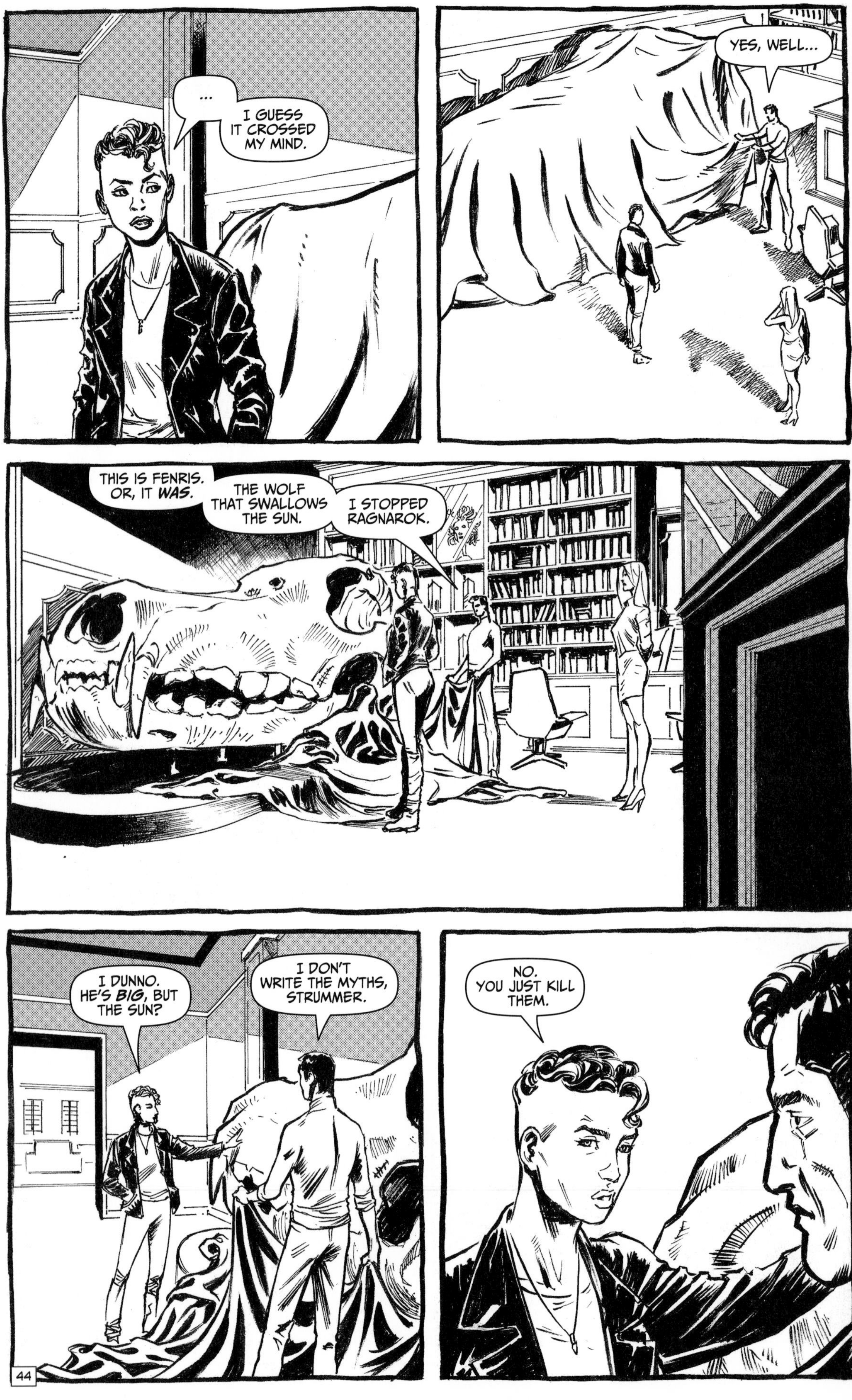
...
I GUESS IT CROSSED MY MIND.
YES, WELL...
THIS IS FENRIS. OR, IT WAS.
THE WOLF THAT SWALLOWS THE SUN.
I STOPPED RAGNAROK.
I DUNNO. HE'S BIG, BUT THE SUN?
I DON'T WRITE THE MYTHS, STRUMMER.
NO. YOU JUST KILL THEM.

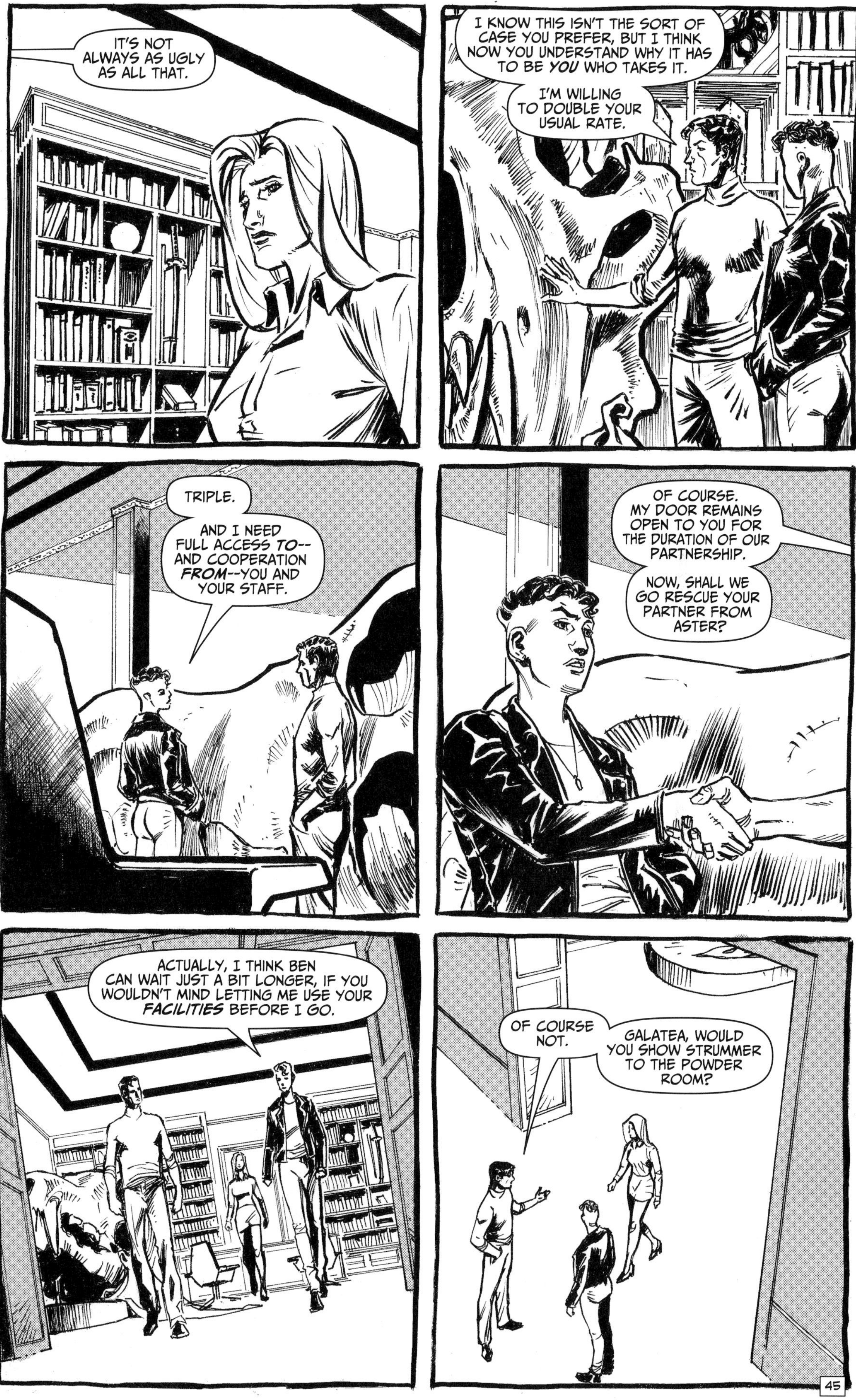
IT'S NOT ALWAYS AS UGLY AS ALL THAT.
I KNOW THIS ISN'T THE SORT OF CASE YOU PREFER, BUT I THINK NOW YOU UNDERSTAND WHY IT HAS TO BE *YOU* WHO TAKES IT.
I'M WILLING TO DOUBLE YOUR USUAL RATE.
TRIPLE.
AND I NEED FULL ACCESS *TO*--AND COOPERATION *FROM*--YOU AND YOUR STAFF.
OF COURSE. MY DOOR REMAINS OPEN TO YOU FOR THE DURATION OF OUR PARTNERSHIP.
NOW, SHALL WE GO RESCUE YOUR PARTNER FROM ASTER?
ACTUALLY, I THINK BEN CAN WAIT JUST A BIT LONGER, IF YOU WOULDN'T MIND LETTING ME USE YOUR *FACILITIES* BEFORE I GO.
OF COURSE NOT.
GALATEA, WOULD YOU SHOW STRUMMER TO THE POWDER ROOM?

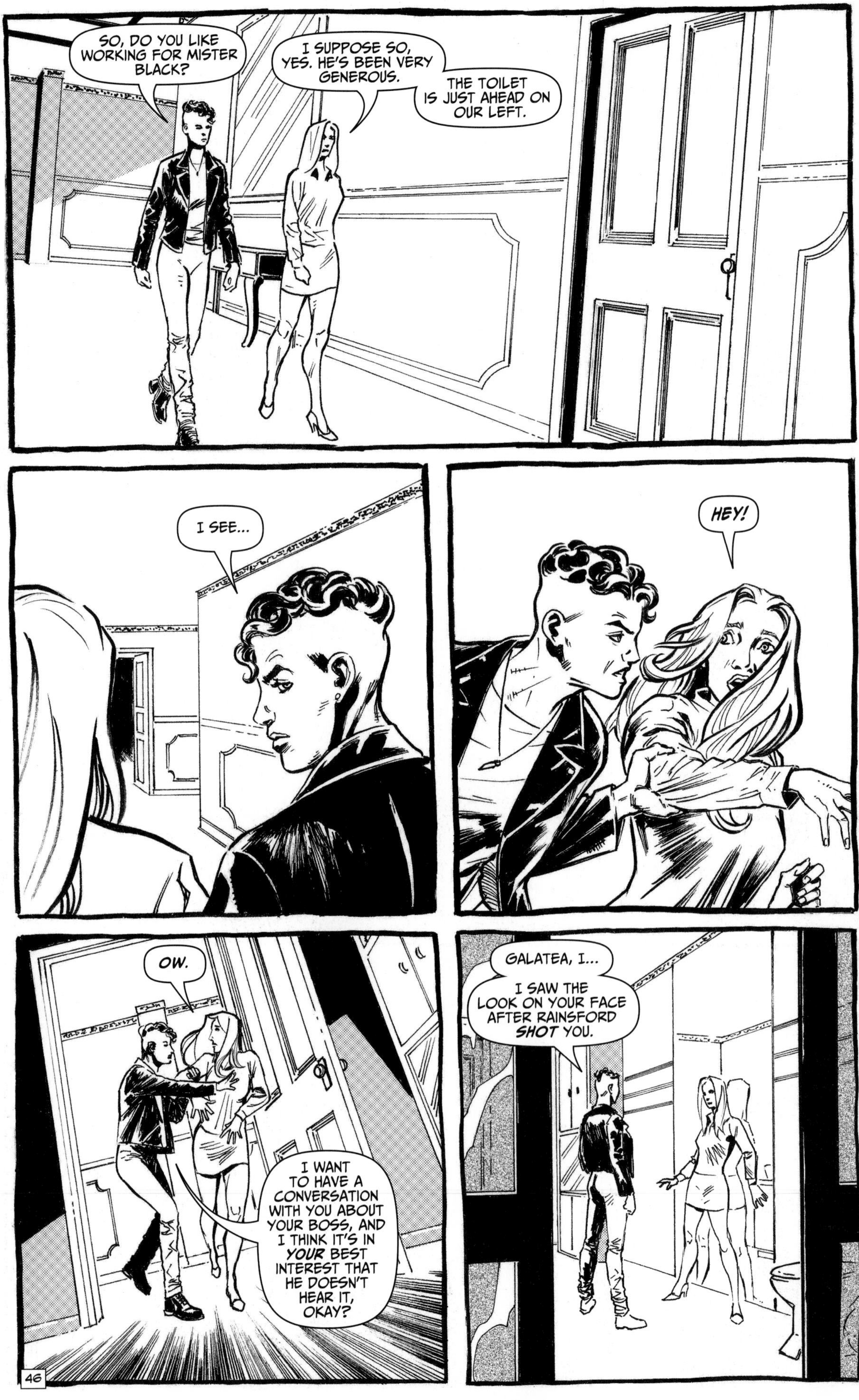
SO, DO YOU LIKE WORKING FOR MISTER BLACK?
I SUPPOSE SO, YES. HE'S BEEN VERY GENEROUS.
THE TOILET IS JUST AHEAD ON OUR LEFT.
I SEE...
HEY!
OW.
I WANT TO HAVE A CONVERSATION WITH YOU ABOUT YOUR BOSS, AND I THINK IT'S IN *YOUR* BEST INTEREST THAT HE DOESN'T HEAR IT, OKAY?
GALATEA, I...
I SAW THE LOOK ON YOUR FACE AFTER RAINSFORD *SHOT* YOU.

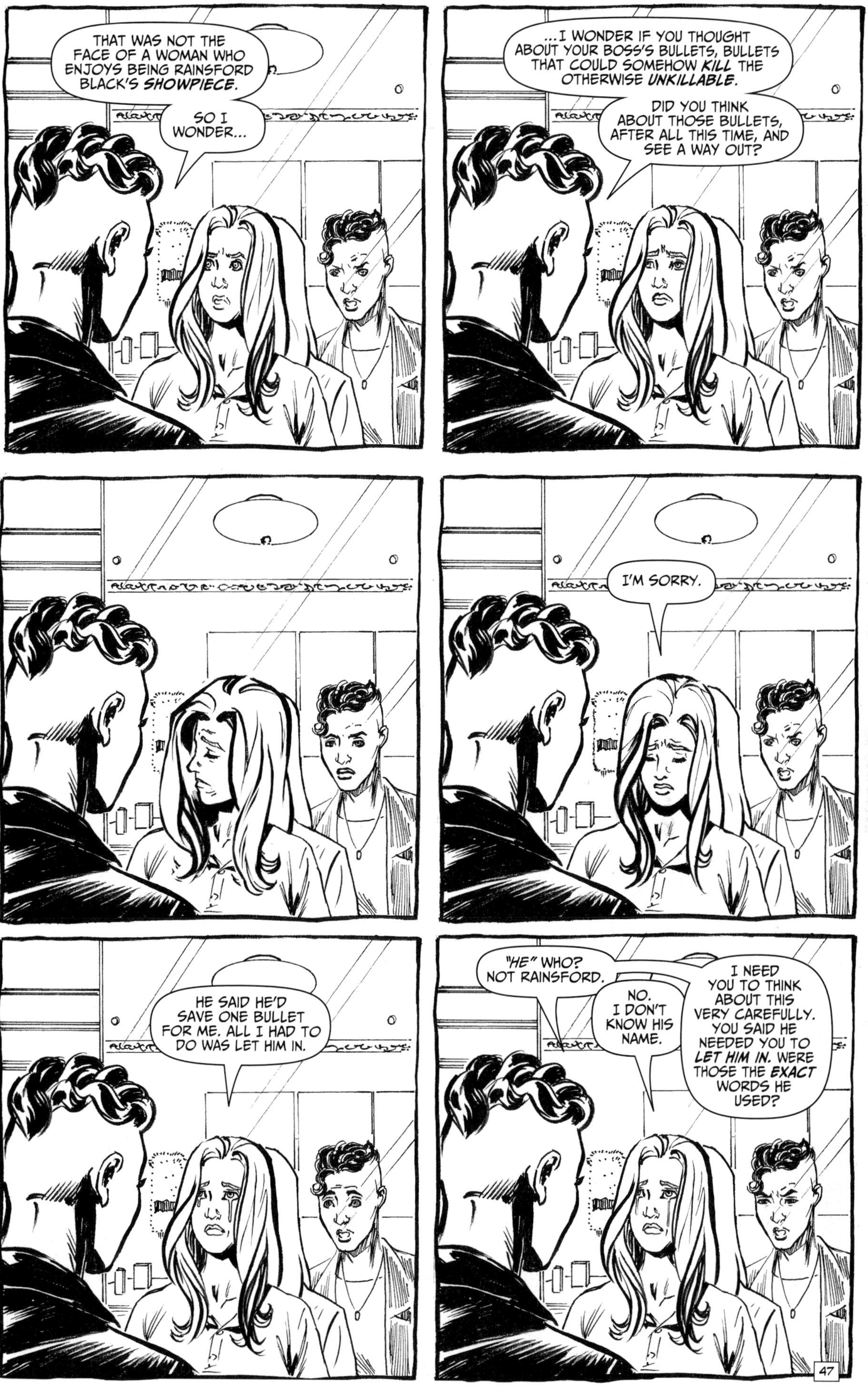
THAT WAS NOT THE FACE OF A WOMAN WHO ENJOYS BEING RAINSFORD BLACK'S SHOWPIECE.
SO I WONDER...
...I WONDER IF YOU THOUGHT ABOUT YOUR BOSS'S BULLETS, BULLETS THAT COULD SOMEHOW KILL THE OTHERWISE UNKILLABLE.
DID YOU THINK ABOUT THOSE BULLETS, AFTER ALL THIS TIME, AND SEE A WAY OUT?
I'M SORRY.
HE SAID HE'D SAVE ONE BULLET FOR ME. ALL I HAD TO DO WAS LET HIM IN.
"HE" WHO? NOT RAINSFORD.
NO. I DON'T KNOW HIS NAME.
I NEED YOU TO THINK ABOUT THIS VERY CAREFULLY. YOU SAID HE NEEDED YOU TO LET HIM IN. WERE THOSE THE EXACT WORDS HE USED?

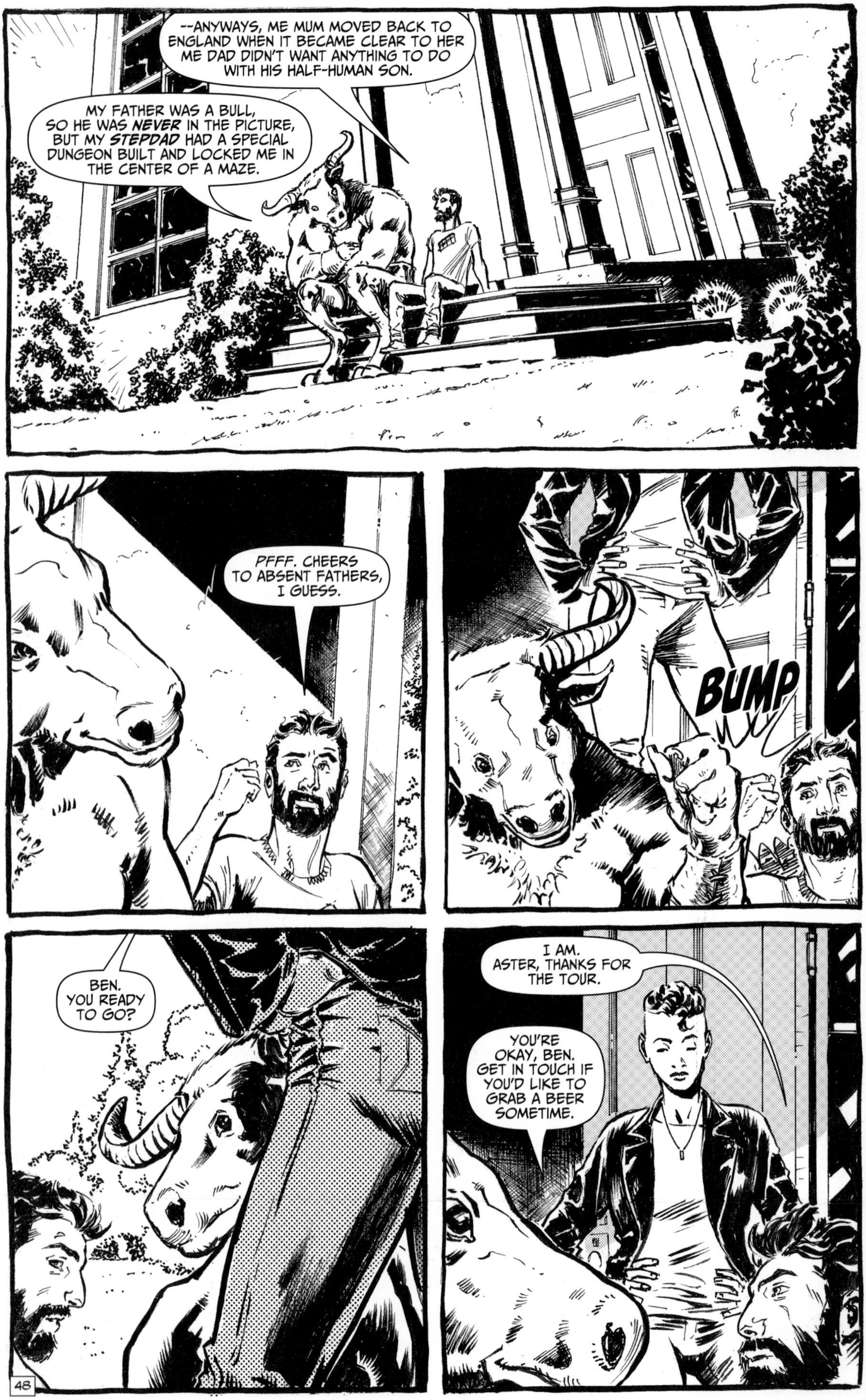
--ANYWAYS, ME MUM MOVED BACK TO ENGLAND WHEN IT BECAME CLEAR TO HER ME DAD DIDN'T WANT ANYTHING TO DO WITH HIS HALF-HUMAN SON.
MY FATHER WAS A BULL, SO HE WAS *NEVER* IN THE PICTURE, BUT MY *STEPDAD* HAD A SPECIAL DUNGEON BUILT AND LOCKED ME IN THE CENTER OF A MAZE.
PFFF. CHEERS TO ABSENT FATHERS, I GUESS.
BUMP
BEN. YOU READY TO GO?
I AM. ASTER, THANKS FOR THE TOUR.
YOU'RE OKAY, BEN. GET IN TOUCH IF YOU'D LIKE TO GRAB A BEER SOMETIME.

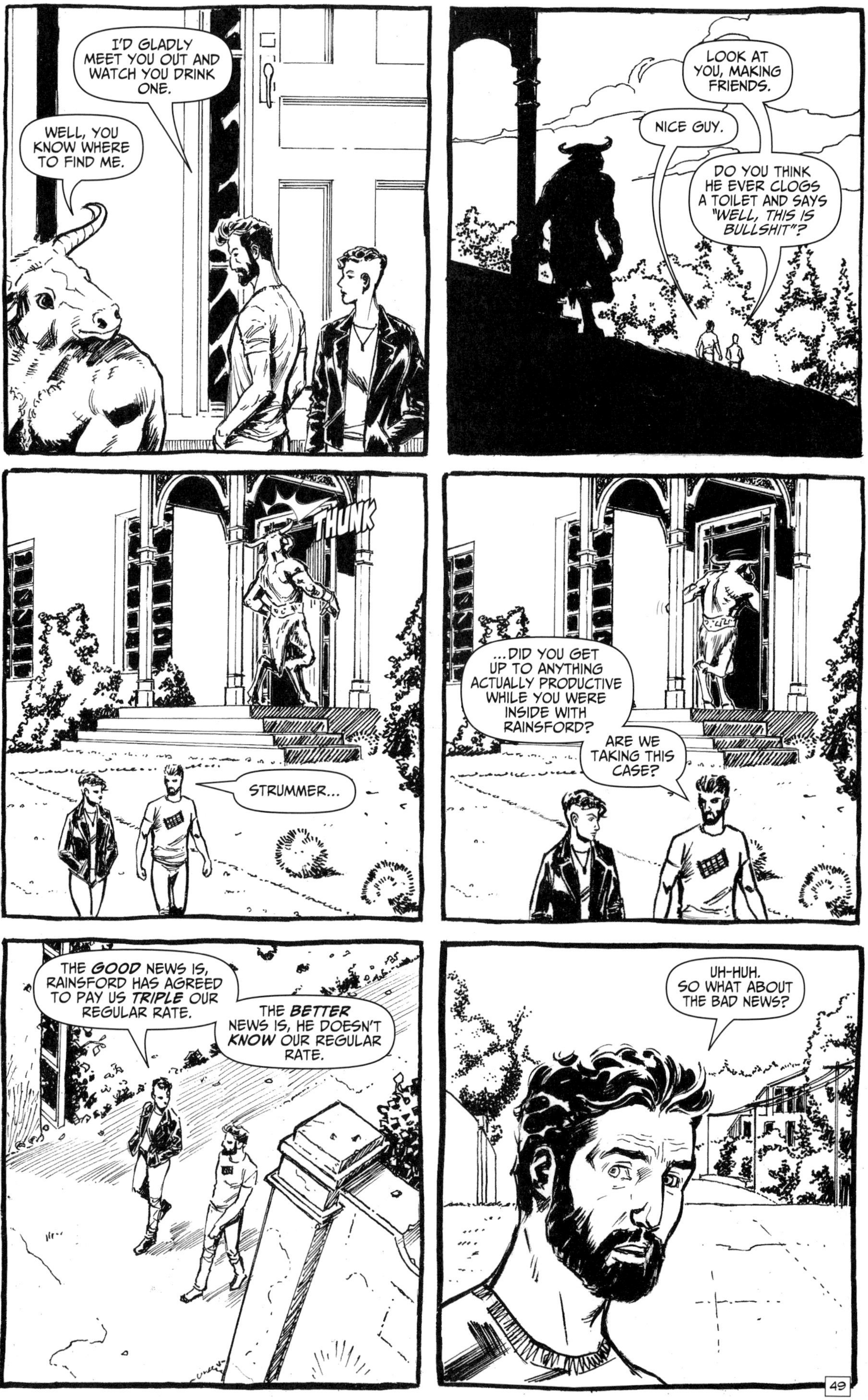
I'D GLADLY MEET YOU OUT AND WATCH YOU DRINK ONE.
WELL, YOU KNOW WHERE TO FIND ME.
LOOK AT YOU, MAKING FRIENDS.
NICE GUY.
DO YOU THINK HE EVER CLOGS A TOILET AND SAYS "WELL, THIS IS BULLSHIT"?
THUNK
STRUMMER...
...DID YOU GET UP TO ANYTHING ACTUALLY PRODUCTIVE WHILE YOU WERE INSIDE WITH RAINSFORD?
ARE WE TAKING THIS CASE?
THE GOOD NEWS IS, RAINSFORD HAS AGREED TO PAY US TRIPLE OUR REGULAR RATE.
THE BETTER NEWS IS, HE DOESN'T KNOW OUR REGULAR RATE.
UH-HUH. SO WHAT ABOUT THE BAD NEWS?

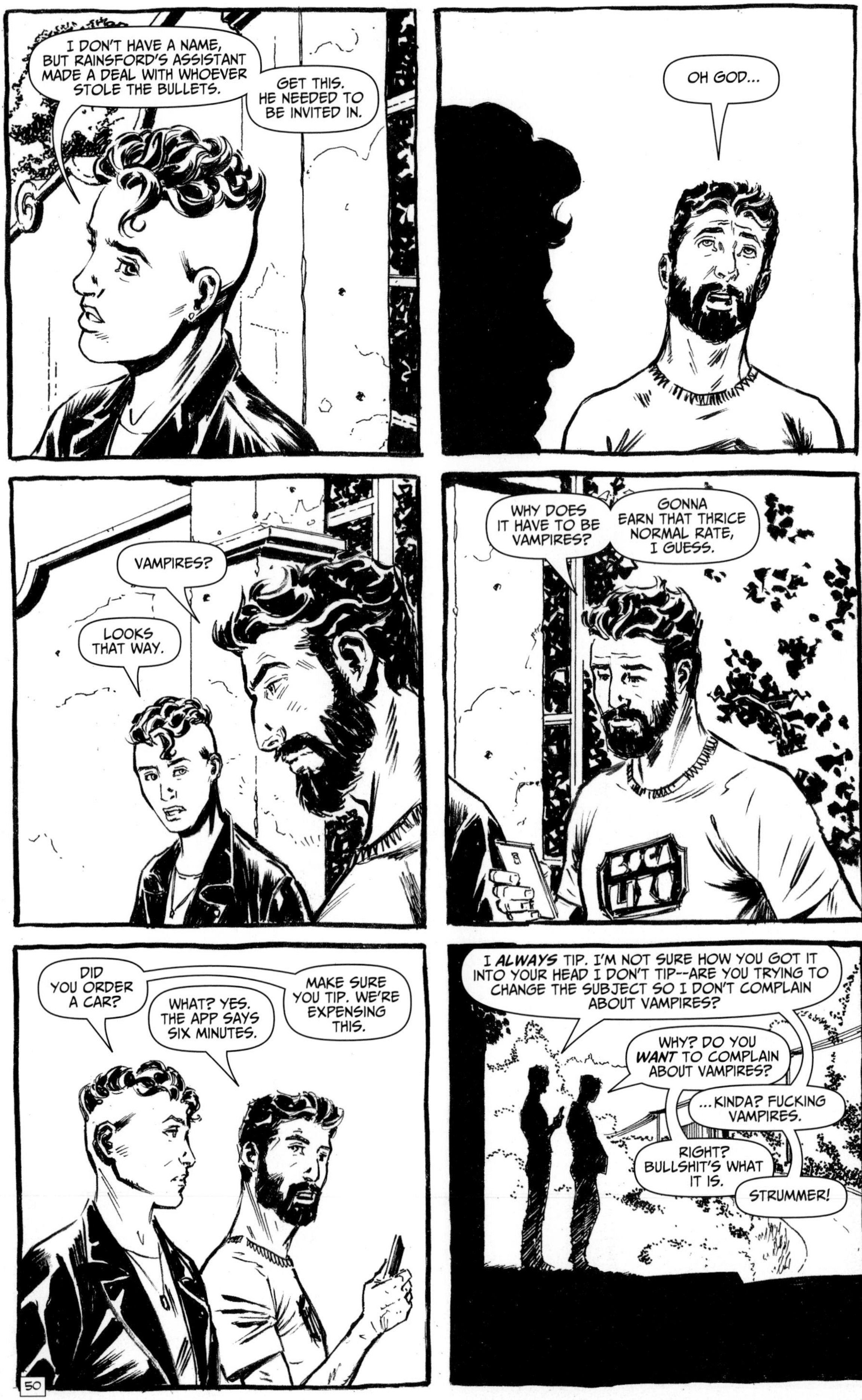
I DON'T HAVE A NAME, BUT RAINSFORD'S ASSISTANT MADE A DEAL WITH WHOEVER STOLE THE BULLETS.
GET THIS. HE NEEDED TO BE INVITED IN.
OH GOD...
VAMPIRES?
LOOKS THAT WAY.
WHY DOES IT HAVE TO BE VAMPIRES?
GONNA EARN THAT THRICE NORMAL RATE, I GUESS.
DID YOU ORDER A CAR?
WHAT? YES. THE APP SAYS SIX MINUTES.
MAKE SURE YOU TIP. WE'RE EXPENSING THIS.
I *ALWAYS* TIP. I'M NOT SURE HOW YOU GOT IT INTO YOUR HEAD I DON'T TIP--ARE YOU TRYING TO CHANGE THE SUBJECT SO I DON'T COMPLAIN ABOUT VAMPIRES?
WHY? DO YOU *WANT* TO COMPLAIN ABOUT VAMPIRES?
...KINDA? FUCKING VAMPIRES.
RIGHT? BULLSHIT'S WHAT IT IS.
STRUMMER!

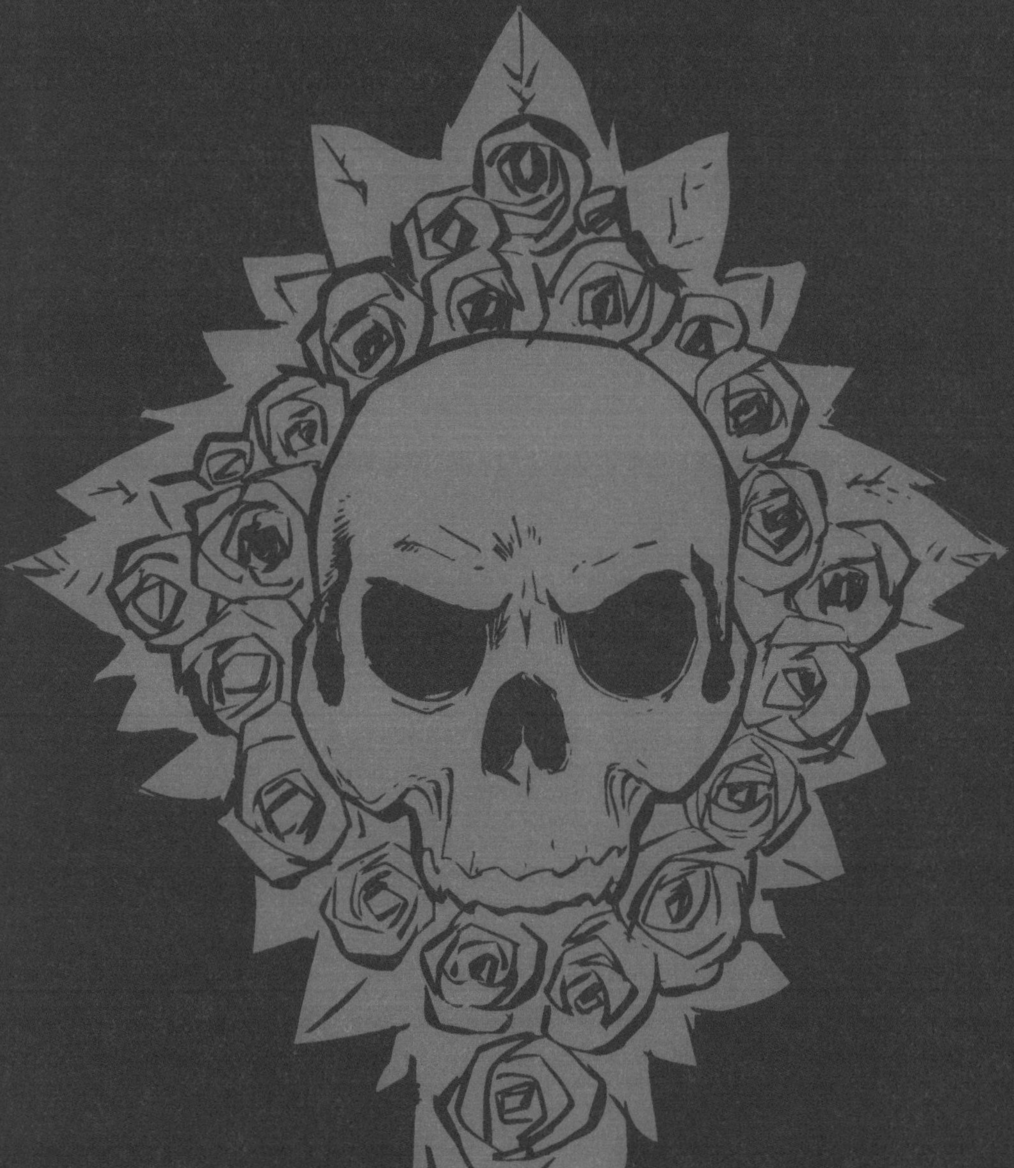

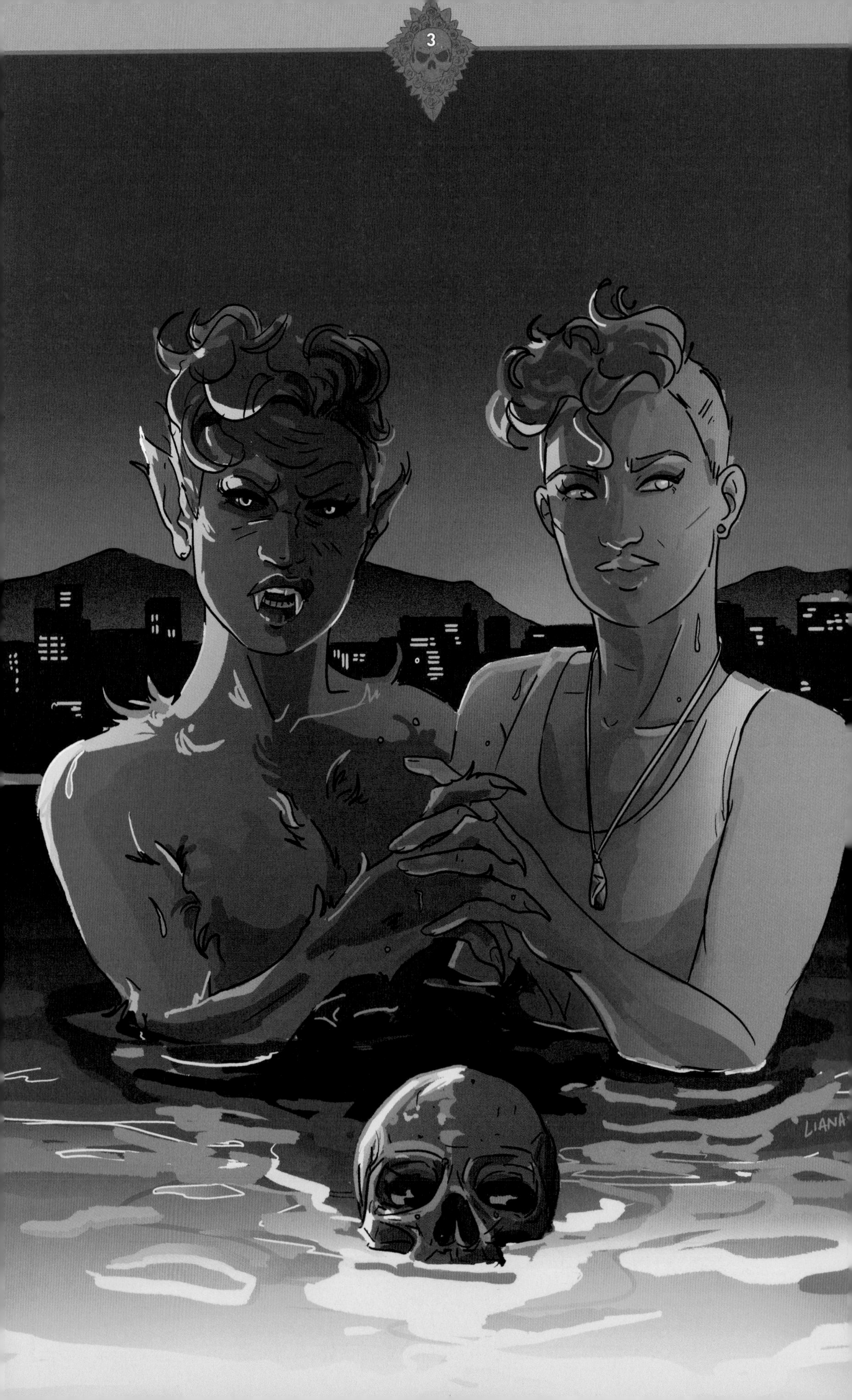
3
LIANA

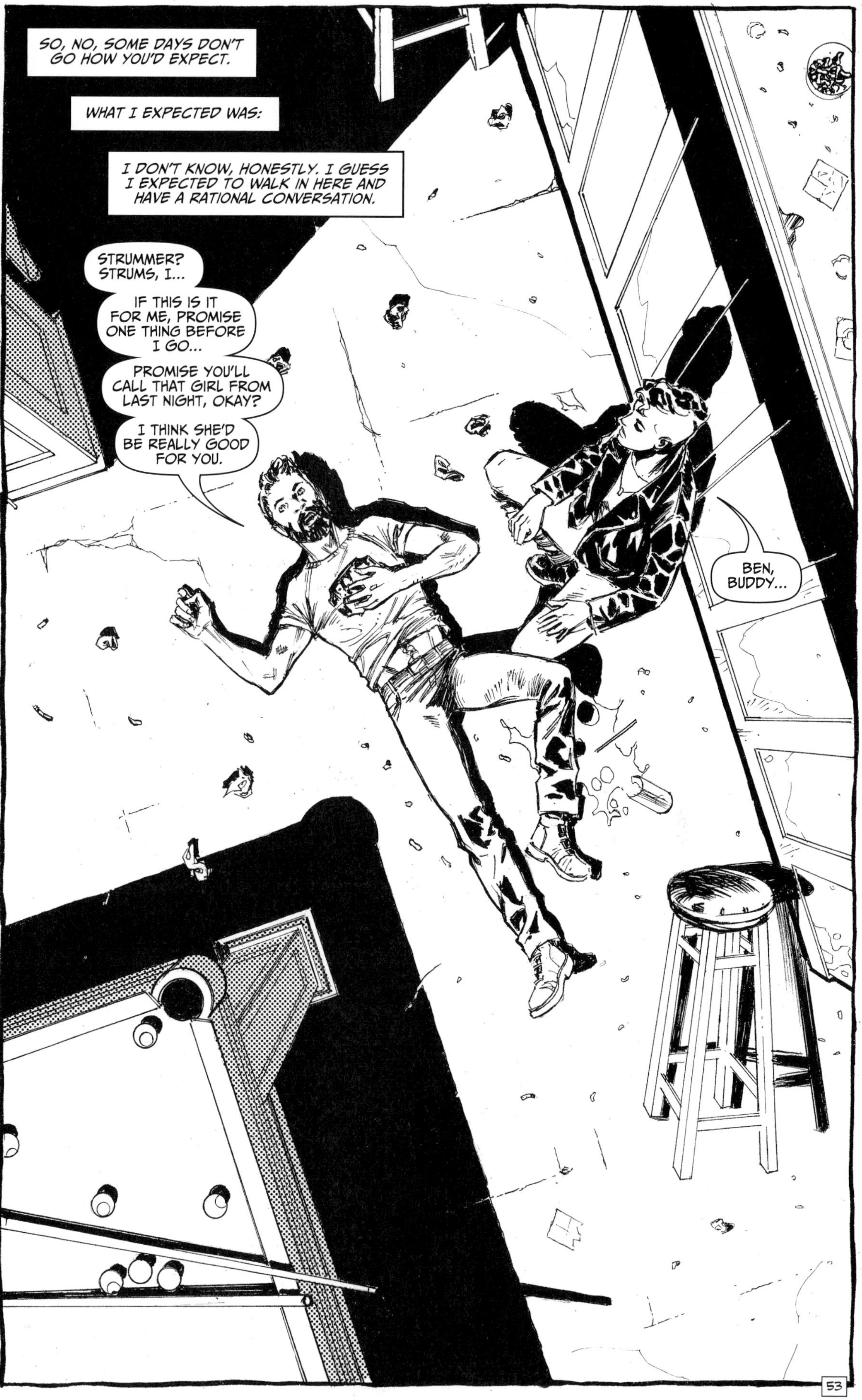
SO, NO, SOME DAYS DON'T GO HOW YOU'D EXPECT.
WHAT I EXPECTED WAS:
I DON'T KNOW, HONESTLY. I GUESS I EXPECTED TO WALK IN HERE AND HAVE A RATIONAL CONVERSATION.
STRUMMER? STRUMS, I...
IF THIS IS IT FOR ME, PROMISE ONE THING BEFORE I GO...
PROMISE YOU'LL CALL THAT GIRL FROM LAST NIGHT, OKAY?
I THINK SHE'D BE REALLY GOOD FOR YOU.
BEN, BUDDY...

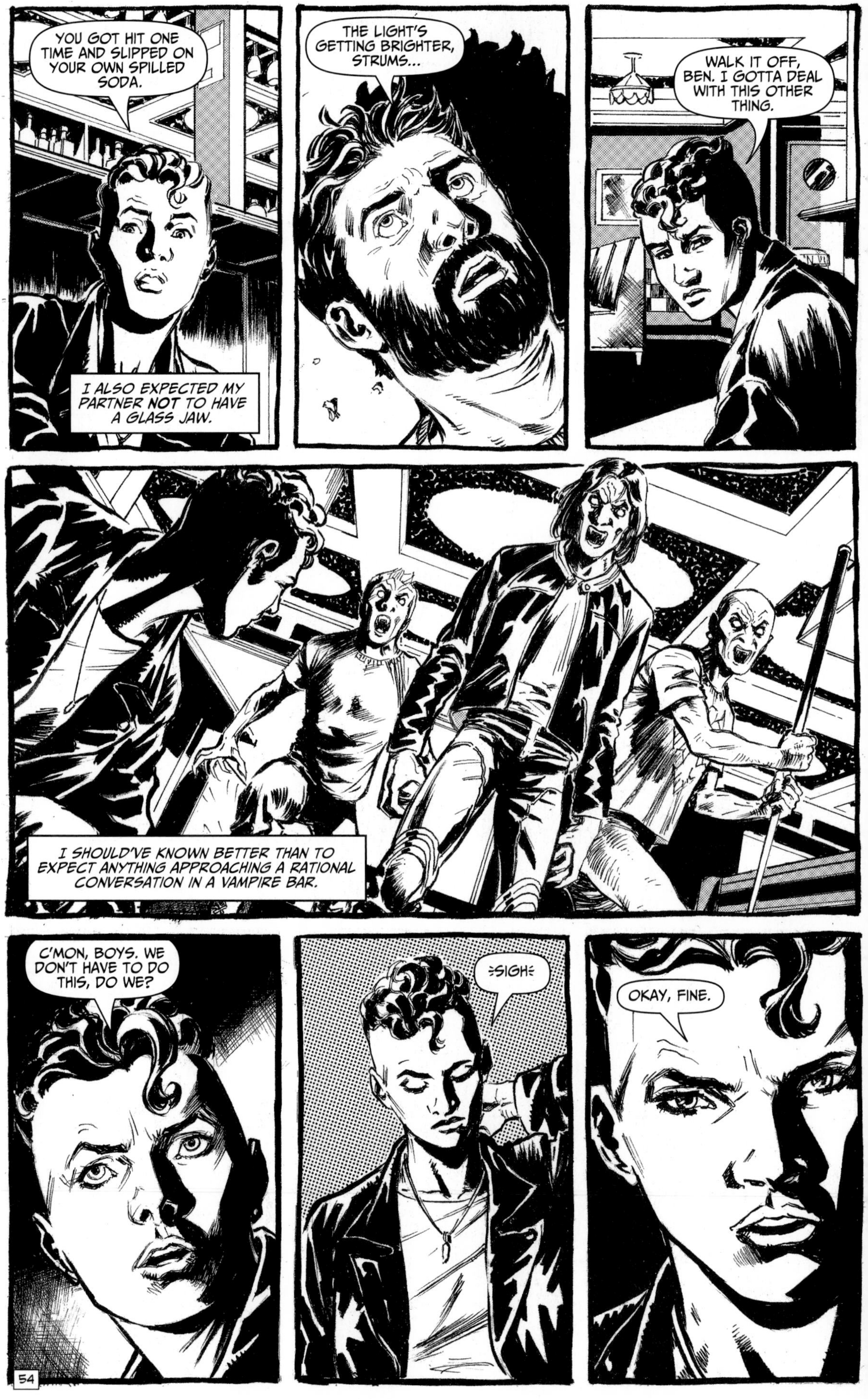
YOU GOT HIT ONE TIME AND SLIPPED ON YOUR OWN SPILLED SODA.
I ALSO EXPECTED MY PARTNER NOT TO HAVE A GLASS JAW.
THE LIGHT'S GETTING BRIGHTER, STRUMS...
WALK IT OFF, BEN. I GOTTA DEAL WITH THIS OTHER THING.
I SHOULD'VE KNOWN BETTER THAN TO EXPECT ANYTHING APPROACHING A RATIONAL CONVERSATION IN A VAMPIRE BAR.
C'MON, BOYS. WE DON'T HAVE TO DO THIS, DO WE?
SIGH
OKAY, FINE.

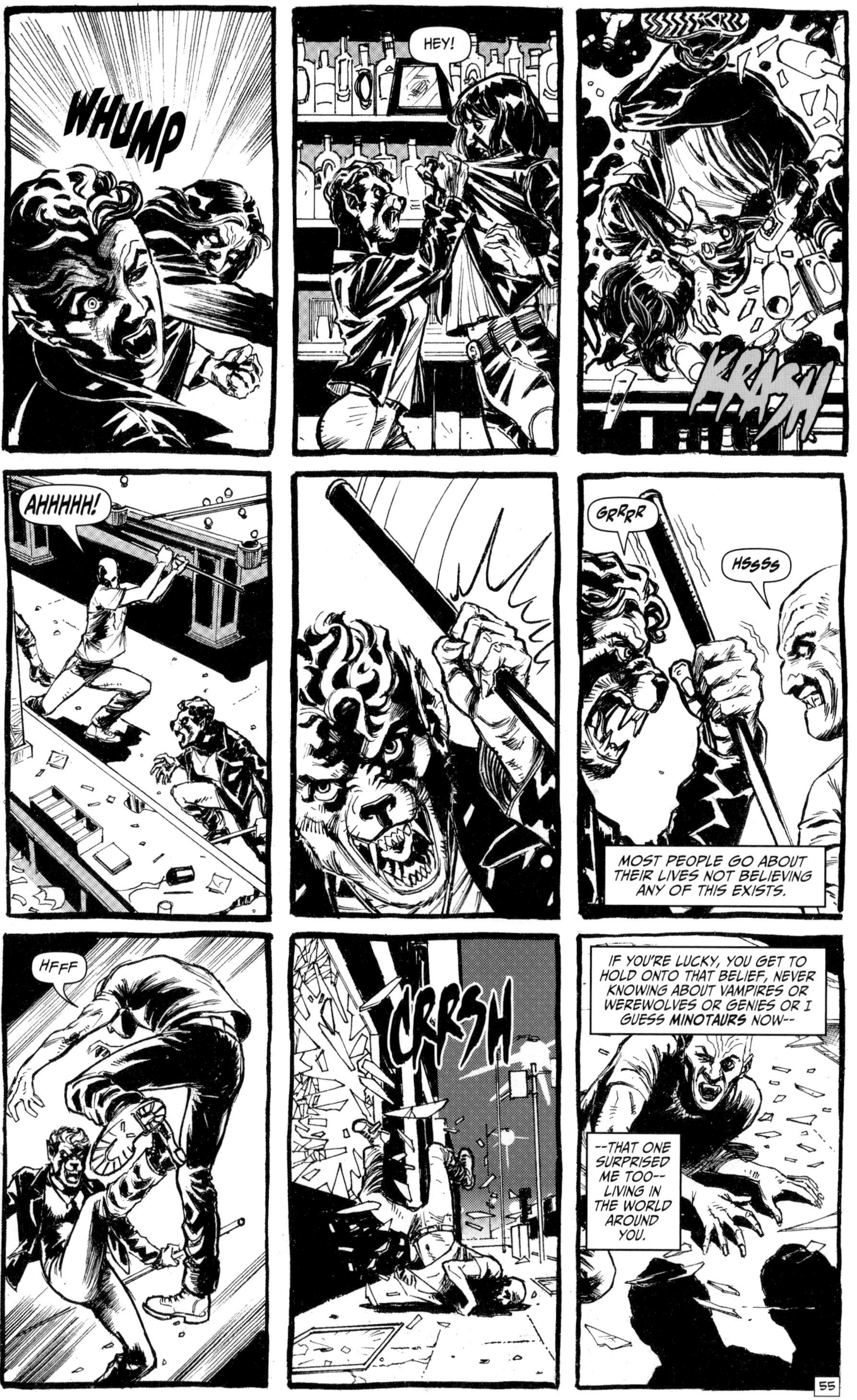
WHUMP
HEY!
KRASH
AHHHHH!
GRRRR
HSSSS
MOST PEOPLE GO ABOUT THEIR LIVES NOT BELIEVING ANY OF THIS EXISTS.
HFFF
CRRSH
IF YOU'RE LUCKY, YOU GET TO HOLD ONTO THAT BELIEF, NEVER KNOWING ABOUT VAMPIRES OR WEREWOLVES OR GENIES OR I GUESS MINOTAURS NOW--
--THAT ONE SURPRISED ME TOO--LIVING IN THE WORLD AROUND YOU.

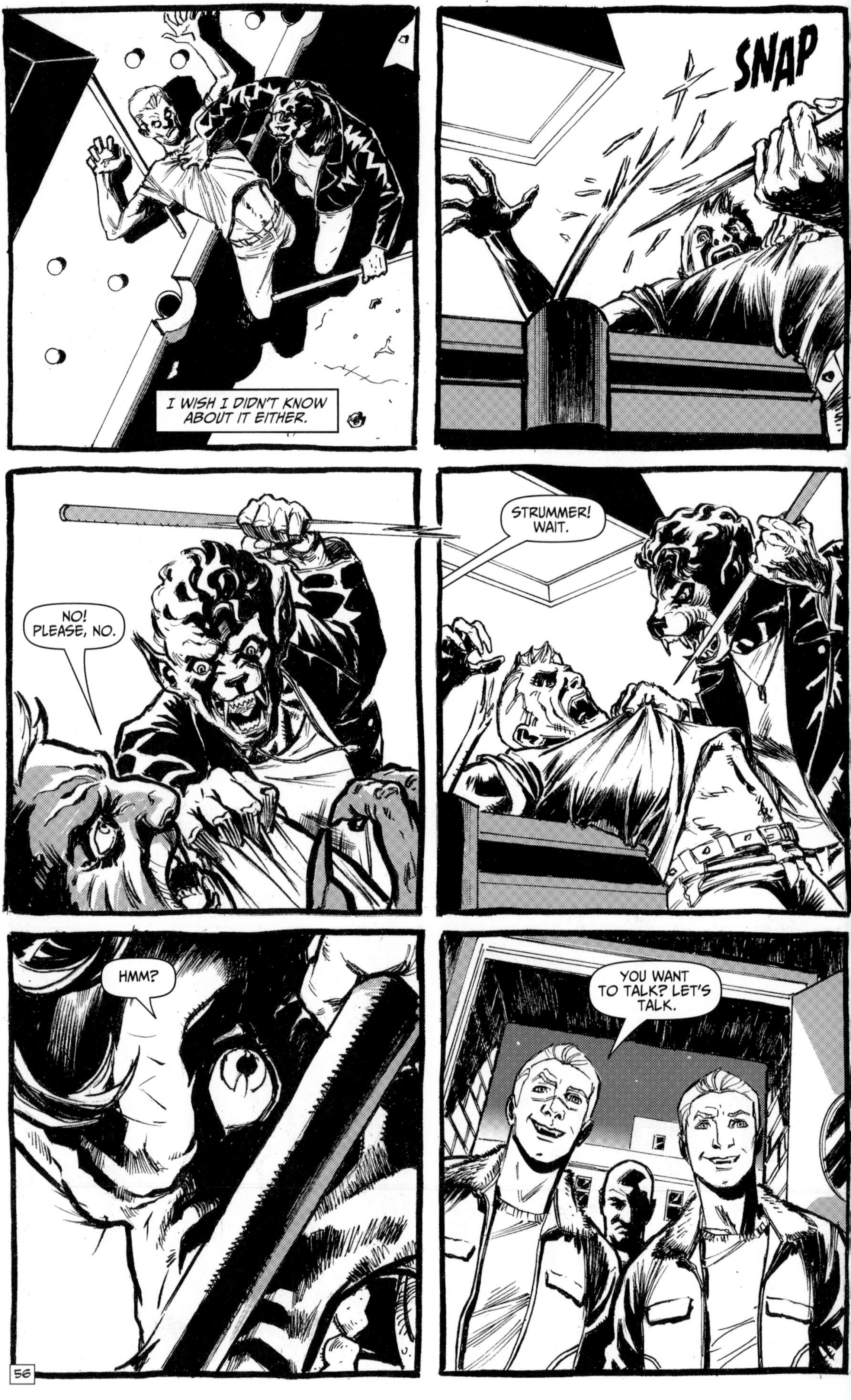
I WISH I DIDN'T KNOW ABOUT IT EITHER.
SNAP
STRUMMER! WAIT.
NO! PLEASE, NO.
HMM?
YOU WANT TO TALK? LET'S TALK.

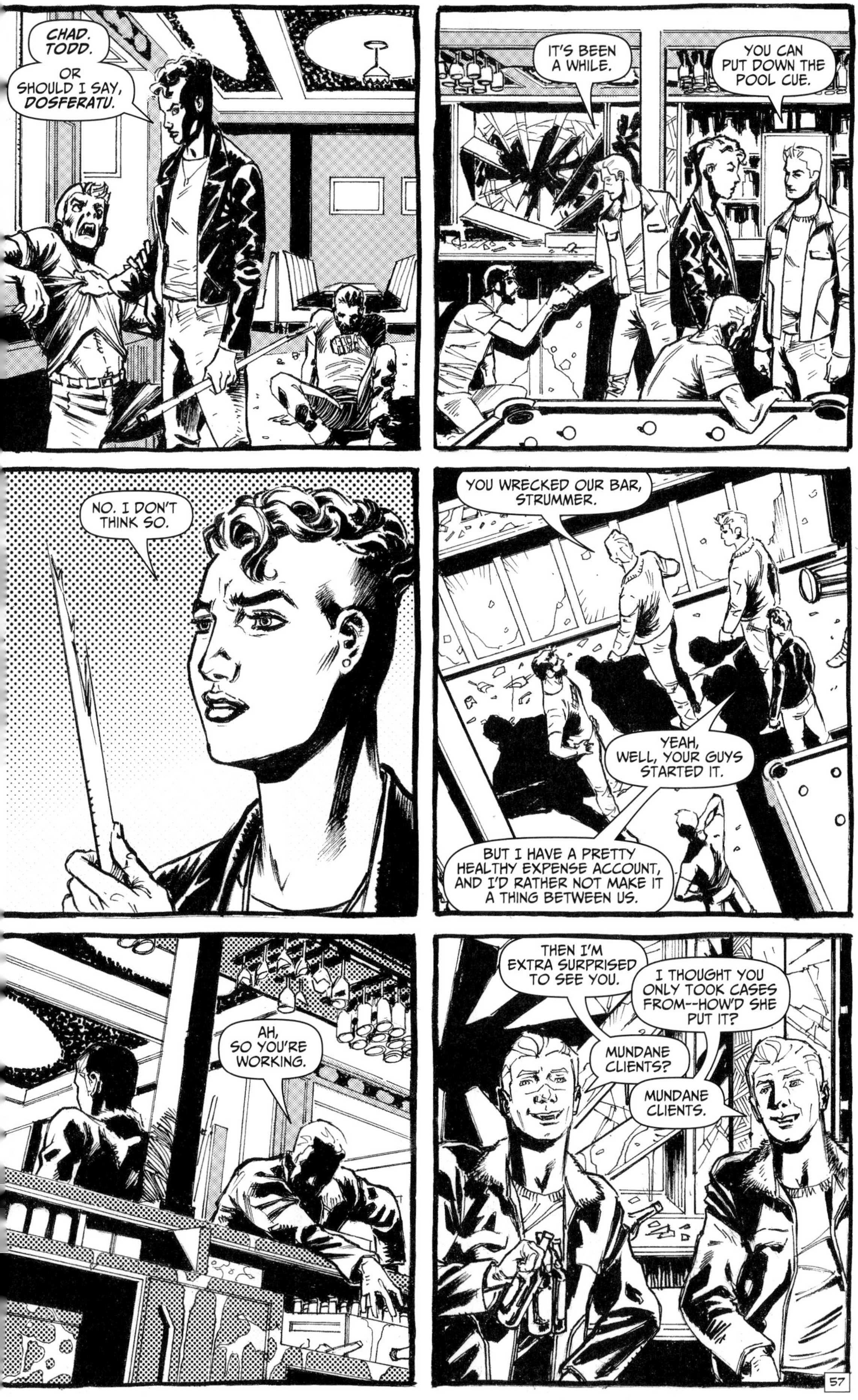
CHAD. TODD.
OR SHOULD I SAY, DOSFERATU.
IT'S BEEN A WHILE.
YOU CAN PUT DOWN THE POOL CUE.
NO. I DON'T THINK SO.
YOU WRECKED OUR BAR, STRUMMER.
YEAH, WELL, YOUR GUYS STARTED IT.
BUT I HAVE A PRETTY HEALTHY EXPENSE ACCOUNT, AND I'D RATHER NOT MAKE IT A THING BETWEEN US.
AH, SO YOU'RE WORKING.
THEN I'M EXTRA SURPRISED TO SEE YOU.
I THOUGHT YOU ONLY TOOK CASES FROM--HOW'D SHE PUT IT?
MUNDANE CLIENTS?
MUNDANE CLIENTS.

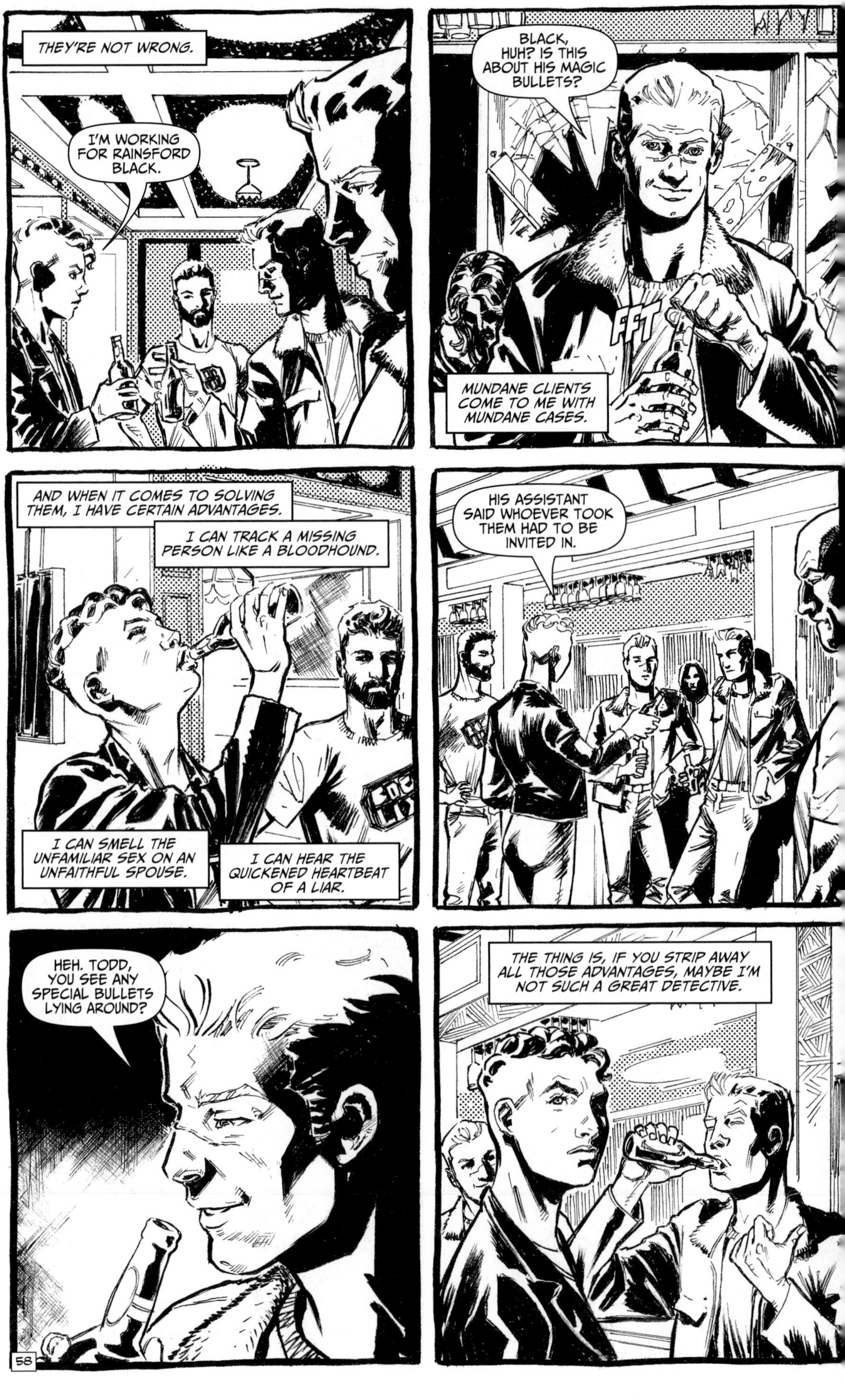

THEY'RE NOT WRONG.
I'M WORKING FOR RAINSFORD BLACK.
BLACK, HUH? IS THIS ABOUT HIS MAGIC BULLETS?
FFT
MUNDANE CLIENTS COME TO ME WITH MUNDANE CASES.
AND WHEN IT COMES TO SOLVING THEM, I HAVE CERTAIN ADVANTAGES.
I CAN TRACK A MISSING PERSON LIKE A BLOODHOUND.
I CAN SMELL THE UNFAMILIAR SEX ON AN UNFAITHFUL SPOUSE.
I CAN HEAR THE QUICKENED HEARTBEAT OF A LIAR.
HIS ASSISTANT SAID WHOEVER TOOK THEM HAD TO BE INVITED IN.
HEH. TODD, YOU SEE ANY SPECIAL BULLETS LYING AROUND?
THE THING IS, IF YOU STRIP AWAY ALL THOSE ADVANTAGES, MAYBE I'M NOT SUCH A GREAT DETECTIVE.

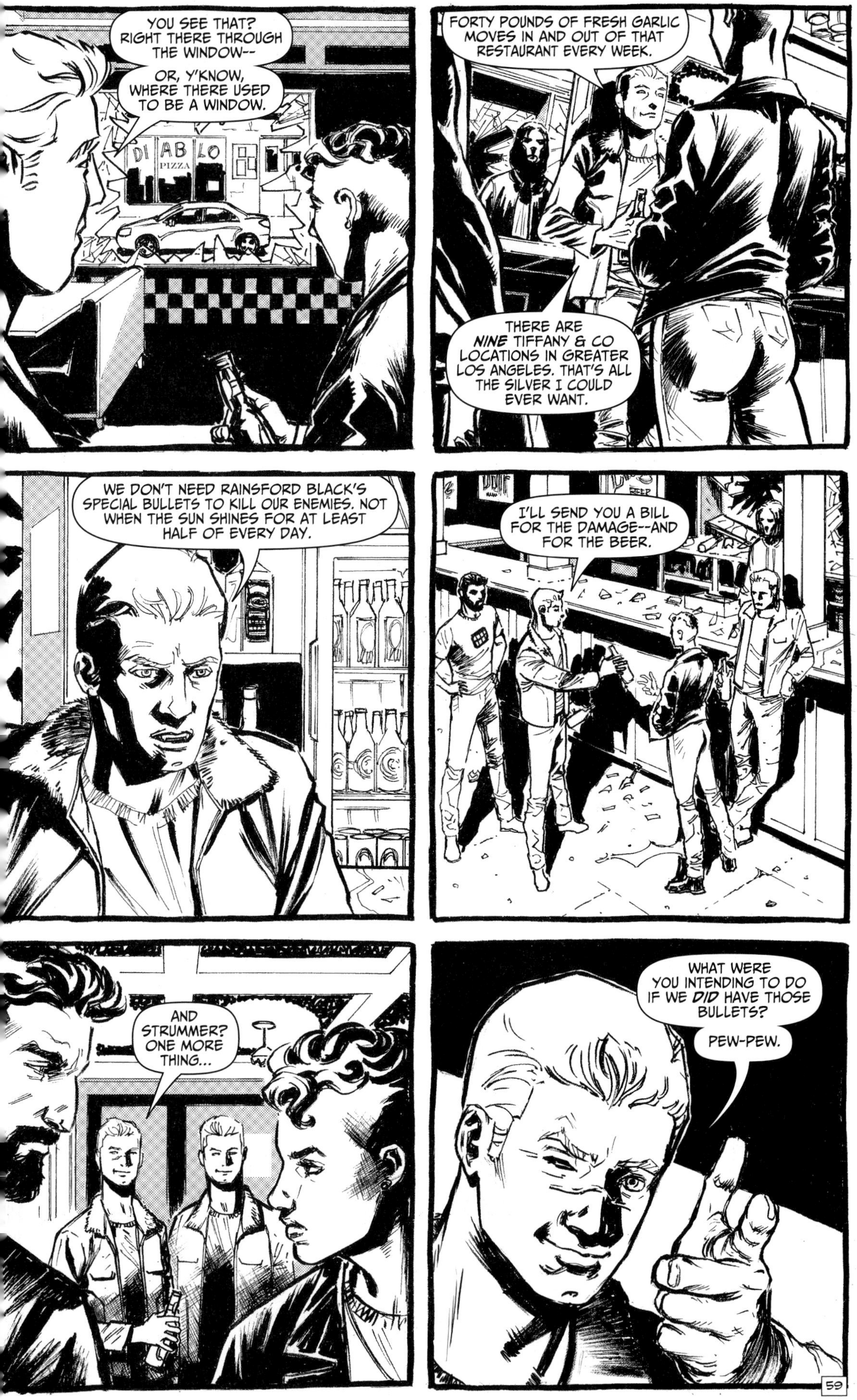
YOU SEE THAT? RIGHT THERE THROUGH THE WINDOW--
OR, Y'KNOW, WHERE THERE USED TO BE A WINDOW.
DIABLO PIZZA
FORTY POUNDS OF FRESH GARLIC MOVES IN AND OUT OF THAT RESTAURANT EVERY WEEK.
THERE ARE NINE TIFFANY & CO LOCATIONS IN GREATER LOS ANGELES. THAT'S ALL THE SILVER I COULD EVER WANT.
WE DON'T NEED RAINSFORD BLACK'S SPECIAL BULLETS TO KILL OUR ENEMIES. NOT WHEN THE SUN SHINES FOR AT LEAST HALF OF EVERY DAY.
I'LL SEND YOU A BILL FOR THE DAMAGE--AND FOR THE BEER.
AND STRUMMER? ONE MORE THING...
WHAT WERE YOU INTENDING TO DO IF WE DID HAVE THOSE BULLETS?
PEW-PEW.

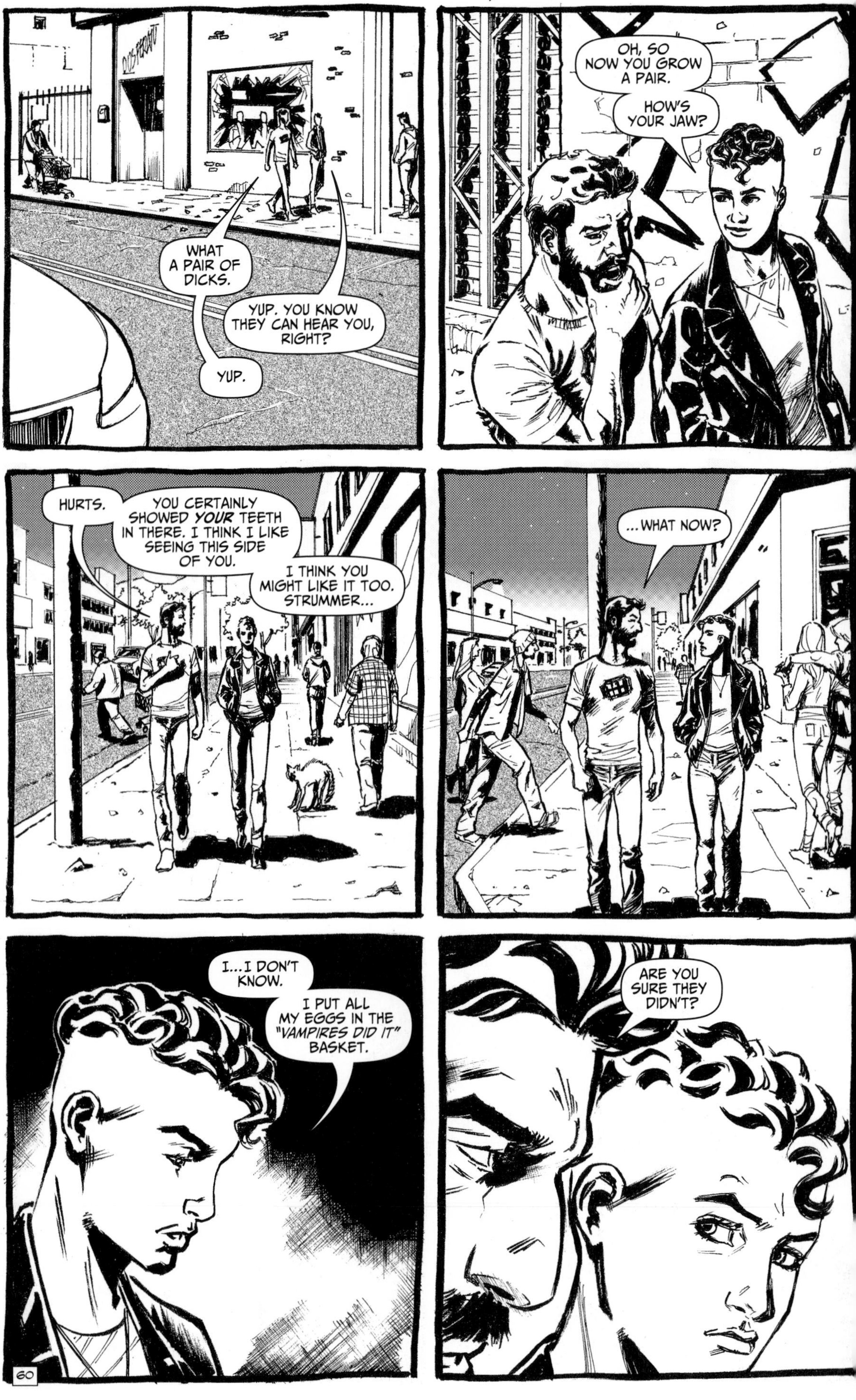
WHAT A PAIR OF DICKS.
YUP. YOU KNOW THEY CAN HEAR YOU, RIGHT?
YUP.
OH, SO NOW YOU GROW A PAIR.
HOW'S YOUR JAW?
HURTS.
YOU CERTAINLY SHOWED *YOUR* TEETH IN THERE. I THINK I LIKE SEEING THIS SIDE OF YOU.
I THINK YOU MIGHT LIKE IT TOO. STRUMMER...
...WHAT NOW?
I...I DON'T KNOW.
I PUT ALL MY EGGS IN THE *"VAMPIRES DID IT"* BASKET.
ARE YOU SURE THEY DIDN'T?

NAH. VAMPIRES ARE KNOWN FOR A LOT OF THINGS, BUT GUILE ISN'T ONE OF THEM.

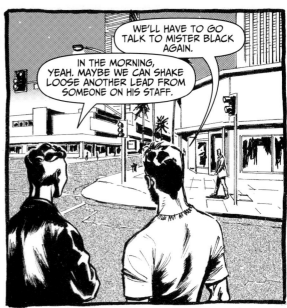

WE'LL HAVE TO GO TALK TO MISTER BLACK AGAIN.

IN THE MORNING, YEAH. MAYBE WE CAN SHAKE LOOSE ANOTHER LEAD FROM SOMEONE ON HIS STAFF.

WE COULD ALWAYS GO SEE THE OLD MAN--HEY!

WHAT THE HELL, MAN! SLOW DOWN AND WATCH WHERE YOU'RE BLOODY GOING!

BEN...

WE ARE NOT GOING TO SEE THE OLD MAN.

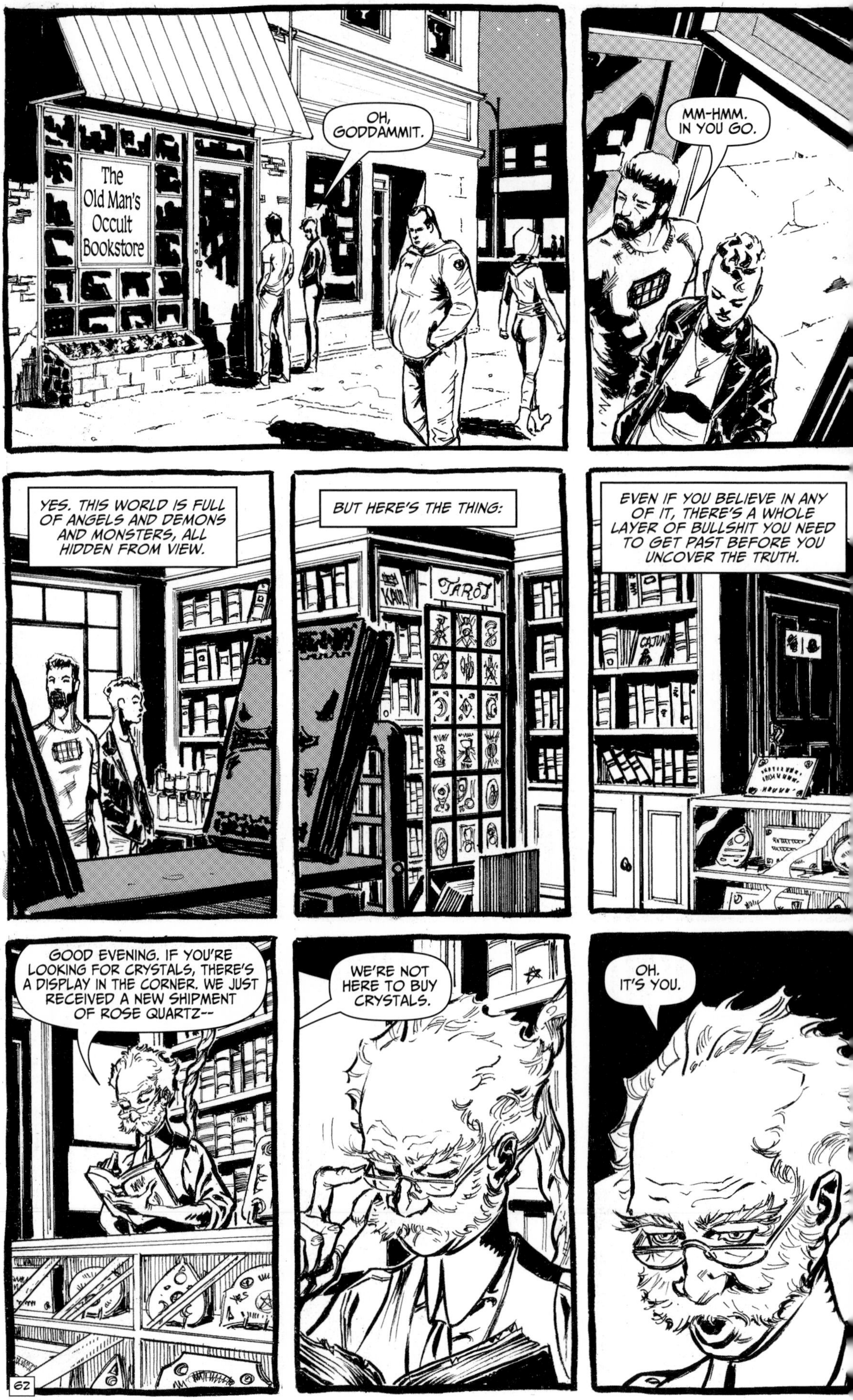
The Old Man's Occult Bookstore
OH, GODDAMMIT.
MM-HMM. IN YOU GO.
YES. THIS WORLD IS FULL OF ANGELS AND DEMONS AND MONSTERS, ALL HIDDEN FROM VIEW.
BUT HERE'S THE THING:
TAROT
EVEN IF YOU BELIEVE IN ANY OF IT, THERE'S A WHOLE LAYER OF BULLSHIT YOU NEED TO GET PAST BEFORE YOU UNCOVER THE TRUTH.
GOOD EVENING. IF YOU'RE LOOKING FOR CRYSTALS, THERE'S A DISPLAY IN THE CORNER. WE JUST RECEIVED A NEW SHIPMENT OF ROSE QUARTZ--
WE'RE NOT HERE TO BUY CRYSTALS.
OH. IT'S YOU.

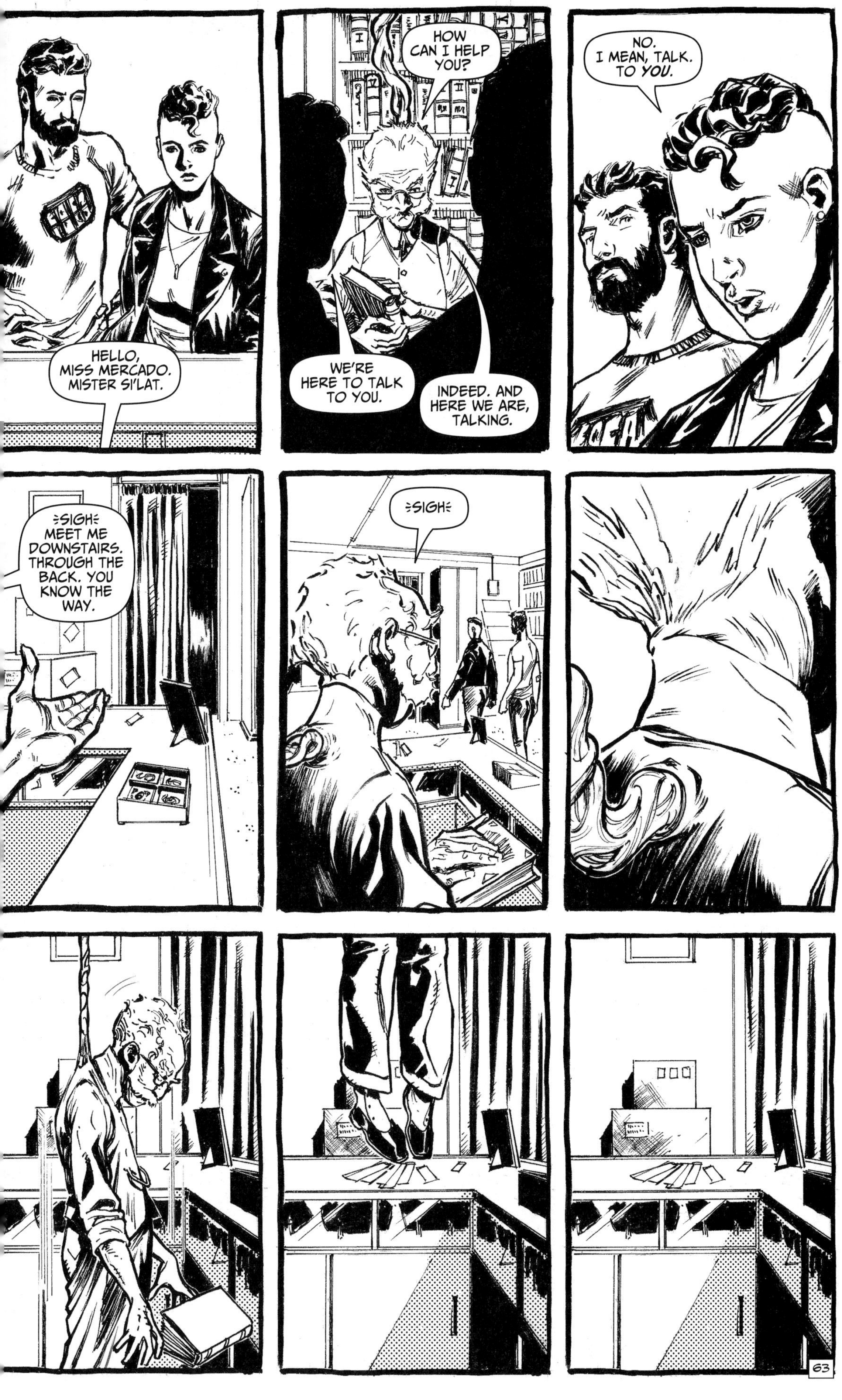
HELLO,
MISS MERCADO.
MISTER SI'LAT.
HOW CAN I HELP YOU?
WE'RE HERE TO TALK TO YOU.
INDEED. AND HERE WE ARE, TALKING.
NO. I MEAN, TALK. TO *YOU*.
≈SIGH≈ MEET ME DOWNSTAIRS. THROUGH THE BACK. YOU KNOW THE WAY.
≈SIGH≈

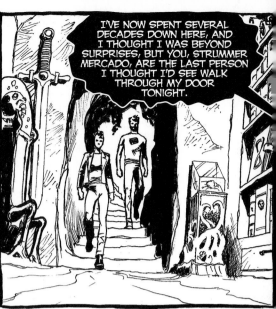

I'VE NOW SPENT SEVERAL DECADES DOWN HERE, AND I THOUGHT I WAS BEYOND SURPRISES, BUT YOU, STRUMMER MERCADO, ARE THE LAST PERSON I THOUGHT I'D SEE WALK THROUGH MY DOOR TONIGHT.

HIS TRUE NAME IS THE STUFF OF NIGHTMARES, SO TO US, HE'S JUST:

HELLO, OLD MAN. IT'S NICE TO SEE YOU AGAIN, TOO.

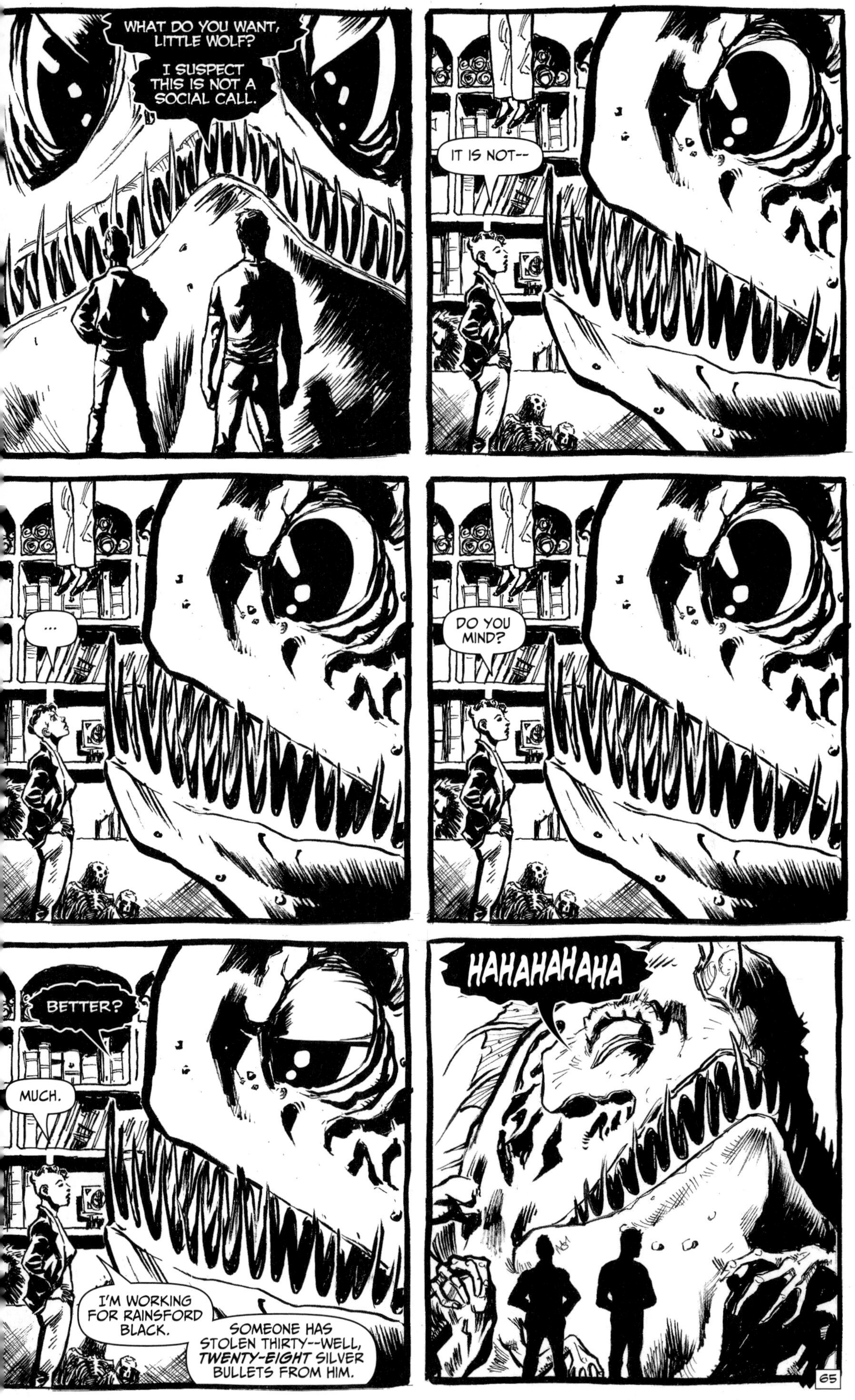
WHAT DO YOU WANT, LITTLE WOLF?
I SUSPECT THIS IS NOT A SOCIAL CALL.
IT IS NOT--
...
DO YOU MIND?
BETTER?
MUCH.
I'M WORKING FOR RAINSFORD BLACK.
SOMEONE HAS STOLEN THIRTY--WELL, *TWENTY-EIGHT* SILVER BULLETS FROM HIM.
HAHAHAHAHA

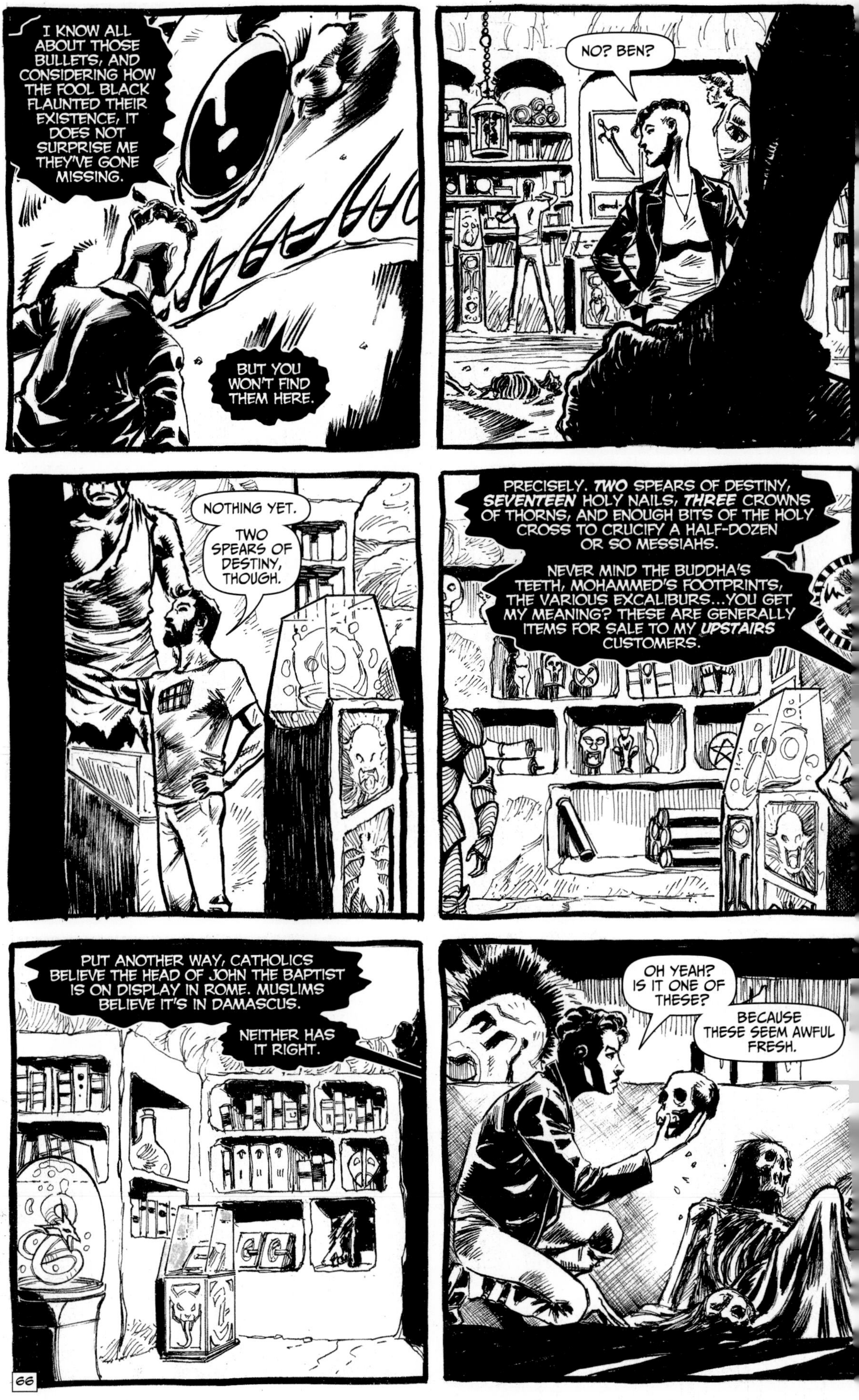
I KNOW ALL ABOUT THOSE BULLETS, AND CONSIDERING HOW THE FOOL BLACK FLAUNTED THEIR EXISTENCE, IT DOES NOT SURPRISE ME THEY'VE GONE MISSING.
BUT YOU WON'T FIND THEM HERE.
NO? BEN?
NOTHING YET.
TWO SPEARS OF DESTINY, THOUGH.
PRECISELY. TWO SPEARS OF DESTINY, SEVENTEEN HOLY NAILS, THREE CROWNS OF THORNS, AND ENOUGH BITS OF THE HOLY CROSS TO CRUCIFY A HALF-DOZEN OR SO MESSIAHS.
NEVER MIND THE BUDDHA'S TEETH, MOHAMMED'S FOOTPRINTS, THE VARIOUS EXCALIBURS...YOU GET MY MEANING? THESE ARE GENERALLY ITEMS FOR SALE TO MY UPSTAIRS CUSTOMERS.
PUT ANOTHER WAY, CATHOLICS BELIEVE THE HEAD OF JOHN THE BAPTIST IS ON DISPLAY IN ROME. MUSLIMS BELIEVE IT'S IN DAMASCUS.
NEITHER HAS IT RIGHT.
OH YEAH? IS IT ONE OF THESE?
BECAUSE THESE SEEM AWFUL FRESH.

I AM WHAT I AM, LITTLE WOLF.

SPEAKING OF, I'VE SEEN THE PAPERS. I KNOW IT WAS YOU WHO KILLED THAT MAN.

≡SIGH≡

IF YOU DON'T HAVE THE BULLETS, ANY IDEA WHO MIGHT?

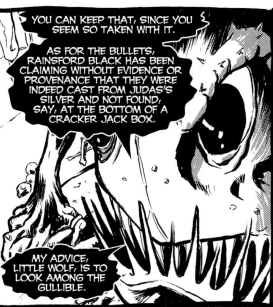

YOU CAN KEEP THAT, SINCE YOU SEEM SO TAKEN WITH IT.

AS FOR THE BULLETS, RAINSFORD BLACK HAS BEEN CLAIMING WITHOUT EVIDENCE OR PROVENANCE THAT THEY WERE INDEED CAST FROM JUDAS'S SILVER AND NOT FOUND, SAY, AT THE BOTTOM OF A CRACKER JACK BOX.

MY ADVICE, LITTLE WOLF, IS TO LOOK AMONG THE GULLIBLE.

THAT DOESN'T NARROW THE POSSIBILITIES MUCH, BUT THANK YOU.

GOOD NIGHT, STRUMMER. BEN.

I HOPE YOU'LL VISIT US AGAIN SOONER RATHER THAN LATER.

GOODBYE, OLD MAN.

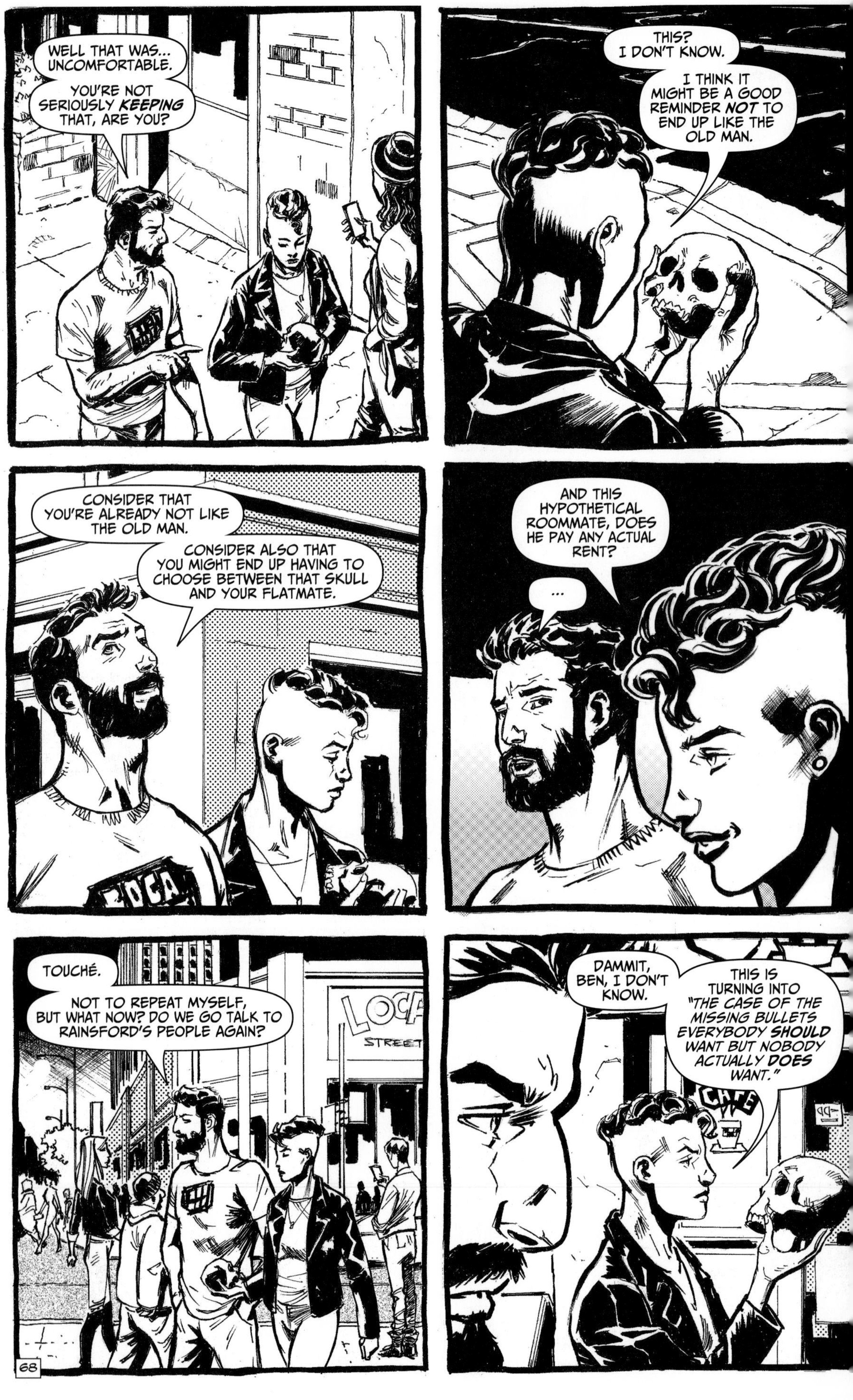
WELL THAT WAS... UNCOMFORTABLE.
YOU'RE NOT SERIOUSLY **KEEPING** THAT, ARE YOU?
THIS? I DON'T KNOW.
I THINK IT MIGHT BE A GOOD REMINDER **NOT** TO END UP LIKE THE OLD MAN.
CONSIDER THAT YOU'RE ALREADY NOT LIKE THE OLD MAN.
CONSIDER ALSO THAT YOU MIGHT END UP HAVING TO CHOOSE BETWEEN THAT SKULL AND YOUR FLATMATE.
AND THIS HYPOTHETICAL ROOMMATE, DOES HE PAY ANY ACTUAL RENT?
...
TOUCHÉ.
NOT TO REPEAT MYSELF, BUT WHAT NOW? DO WE GO TALK TO RAINSFORD'S PEOPLE AGAIN?
STREET
DAMMIT, BEN, I DON'T KNOW.
THIS IS TURNING INTO *"THE CASE OF THE MISSING BULLETS EVERYBODY **SHOULD** WANT BUT NOBODY ACTUALLY **DOES** WANT."*
CAFE

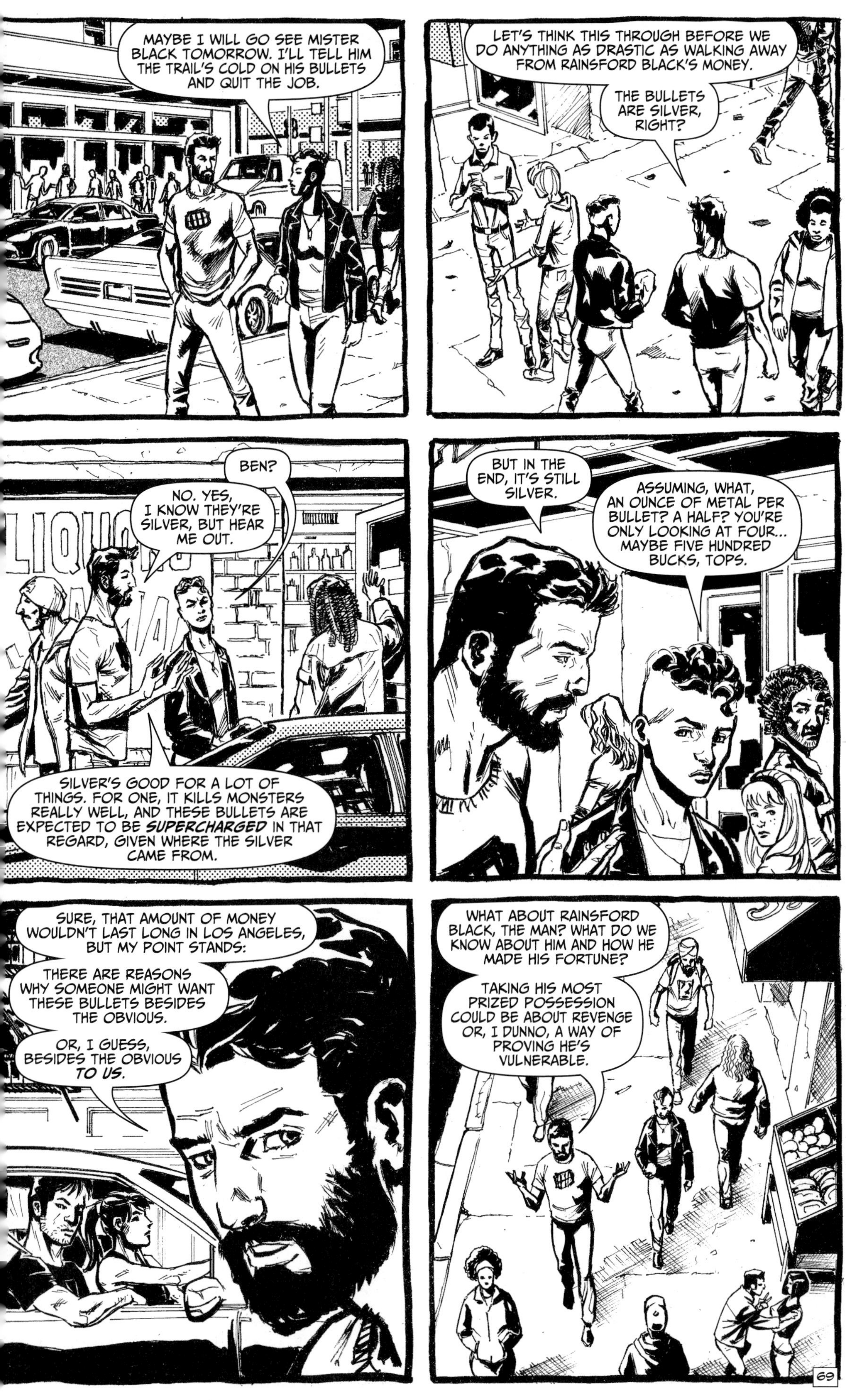
MAYBE I WILL GO SEE MISTER BLACK TOMORROW. I'LL TELL HIM THE TRAIL'S COLD ON HIS BULLETS AND QUIT THE JOB.
LET'S THINK THIS THROUGH BEFORE WE DO ANYTHING AS DRASTIC AS WALKING AWAY FROM RAINSFORD BLACK'S MONEY.
THE BULLETS ARE SILVER, RIGHT?
BEN?
NO. YES, I KNOW THEY'RE SILVER, BUT HEAR ME OUT.
SILVER'S GOOD FOR A LOT OF THINGS. FOR ONE, IT KILLS MONSTERS REALLY WELL, AND THESE BULLETS ARE EXPECTED TO BE ***SUPERCHARGED*** IN THAT REGARD, GIVEN WHERE THE SILVER CAME FROM.
BUT IN THE END, IT'S STILL SILVER.
ASSUMING, WHAT, AN OUNCE OF METAL PER BULLET? A HALF? YOU'RE ONLY LOOKING AT FOUR... MAYBE FIVE HUNDRED BUCKS, TOPS.
SURE, THAT AMOUNT OF MONEY WOULDN'T LAST LONG IN LOS ANGELES, BUT MY POINT STANDS:
THERE ARE REASONS WHY SOMEONE MIGHT WANT THESE BULLETS BESIDES THE OBVIOUS.
OR, I GUESS, BESIDES THE OBVIOUS ***TO US***.
WHAT ABOUT RAINSFORD BLACK, THE MAN? WHAT DO WE KNOW ABOUT HIM AND HOW HE MADE HIS FORTUNE?
TAKING HIS MOST PRIZED POSSESSION COULD BE ABOUT REVENGE OR, I DUNNO, A WAY OF PROVING HE'S VULNERABLE.

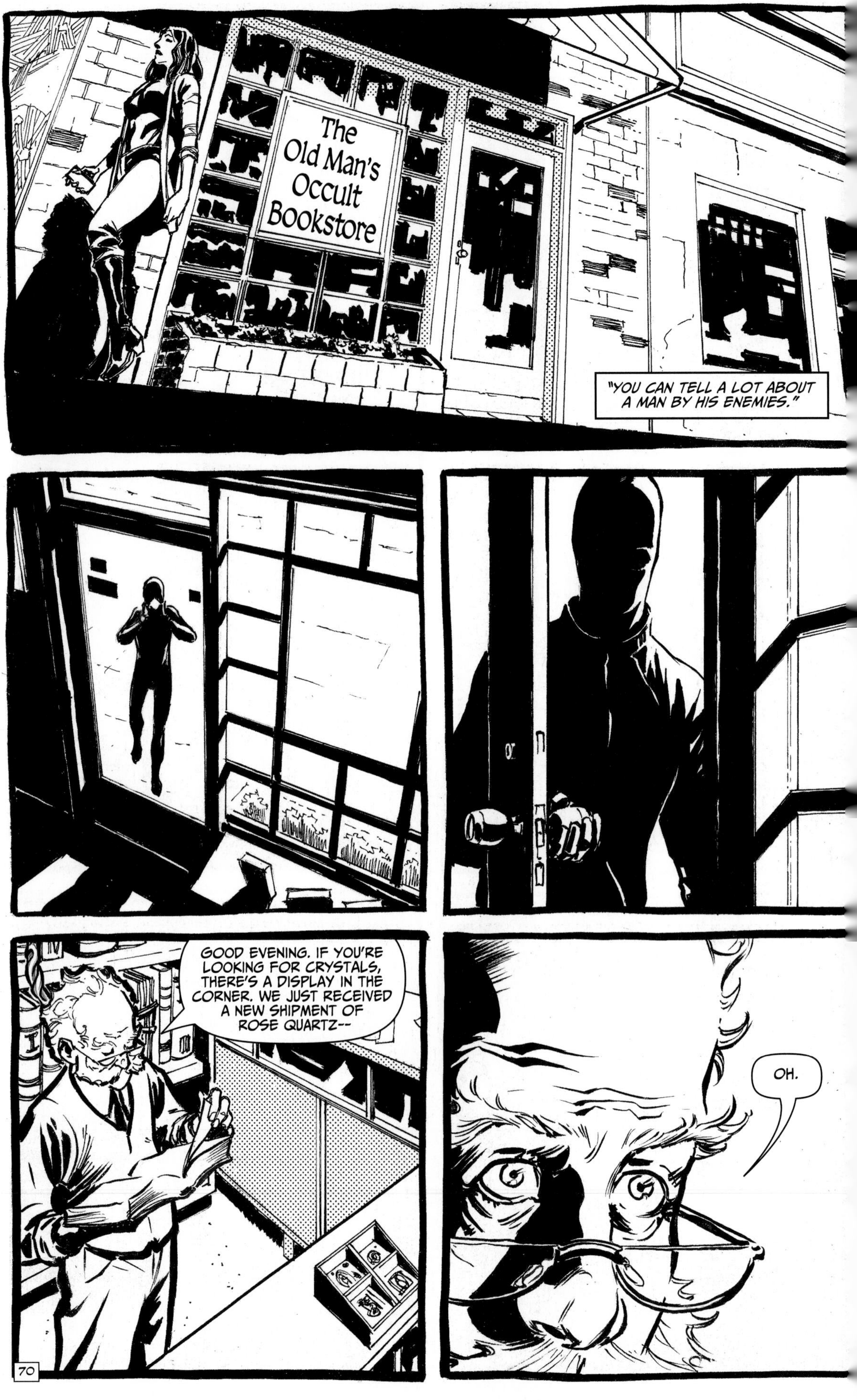
The Old Man's Occult Bookstore
"YOU CAN TELL A LOT ABOUT A MAN BY HIS ENEMIES."
GOOD EVENING. IF YOU'RE LOOKING FOR CRYSTALS, THERE'S A DISPLAY IN THE CORNER. WE JUST RECEIVED A NEW SHIPMENT OF ROSE QUARTZ--
OH.

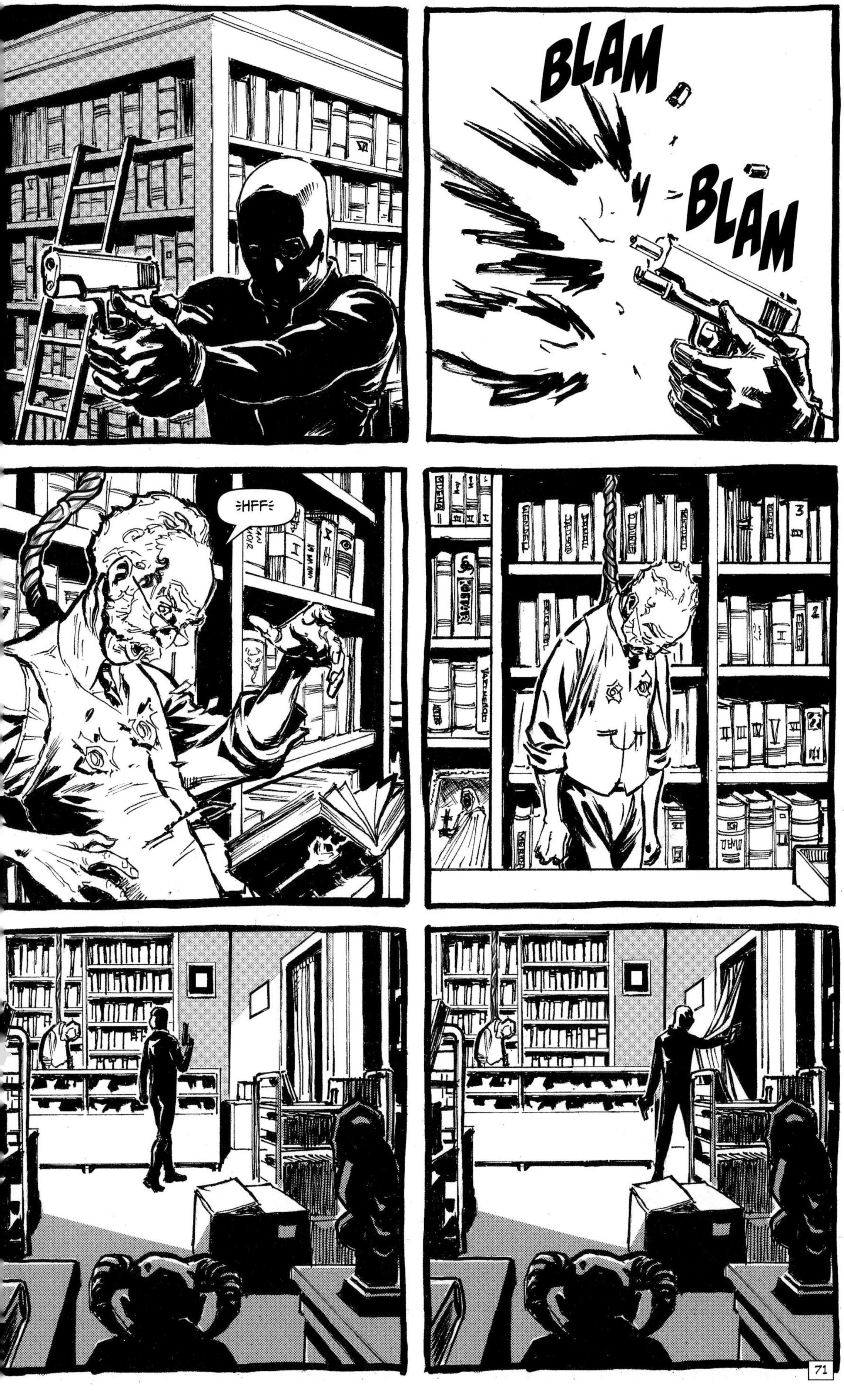
BLAM
BLAM
HFF

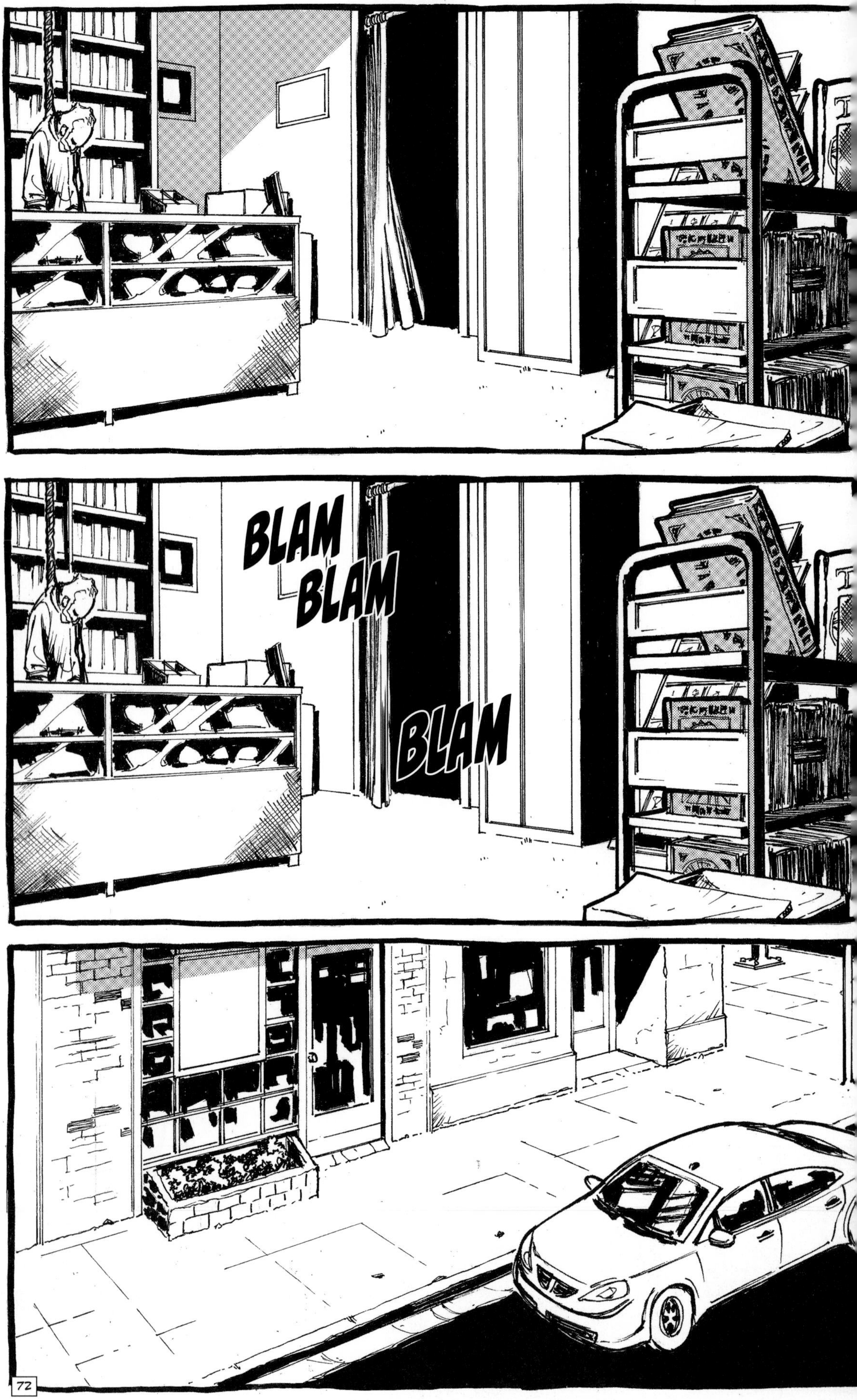
BLAM
BLAM
BLAM

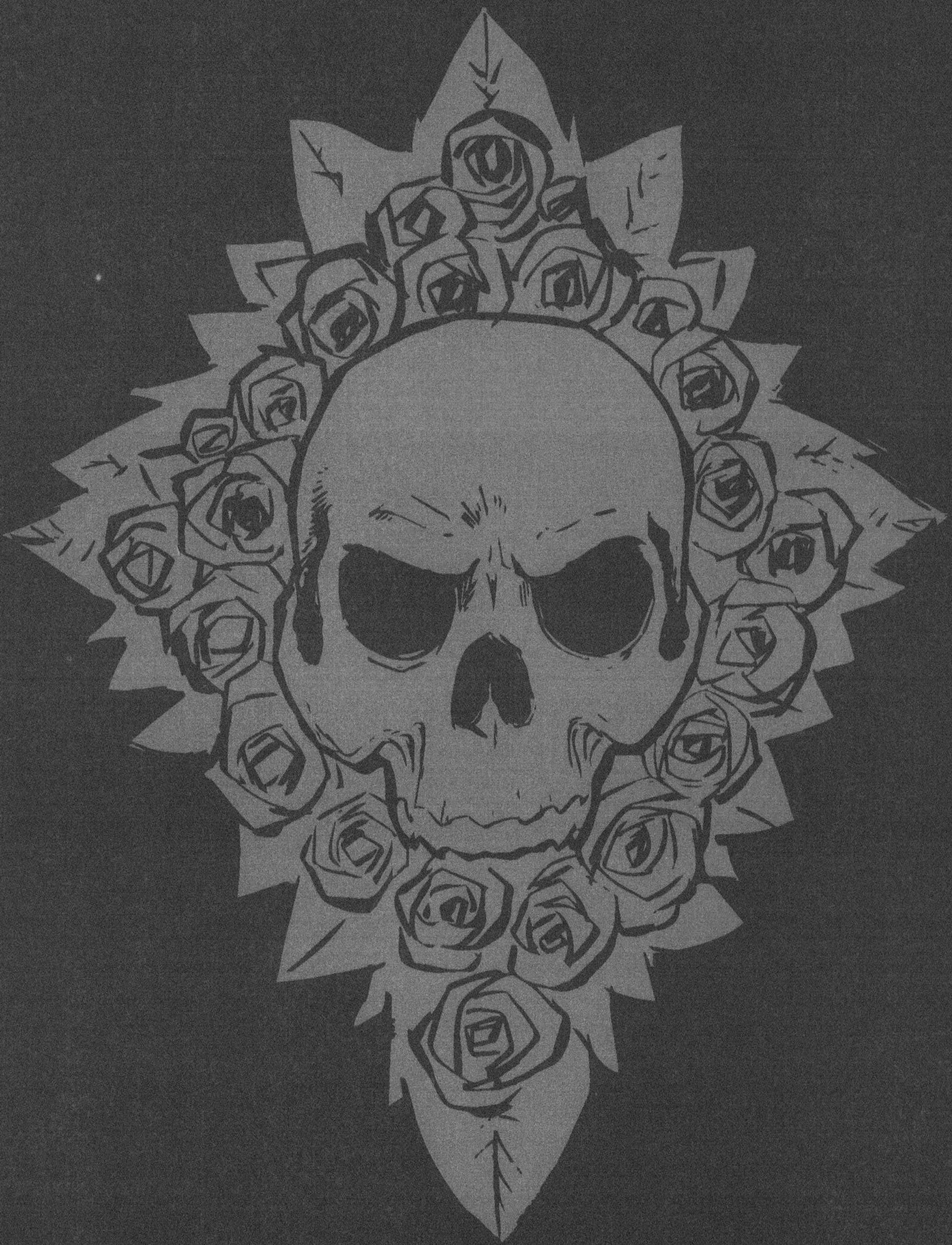

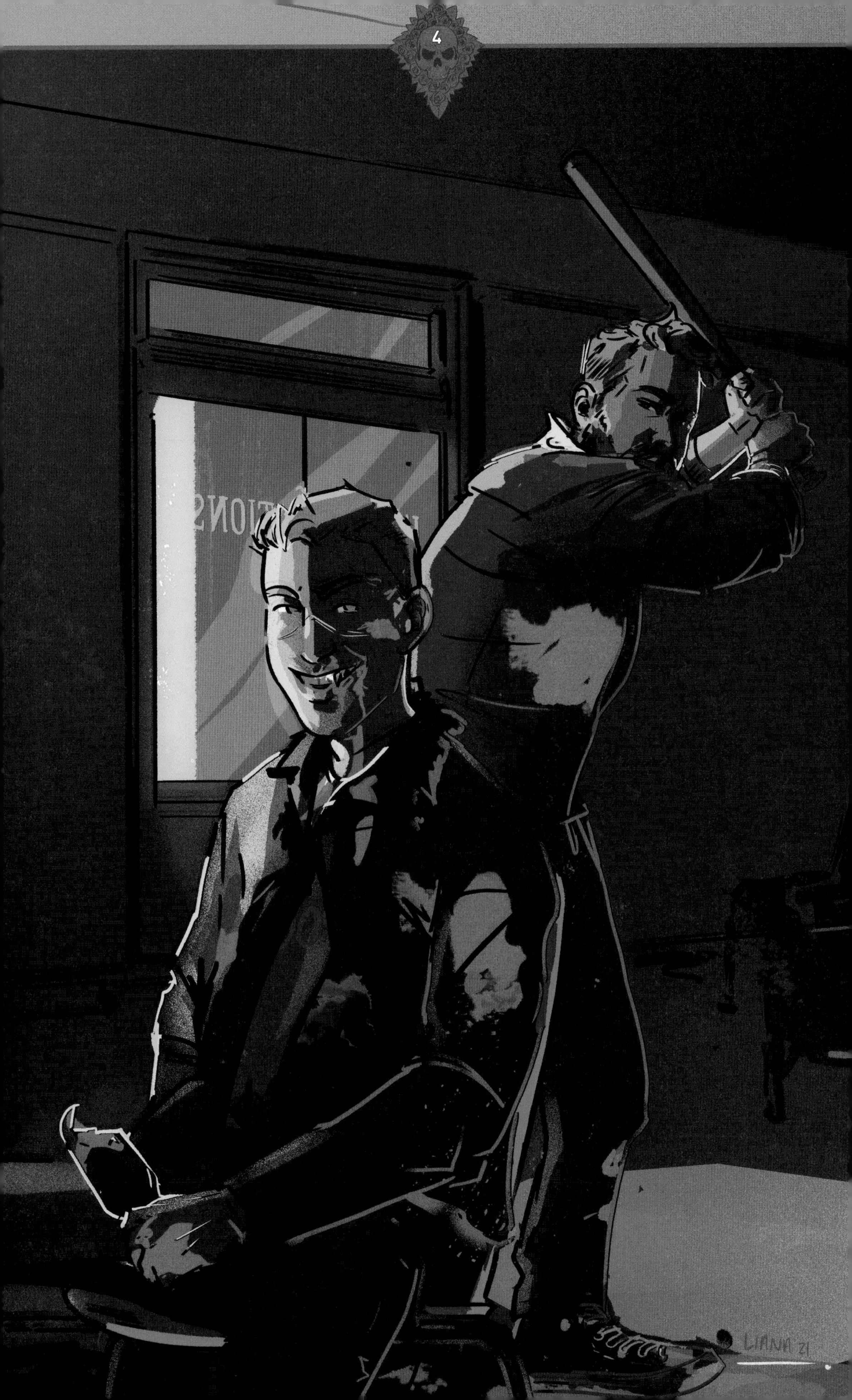
4
LIANA '21

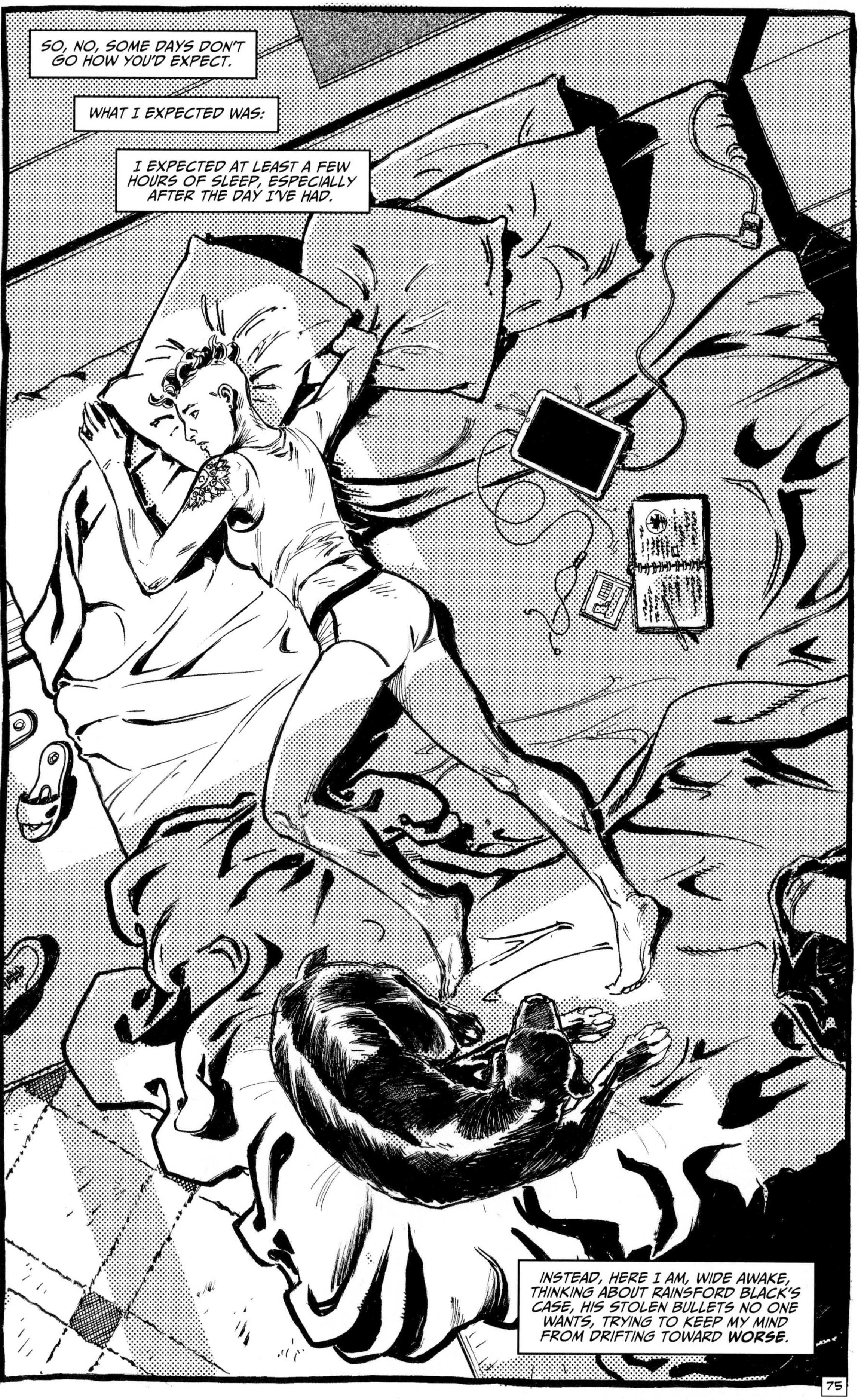
SO, NO, SOME DAYS DON'T GO HOW YOU'D EXPECT.
WHAT I EXPECTED WAS:
I EXPECTED AT LEAST A FEW HOURS OF SLEEP, ESPECIALLY AFTER THE DAY I'VE HAD.
INSTEAD, HERE I AM, WIDE AWAKE, THINKING ABOUT RAINSFORD BLACK'S CASE, HIS STOLEN BULLETS NO ONE WANTS, TRYING TO KEEP MY MIND FROM DRIFTING TOWARD **WORSE**.

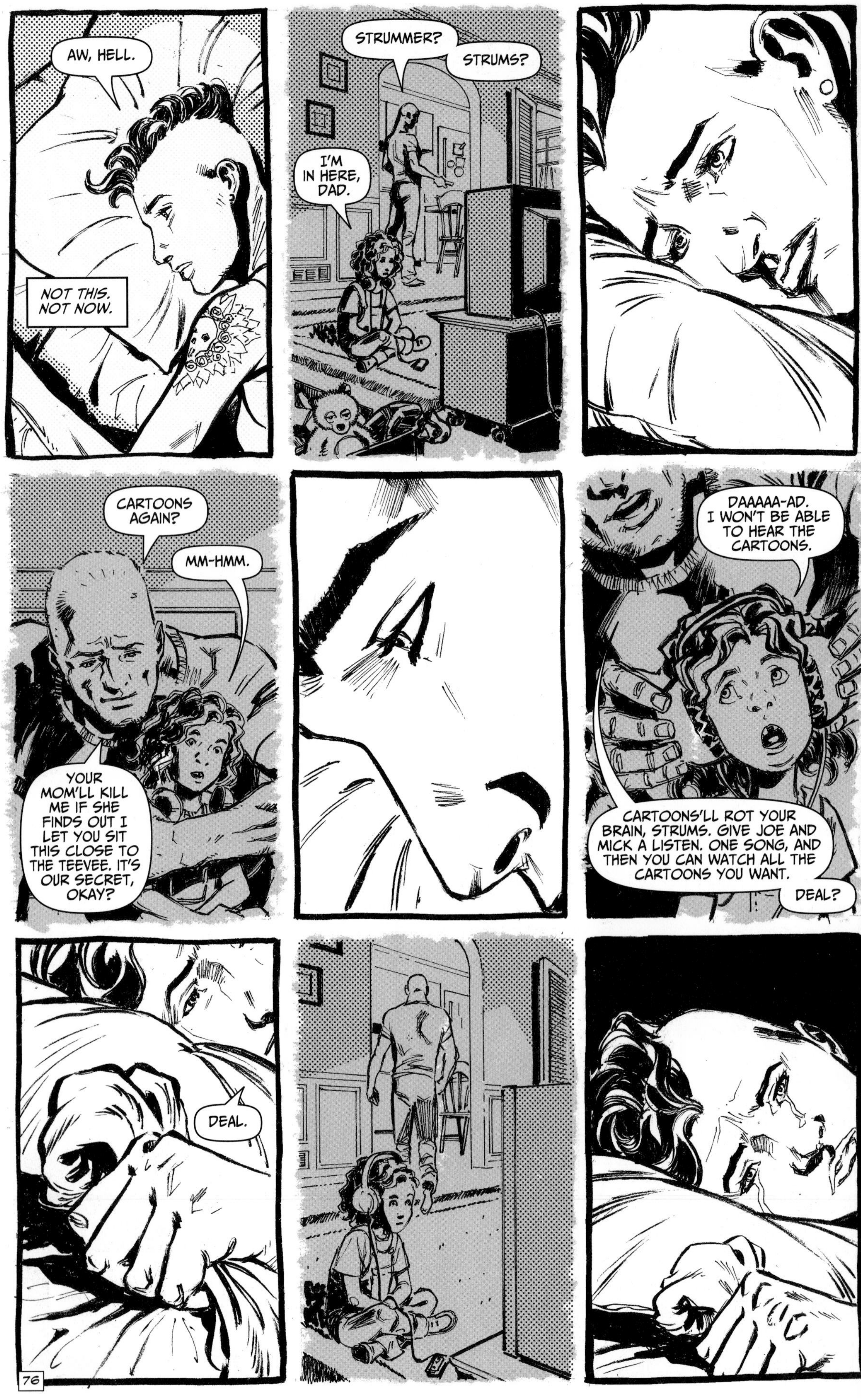
AW, HELL.
NOT THIS. NOT NOW.
STRUMMER?
STRUMS?
I'M IN HERE, DAD.
CARTOONS AGAIN?
MM-HMM.
YOUR MOM'LL KILL ME IF SHE FINDS OUT I LET YOU SIT THIS CLOSE TO THE TEEVEE. IT'S OUR SECRET, OKAY?
DAAAAA-AD. I WON'T BE ABLE TO HEAR THE CARTOONS.
CARTOONS'LL ROT YOUR BRAIN, STRUMS. GIVE JOE AND MICK A LISTEN. ONE SONG, AND THEN YOU CAN WATCH ALL THE CARTOONS YOU WANT.
DEAL?
DEAL.

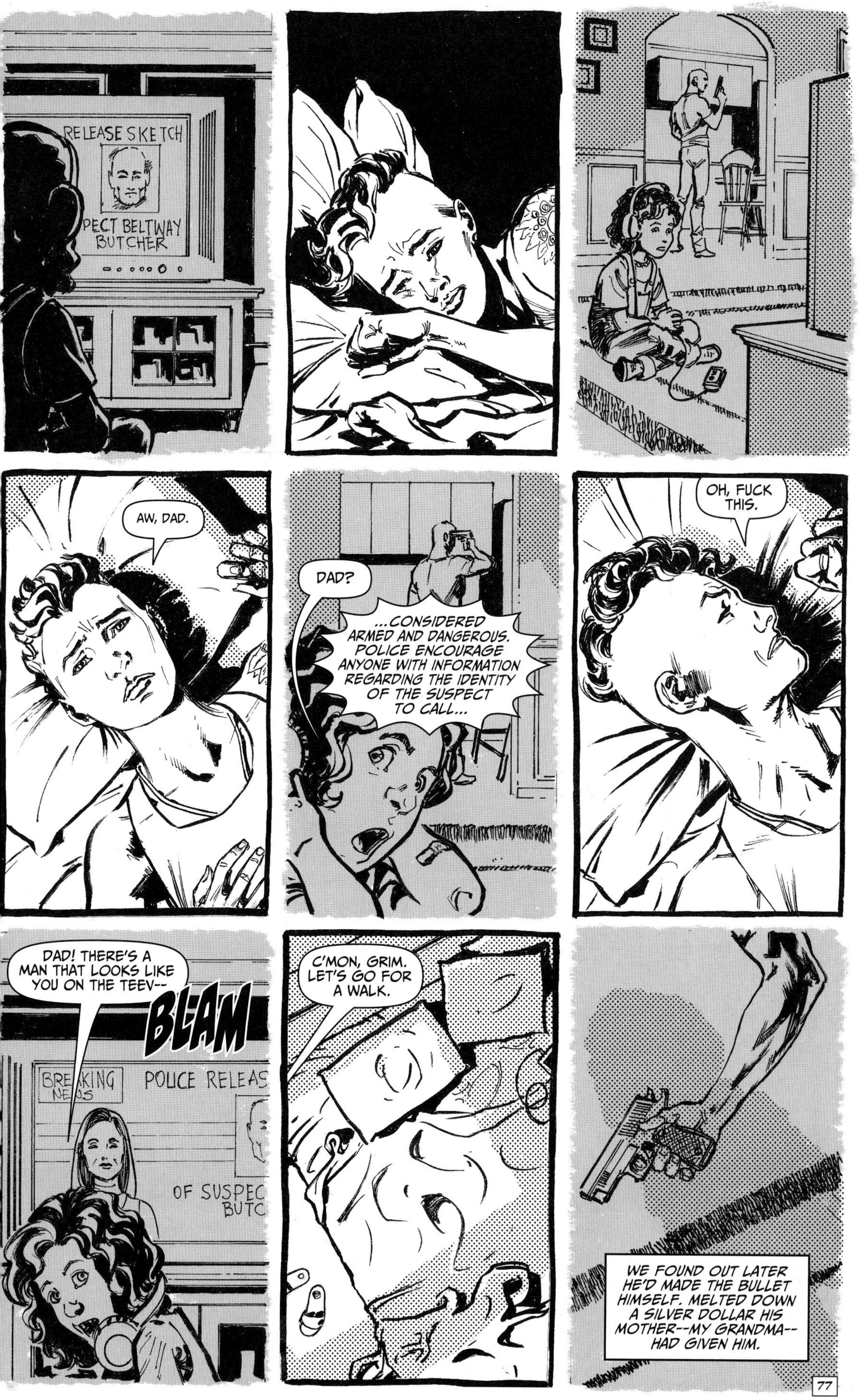
RELEASE SKETCH
PECT BELTWAY BUTCHER
AW, DAD.
DAD?
...CONSIDERED ARMED AND DANGEROUS. POLICE ENCOURAGE ANYONE WITH INFORMATION REGARDING THE IDENTITY OF THE SUSPECT TO CALL...
OH, FUCK THIS.
DAD! THERE'S A MAN THAT LOOKS LIKE YOU ON THE TEEV--
BLAM
BREAKING NEWS
POLICE RELEAS
OF SUSPEC
BUTC
C'MON, GRIM. LET'S GO FOR A WALK.
WE FOUND OUT LATER HE'D MADE THE BULLET HIMSELF. MELTED DOWN A SILVER DOLLAR HIS MOTHER--MY GRANDMA--HAD GIVEN HIM.

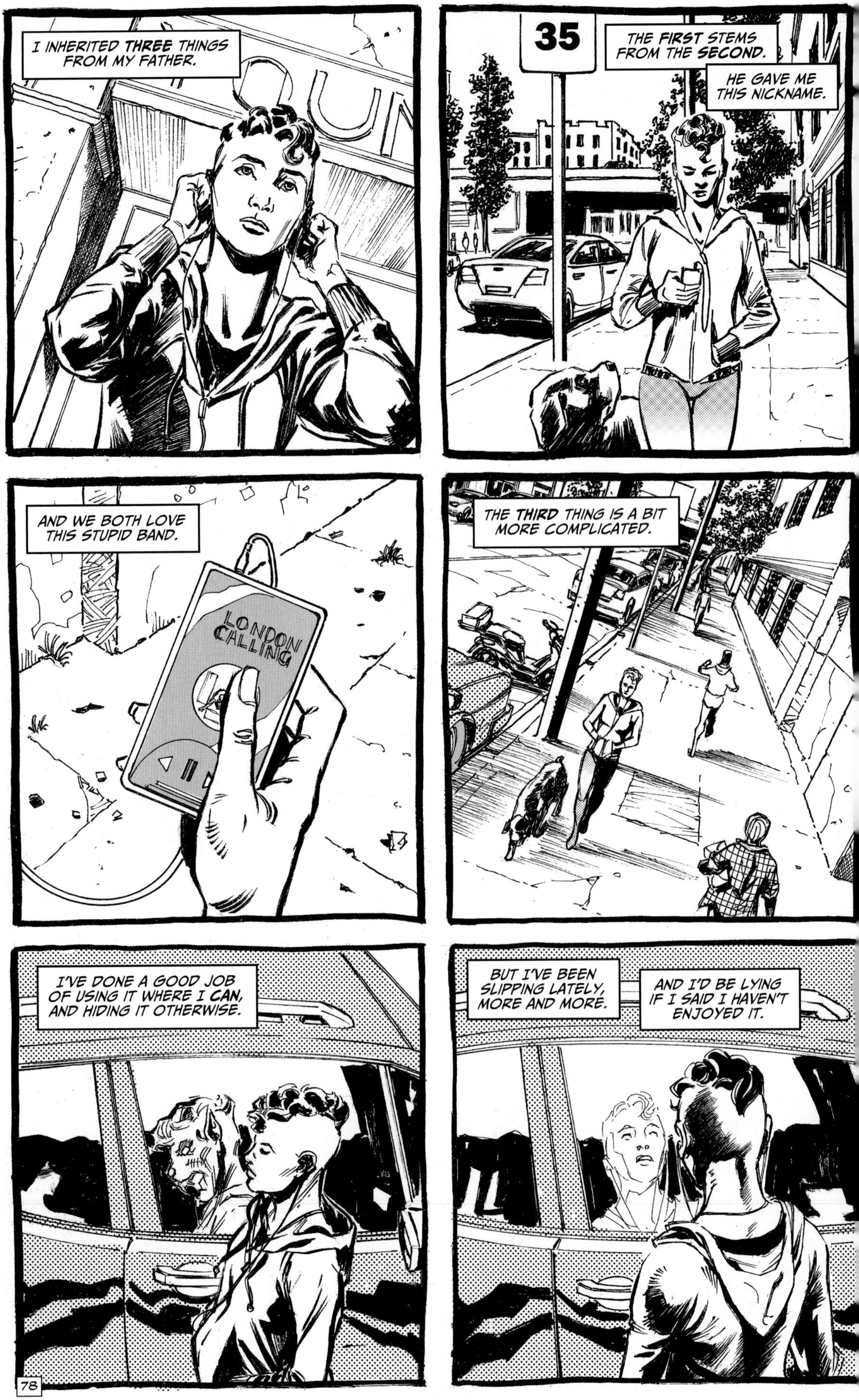
I INHERITED THREE THINGS FROM MY FATHER.
35
THE FIRST STEMS FROM THE SECOND.
HE GAVE ME THIS NICKNAME.
AND WE BOTH LOVE THIS STUPID BAND.
LONDON CALLING
THE THIRD THING IS A BIT MORE COMPLICATED.
I'VE DONE A GOOD JOB OF USING IT WHERE I CAN, AND HIDING IT OTHERWISE.
BUT I'VE BEEN SLIPPING LATELY, MORE AND MORE.
AND I'D BE LYING IF I SAID I HAVEN'T ENJOYED IT.

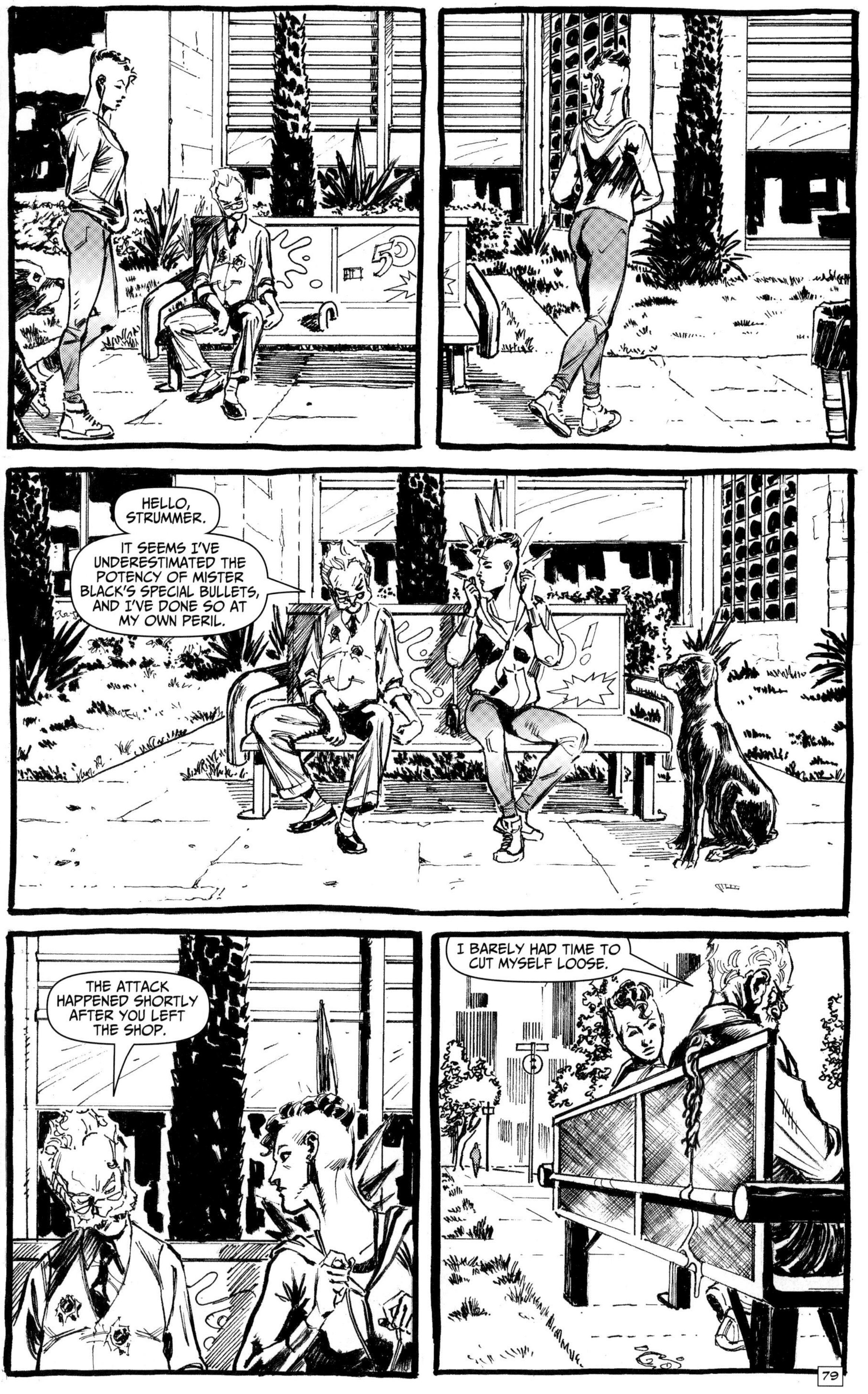
HELLO, STRUMMER.
IT SEEMS I'VE UNDERESTIMATED THE POTENCY OF MISTER BLACK'S SPECIAL BULLETS, AND I'VE DONE SO AT MY OWN PERIL.
THE ATTACK HAPPENED SHORTLY AFTER YOU LEFT THE SHOP.
I BARELY HAD TIME TO CUT MYSELF LOOSE.

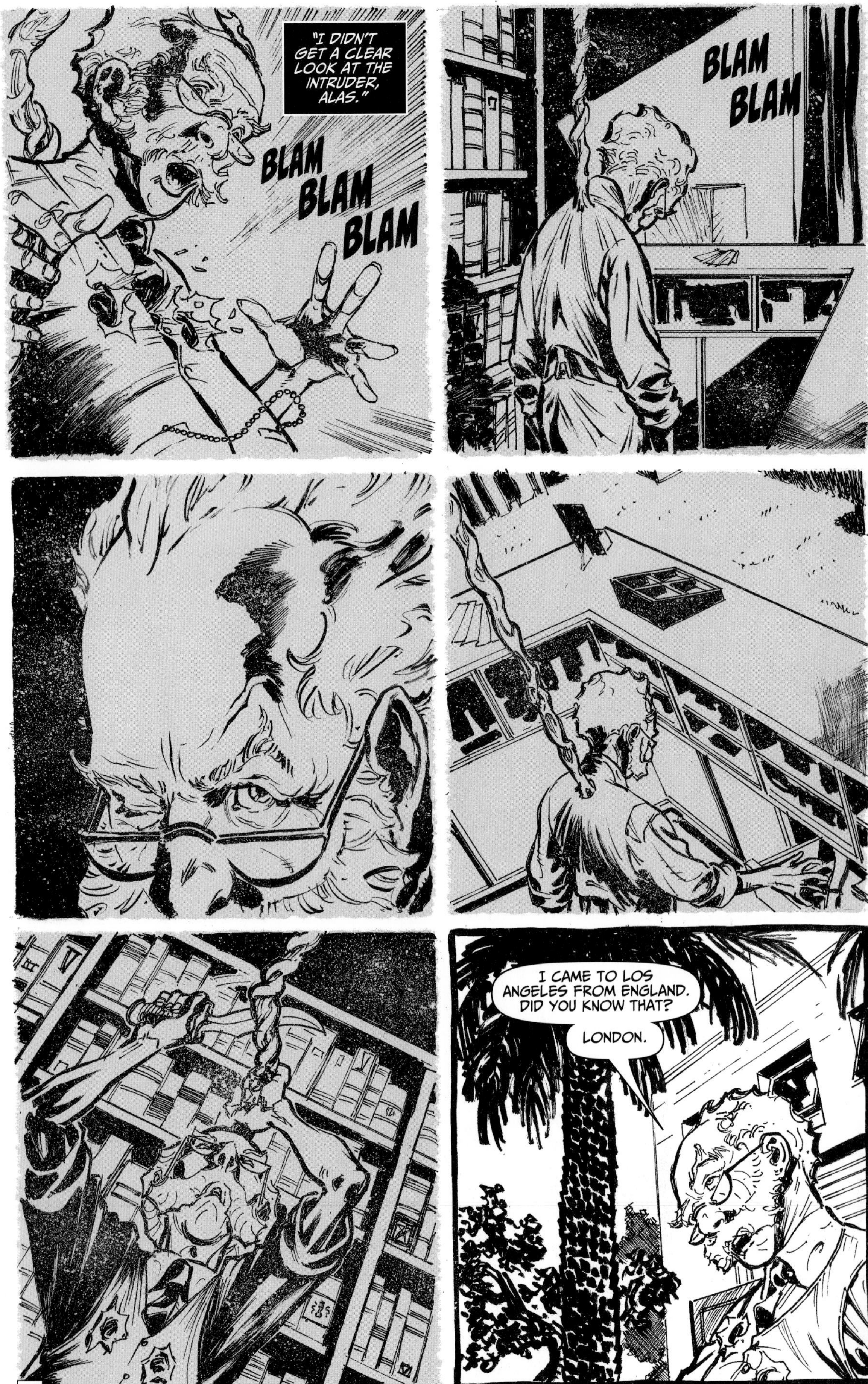
"I DIDN'T GET A CLEAR LOOK AT THE INTRUDER, ALAS."
BLAM BLAM BLAM
BLAM BLAM
I CAME TO LOS ANGELES FROM ENGLAND. DID YOU KNOW THAT?
LONDON.

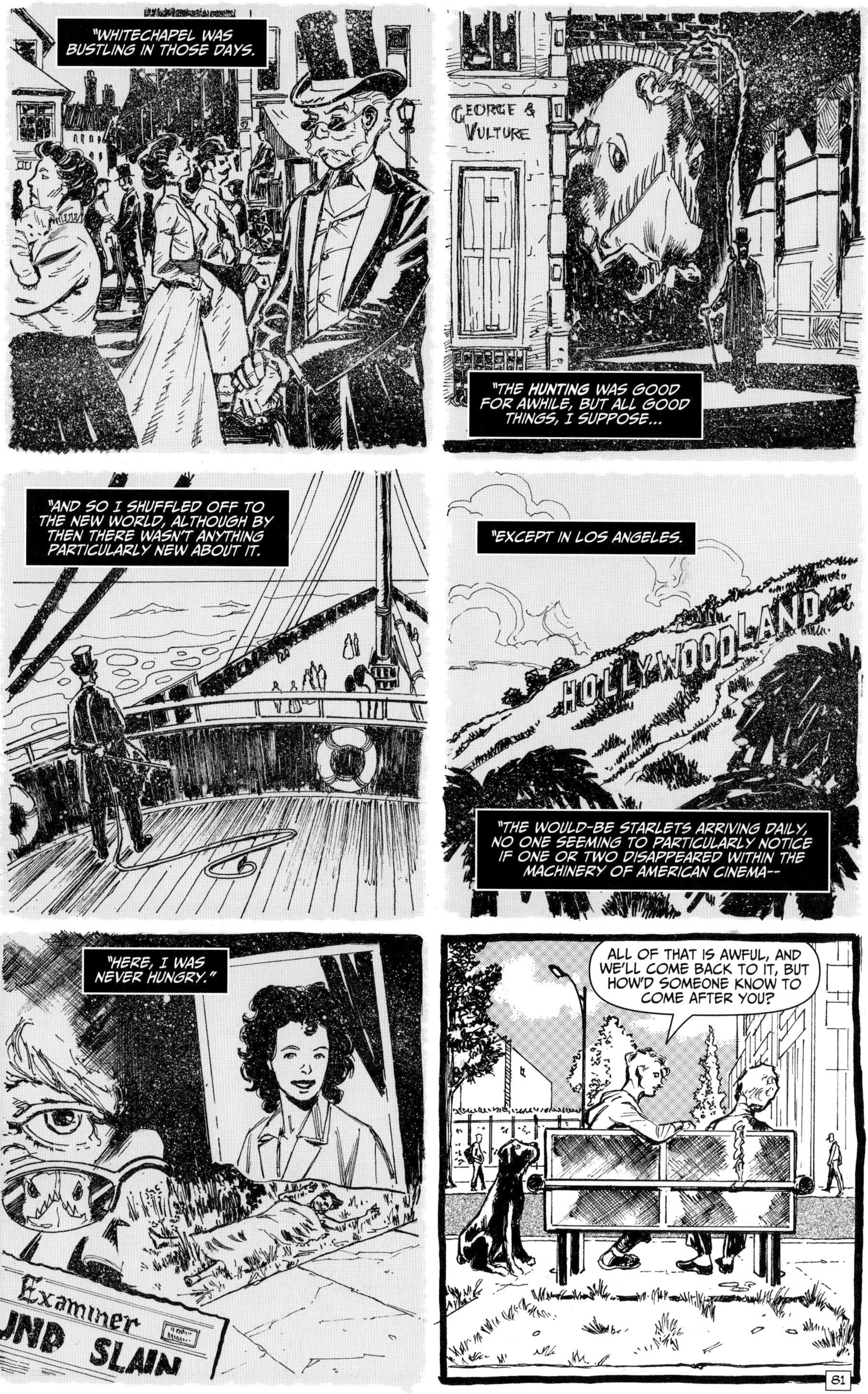
"WHITECHAPEL WAS BUSTLING IN THOSE DAYS.
GEORGE & VULTURE
"THE HUNTING WAS GOOD FOR AWHILE, BUT ALL GOOD THINGS, I SUPPOSE...
"AND SO I SHUFFLED OFF TO THE NEW WORLD, ALTHOUGH BY THEN THERE WASN'T ANYTHING PARTICULARLY NEW ABOUT IT.
"EXCEPT IN LOS ANGELES.
HOLLYWOODLAND
"THE WOULD-BE STARLETS ARRIVING DAILY, NO ONE SEEMING TO PARTICULARLY NOTICE IF ONE OR TWO DISAPPEARED WITHIN THE MACHINERY OF AMERICAN CINEMA--
"HERE, I WAS NEVER HUNGRY."
Examiner
JND SLAIN
ALL OF THAT IS AWFUL, AND WE'LL COME BACK TO IT, BUT HOW'D SOMEONE KNOW TO COME AFTER YOU?

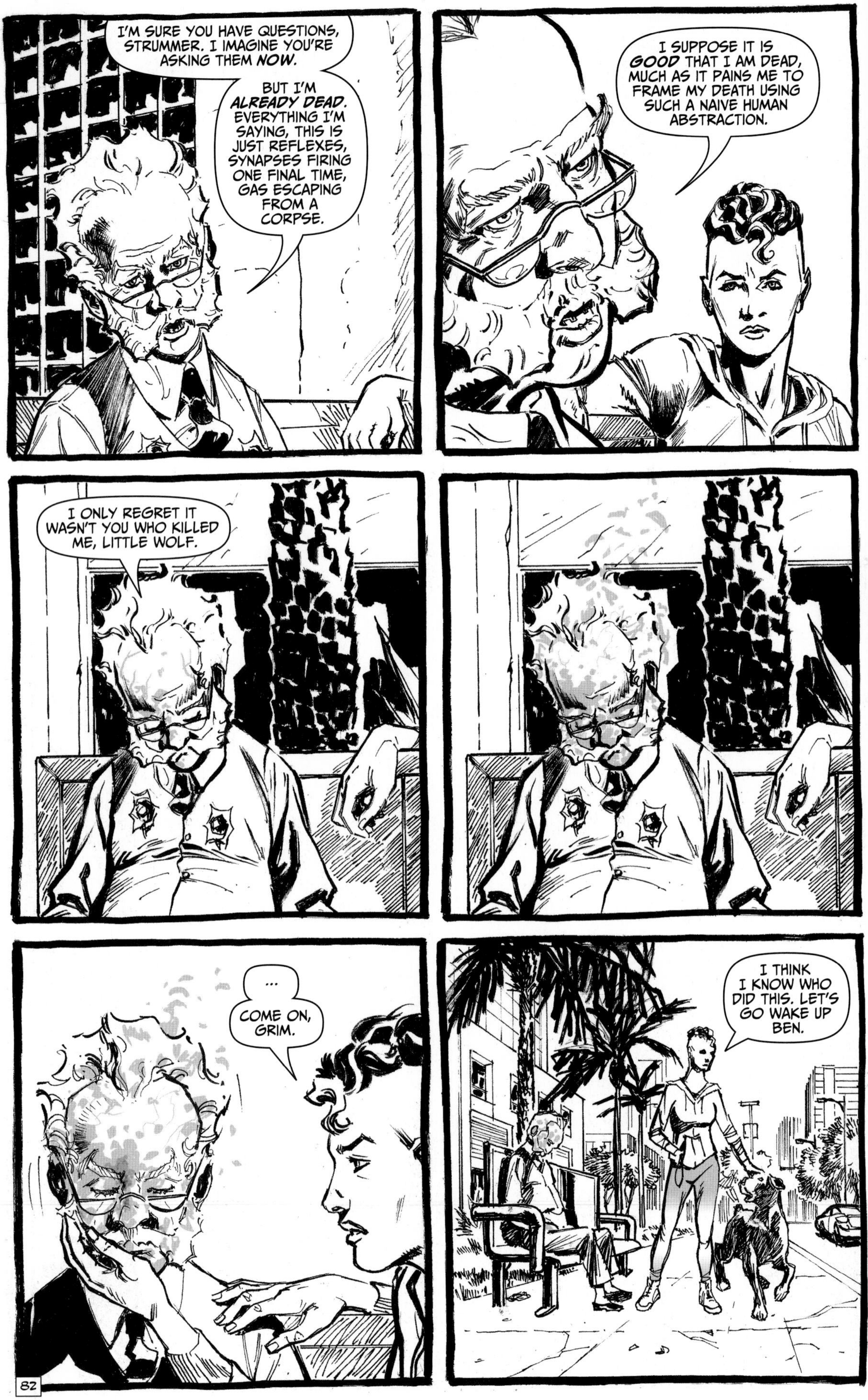
I'M SURE YOU HAVE QUESTIONS, STRUMMER. I IMAGINE YOU'RE ASKING THEM NOW.
BUT I'M ALREADY DEAD. EVERYTHING I'M SAYING, THIS IS JUST REFLEXES, SYNAPSES FIRING ONE FINAL TIME, GAS ESCAPING FROM A CORPSE.
I SUPPOSE IT IS GOOD THAT I AM DEAD, MUCH AS IT PAINS ME TO FRAME MY DEATH USING SUCH A NAIVE HUMAN ABSTRACTION.
I ONLY REGRET IT WASN'T YOU WHO KILLED ME, LITTLE WOLF.
...
COME ON, GRIM.
I THINK I KNOW WHO DID THIS. LET'S GO WAKE UP BEN.

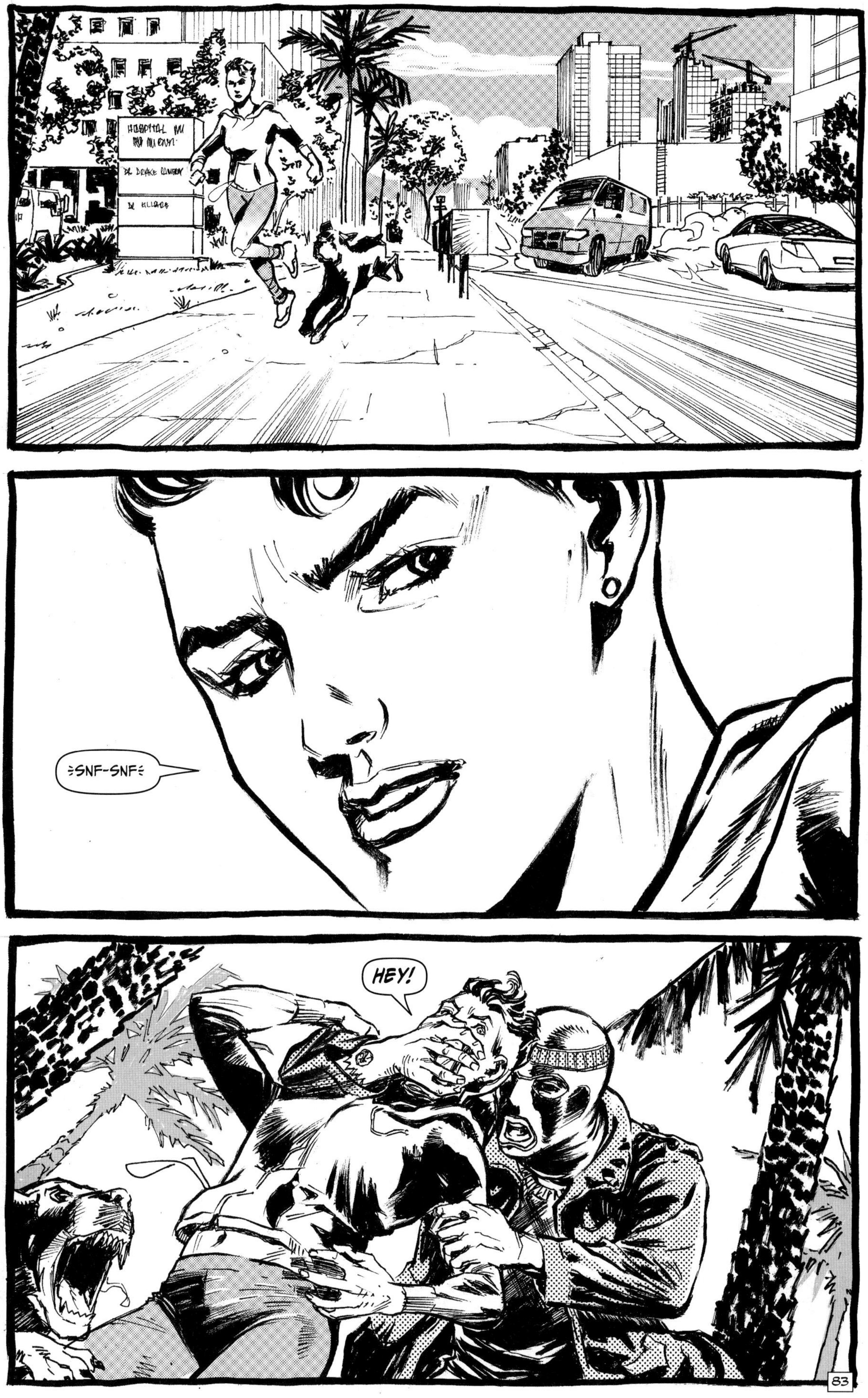
SNF-SNF
HEY!

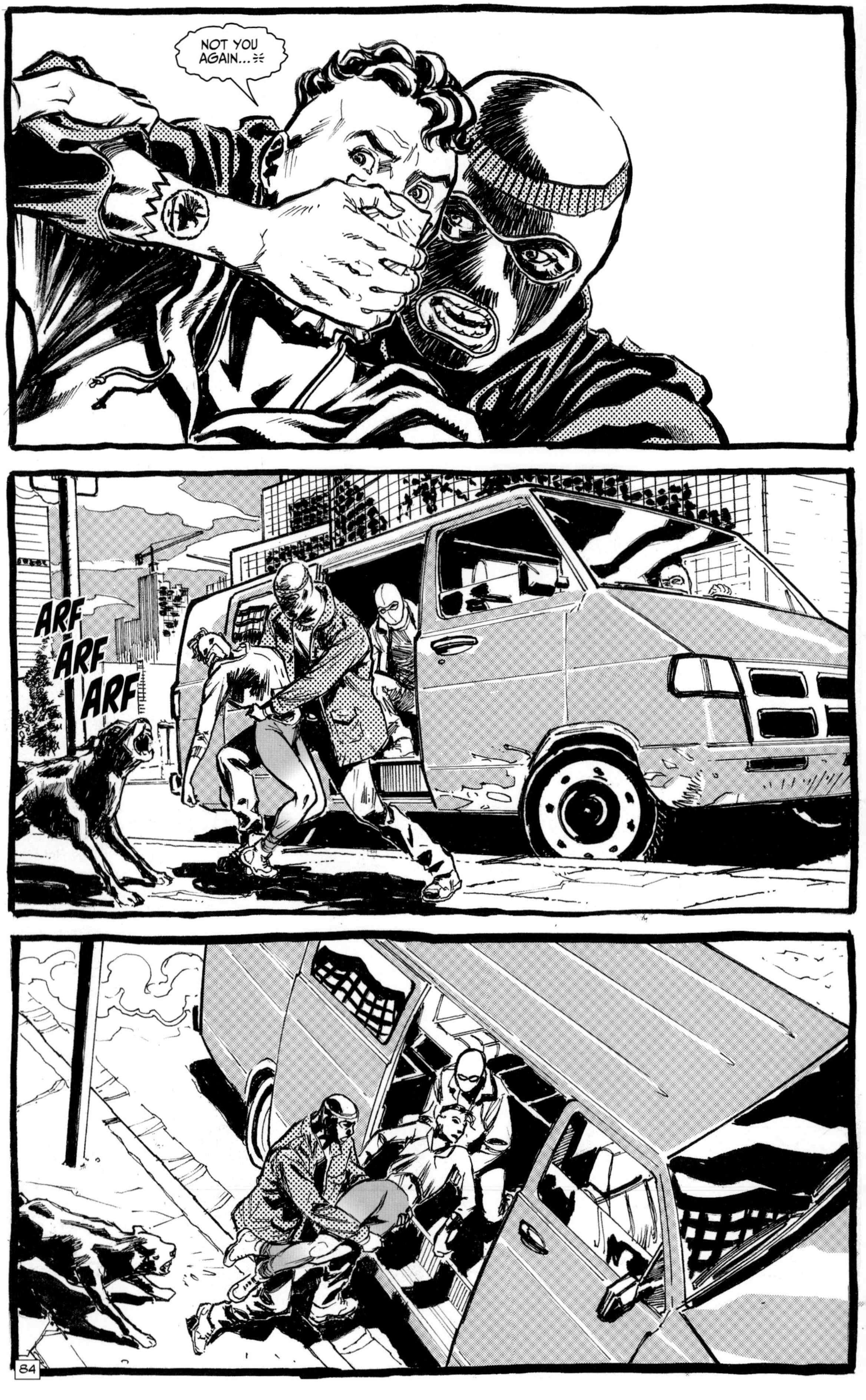
NOT YOU AGAIN...
ARF
ARF
ARF

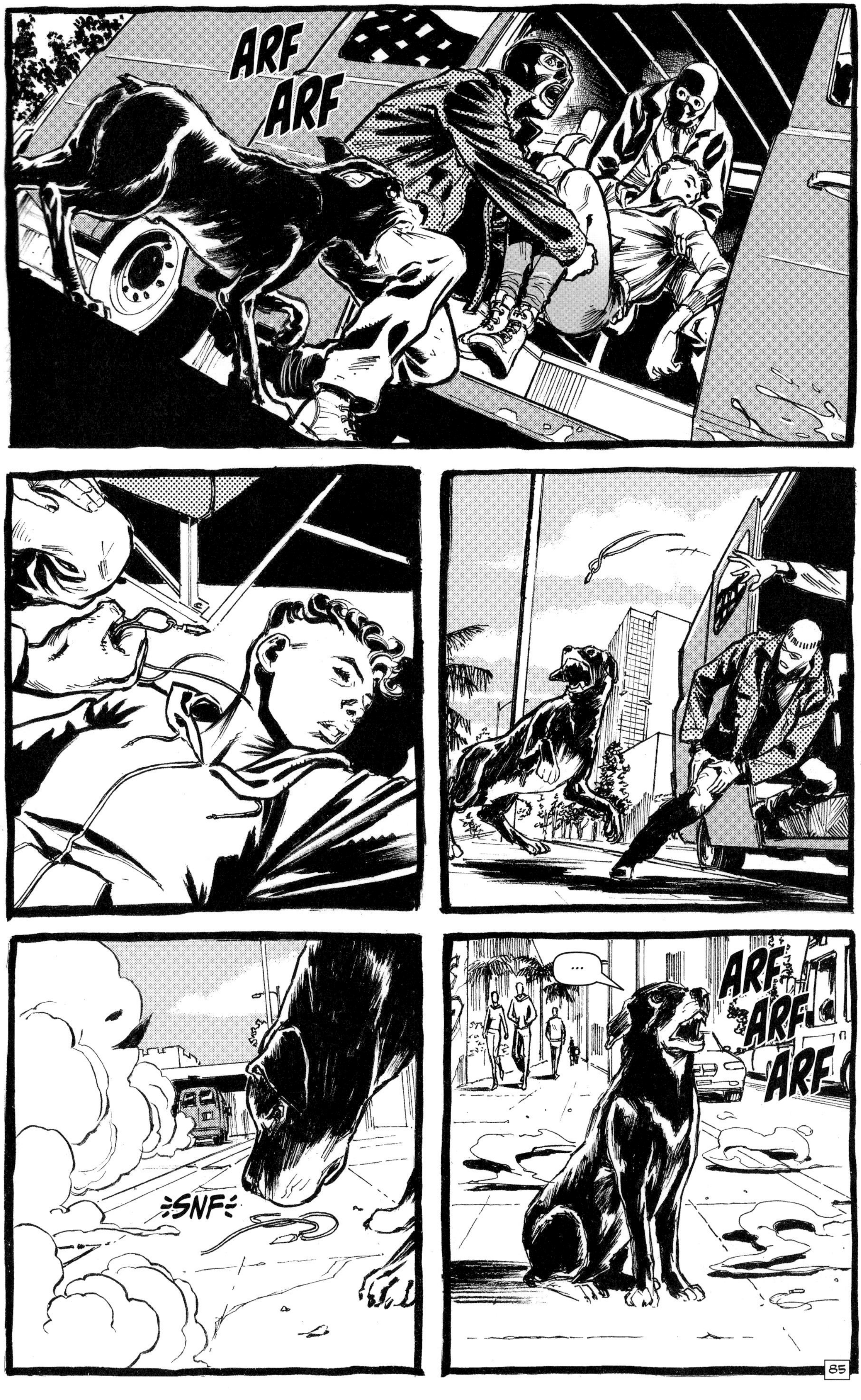
ARF
ARF
SNF
...
ARF
ARF
ARF

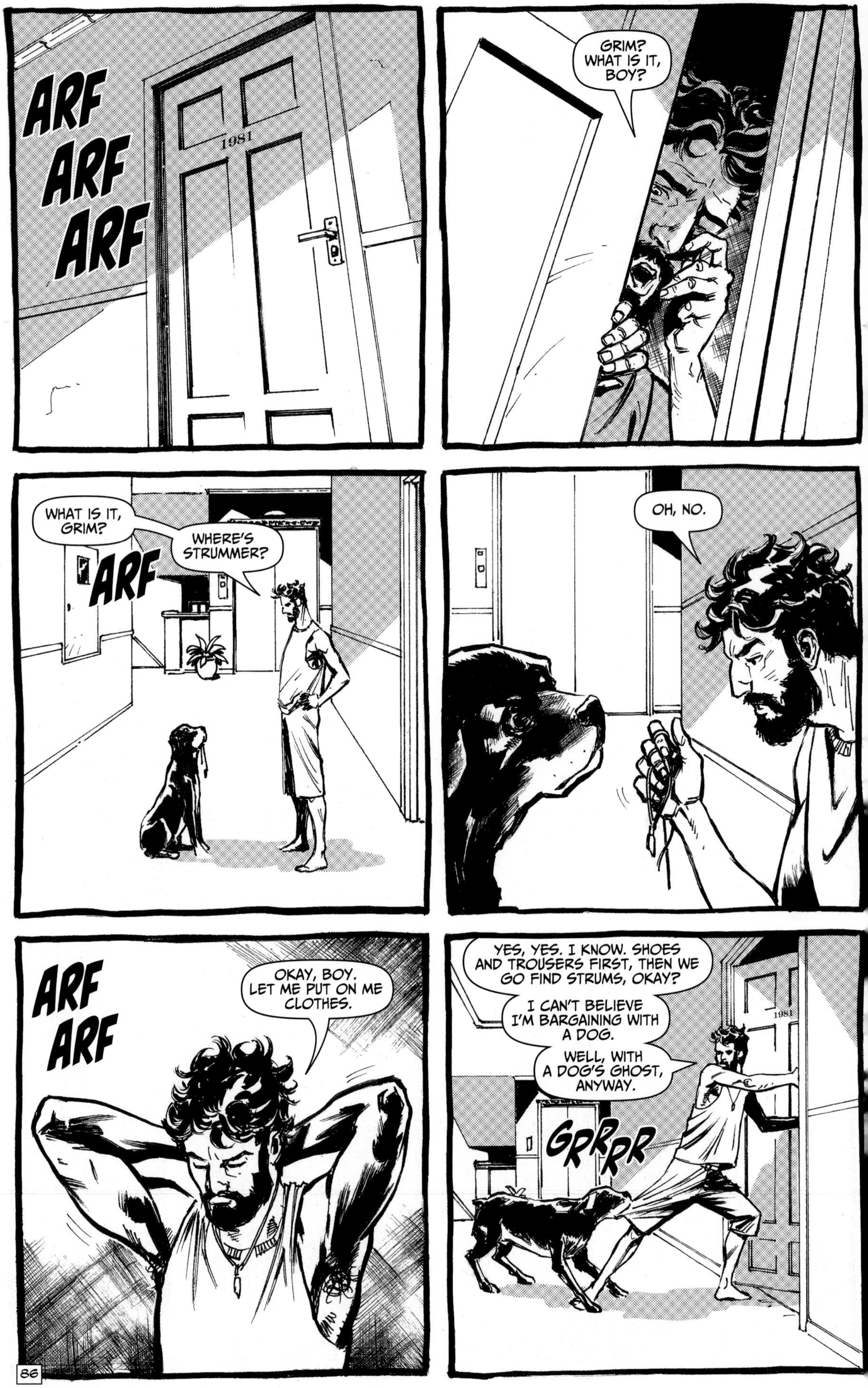
ARF
ARF
ARF
1981
GRIM? WHAT IS IT, BOY?
WHAT IS IT, GRIM?
ARF
WHERE'S STRUMMER?
OH, NO.
ARF
ARF
OKAY, BOY. LET ME PUT ON ME CLOTHES.
YES, YES. I KNOW. SHOES AND TROUSERS FIRST, THEN WE GO FIND STRUMS, OKAY?
I CAN'T BELIEVE I'M BARGAINING WITH A DOG.
WELL, WITH A DOG'S GHOST, ANYWAY.
1981
GRRRRR

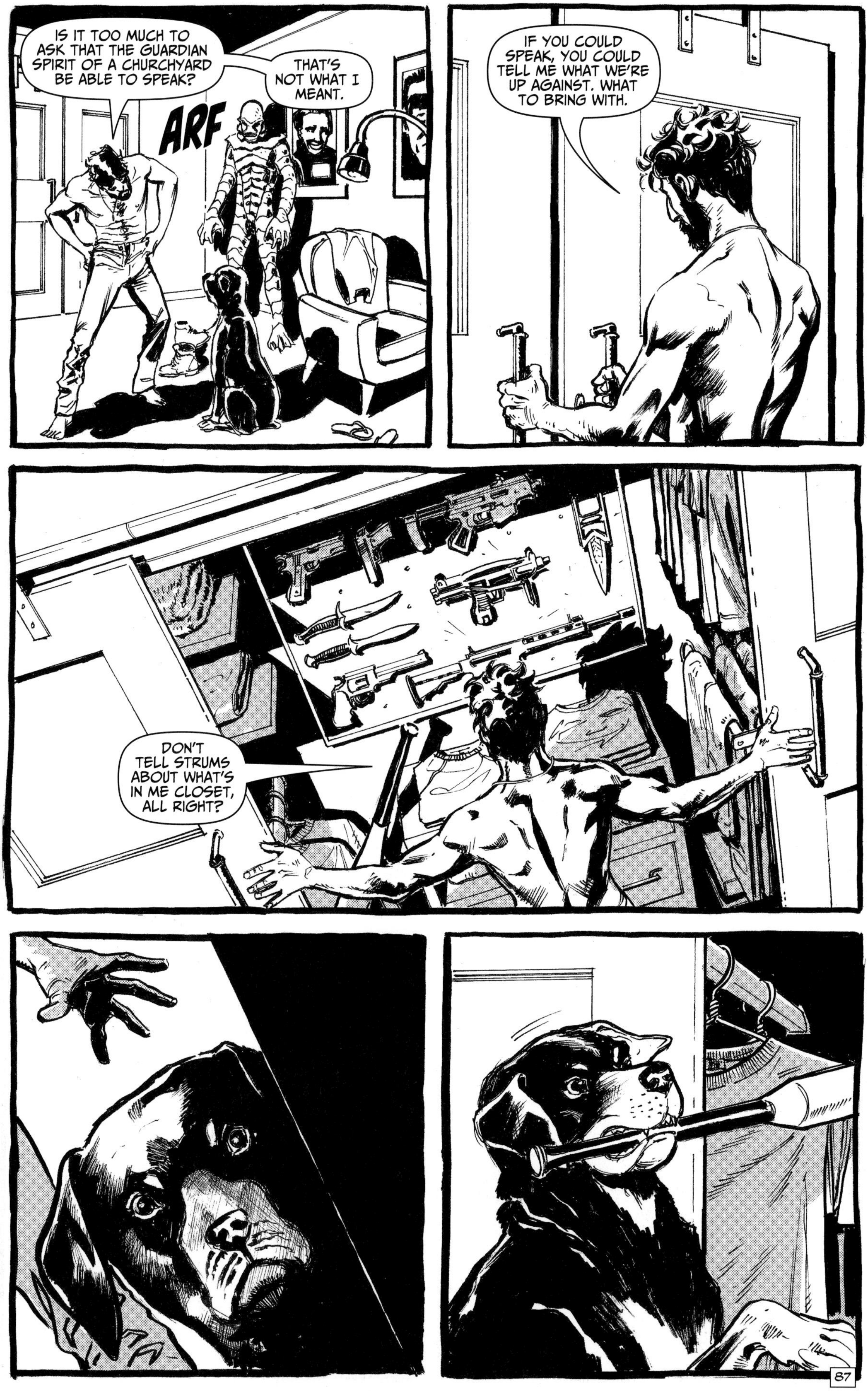
IS IT TOO MUCH TO ASK THAT THE GUARDIAN SPIRIT OF A CHURCHYARD BE ABLE TO SPEAK?
ARF
THAT'S NOT WHAT I MEANT.
IF YOU COULD SPEAK, YOU COULD TELL ME WHAT WE'RE UP AGAINST. WHAT TO BRING WITH.
DON'T TELL STRUMS ABOUT WHAT'S IN ME CLOSET, ALL RIGHT?

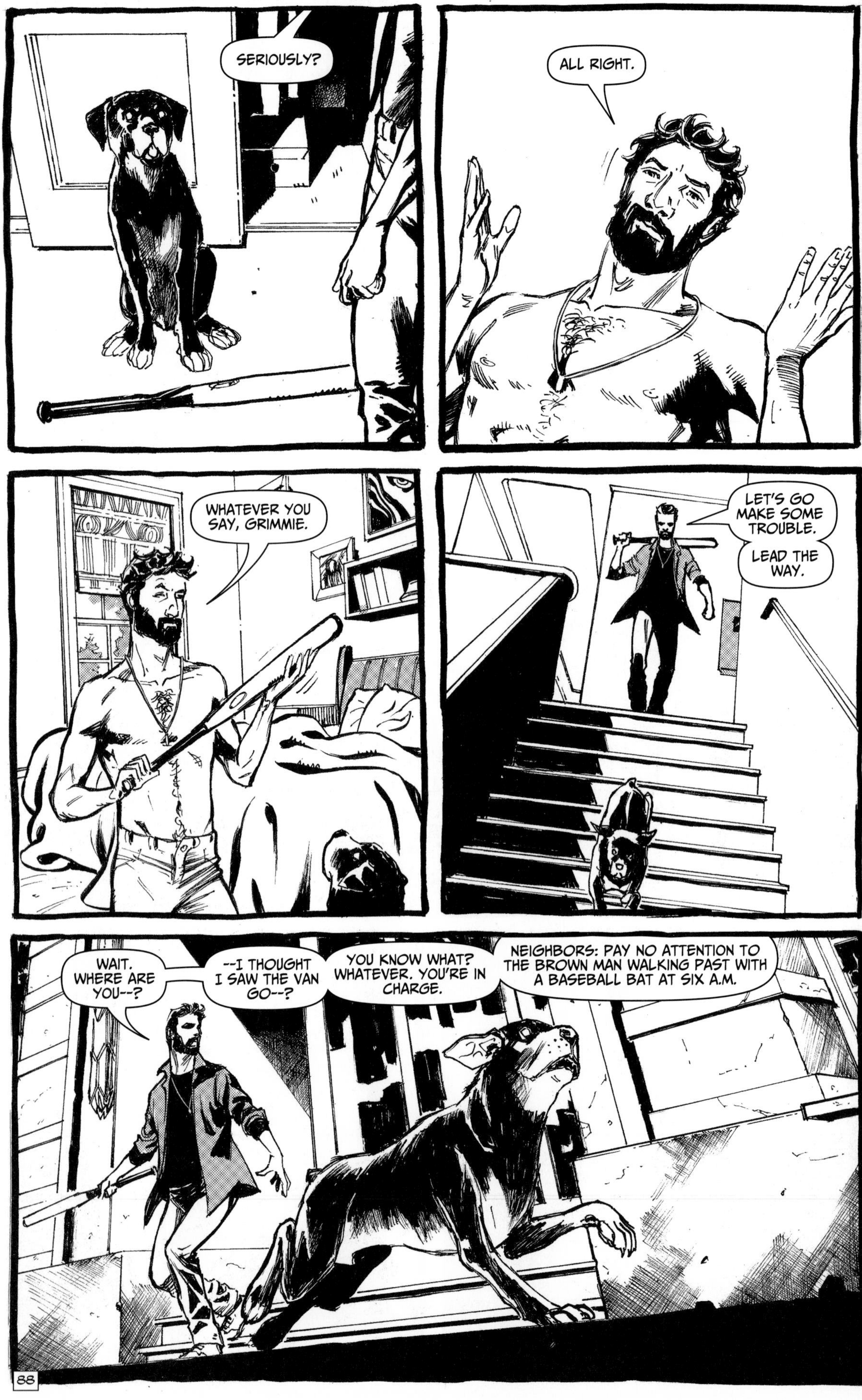
SERIOUSLY?
ALL RIGHT.
WHATEVER YOU SAY, GRIMMIE.
LET'S GO MAKE SOME TROUBLE.
LEAD THE WAY.
WAIT. WHERE ARE YOU--?
--I THOUGHT I SAW THE VAN GO--?
YOU KNOW WHAT? WHATEVER. YOU'RE IN CHARGE.
NEIGHBORS: PAY NO ATTENTION TO THE BROWN MAN WALKING PAST WITH A BASEBALL BAT AT SIX A.M.

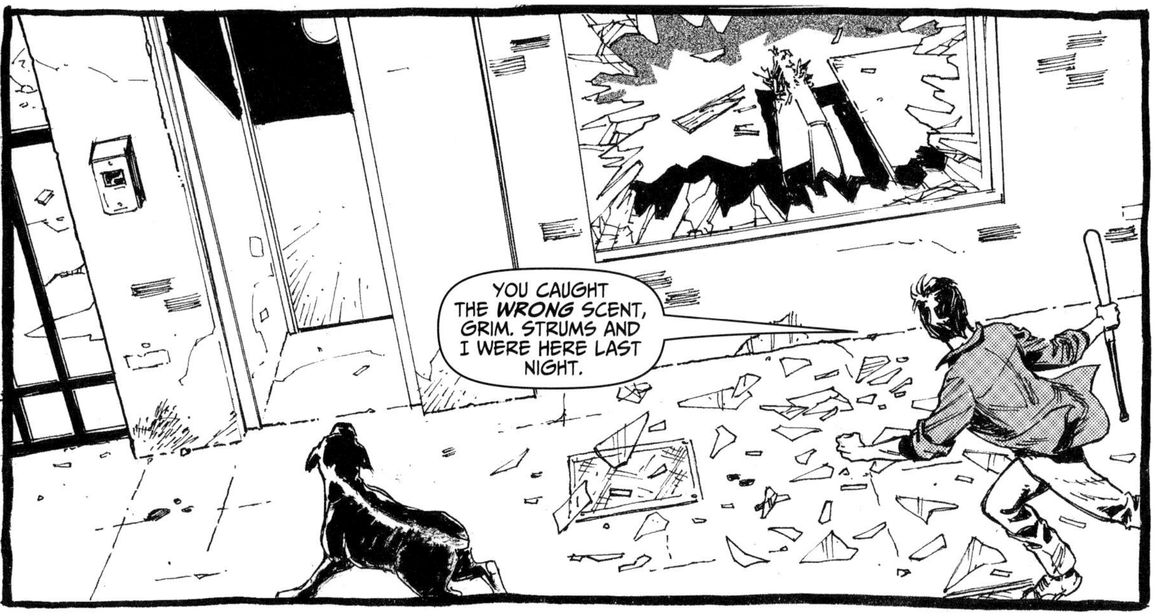
YOU CAUGHT THE WRONG SCENT, GRIM. STRUMS AND I WERE HERE LAST NIGHT.

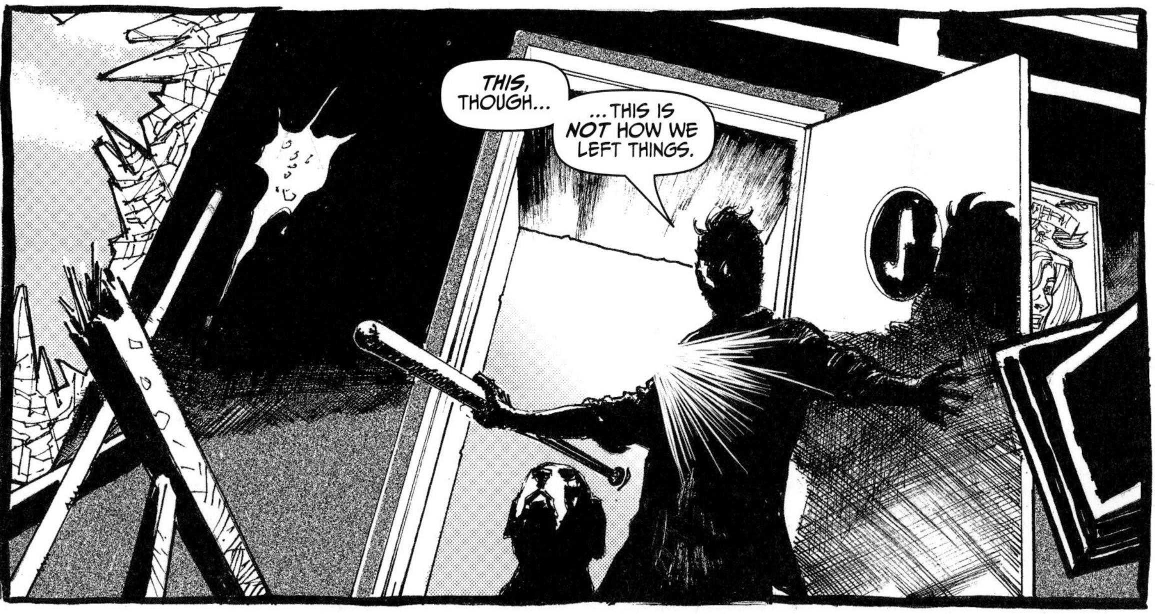
THIS, THOUGH...
...THIS IS NOT HOW WE LEFT THINGS.

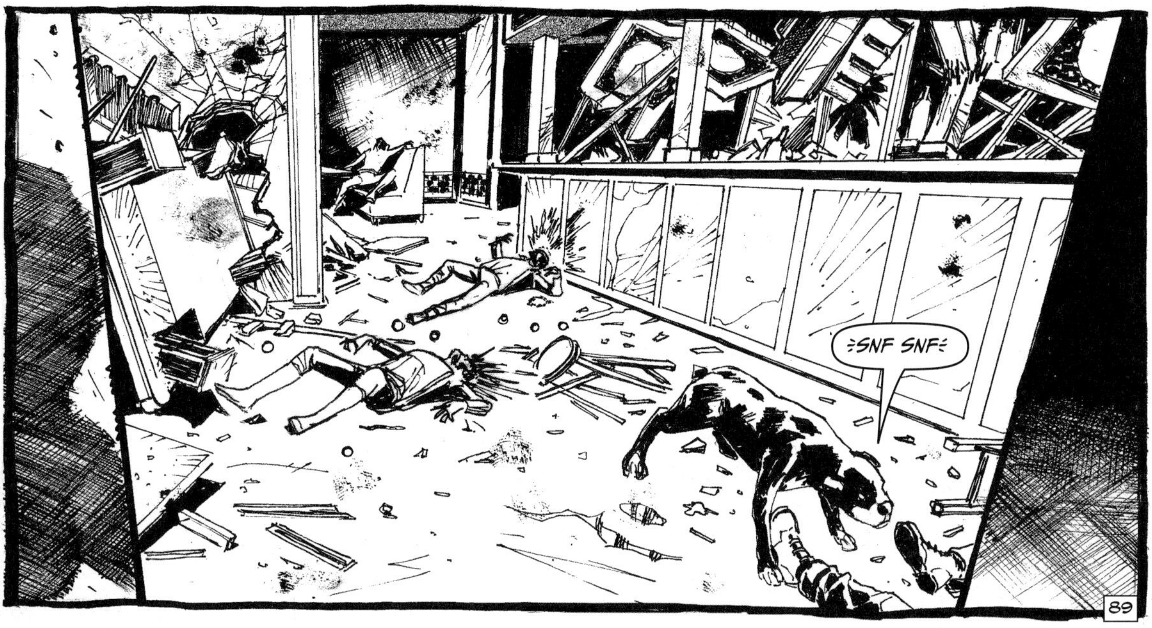
SNF SNF

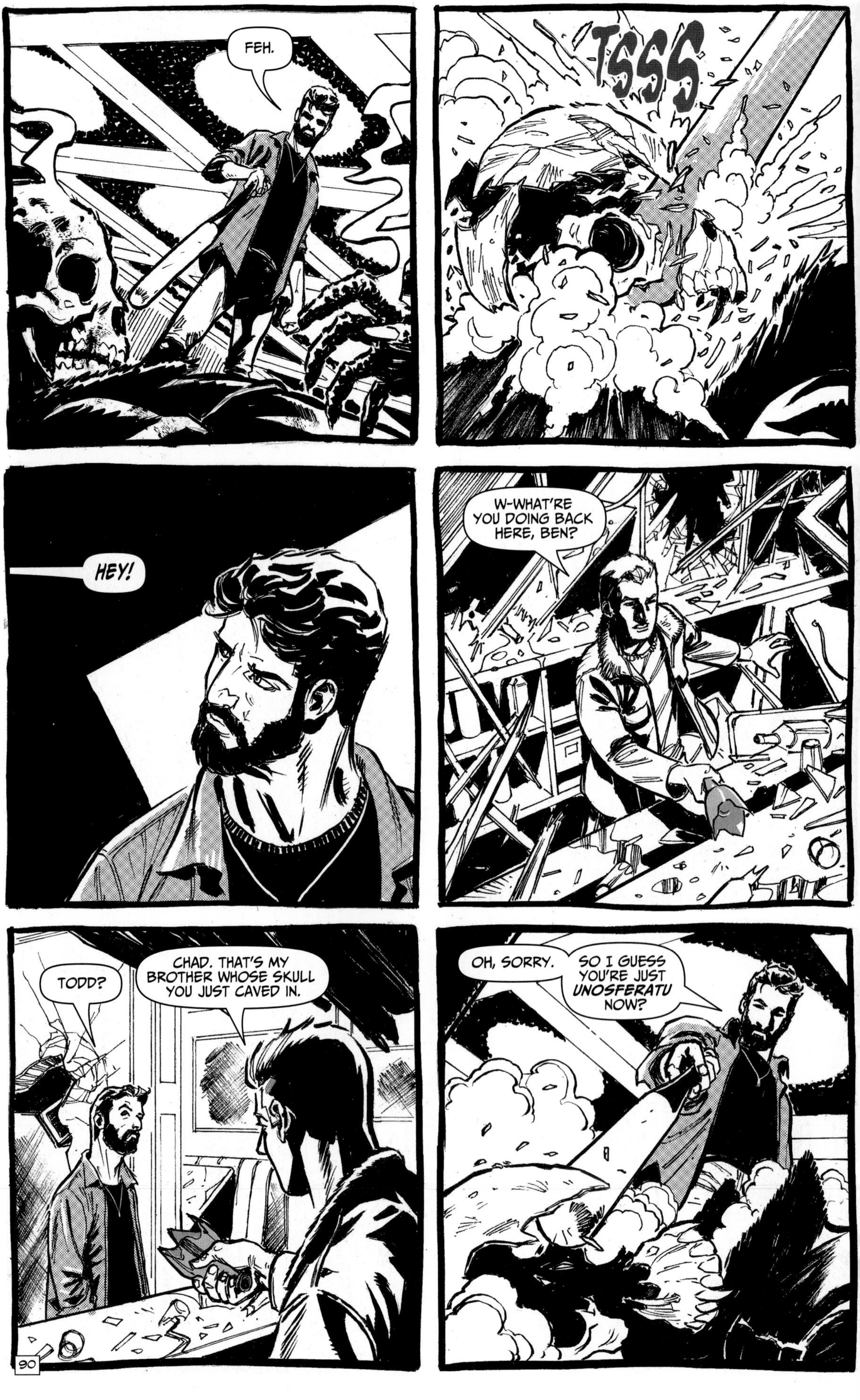
FEH.
TSSS
HEY!
W-WHAT'RE YOU DOING BACK HERE, BEN?
TODD?
CHAD. THAT'S MY BROTHER WHOSE SKULL YOU JUST CAVED IN.
OH, SORRY.
SO I GUESS YOU'RE JUST UNOSFERATU NOW?

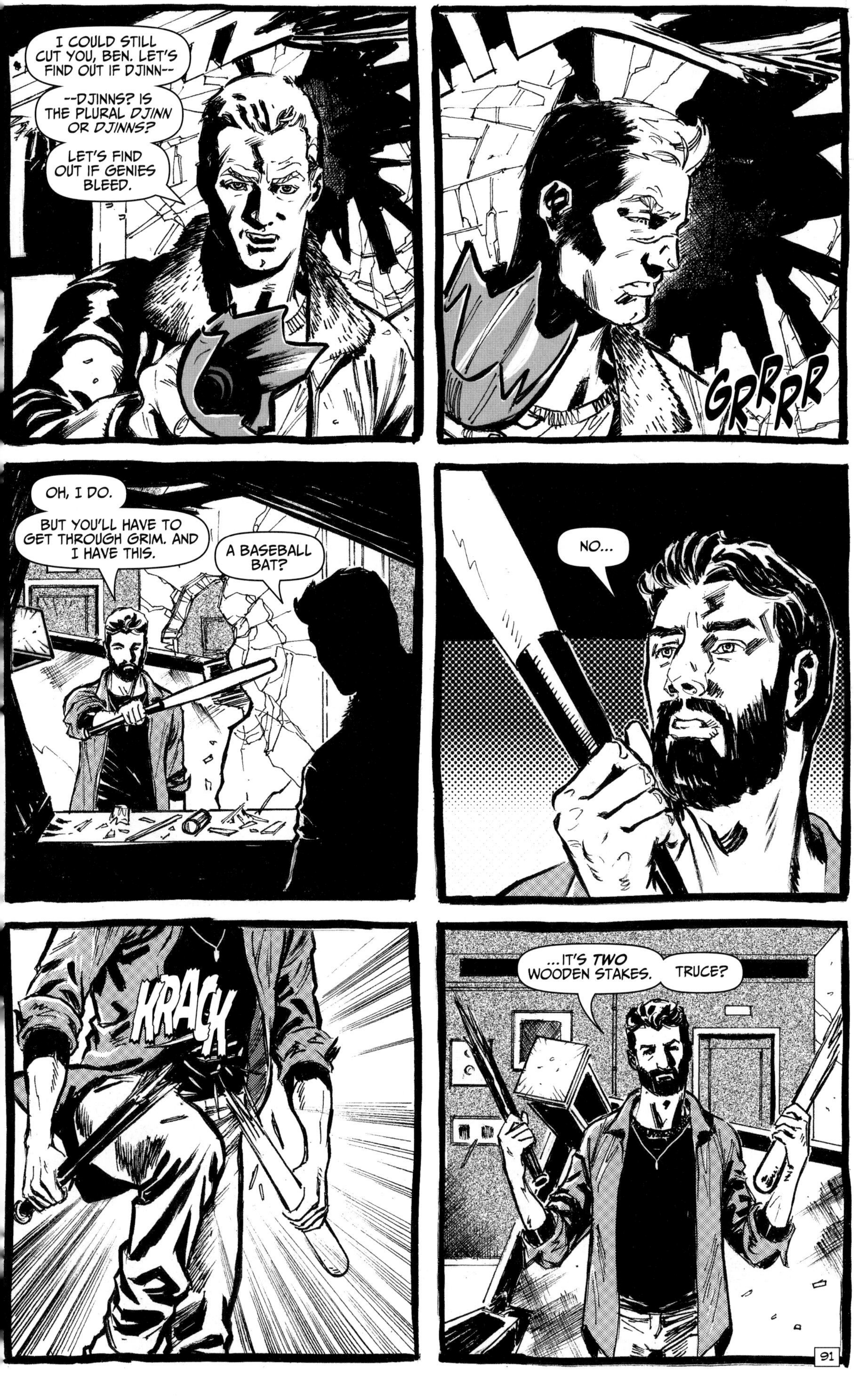
I COULD STILL CUT YOU, BEN. LET'S FIND OUT IF DJINN--
--DJINNS? IS THE PLURAL *DJINN* OR *DJINNS?*
LET'S FIND OUT IF GENIES BLEED.
GRRRR
OH, I DO.
BUT YOU'LL HAVE TO GET THROUGH GRIM. AND I HAVE THIS.
A BASEBALL BAT?
NO...
KRACK
...IT'S *TWO* WOODEN STAKES.
TRUCE?

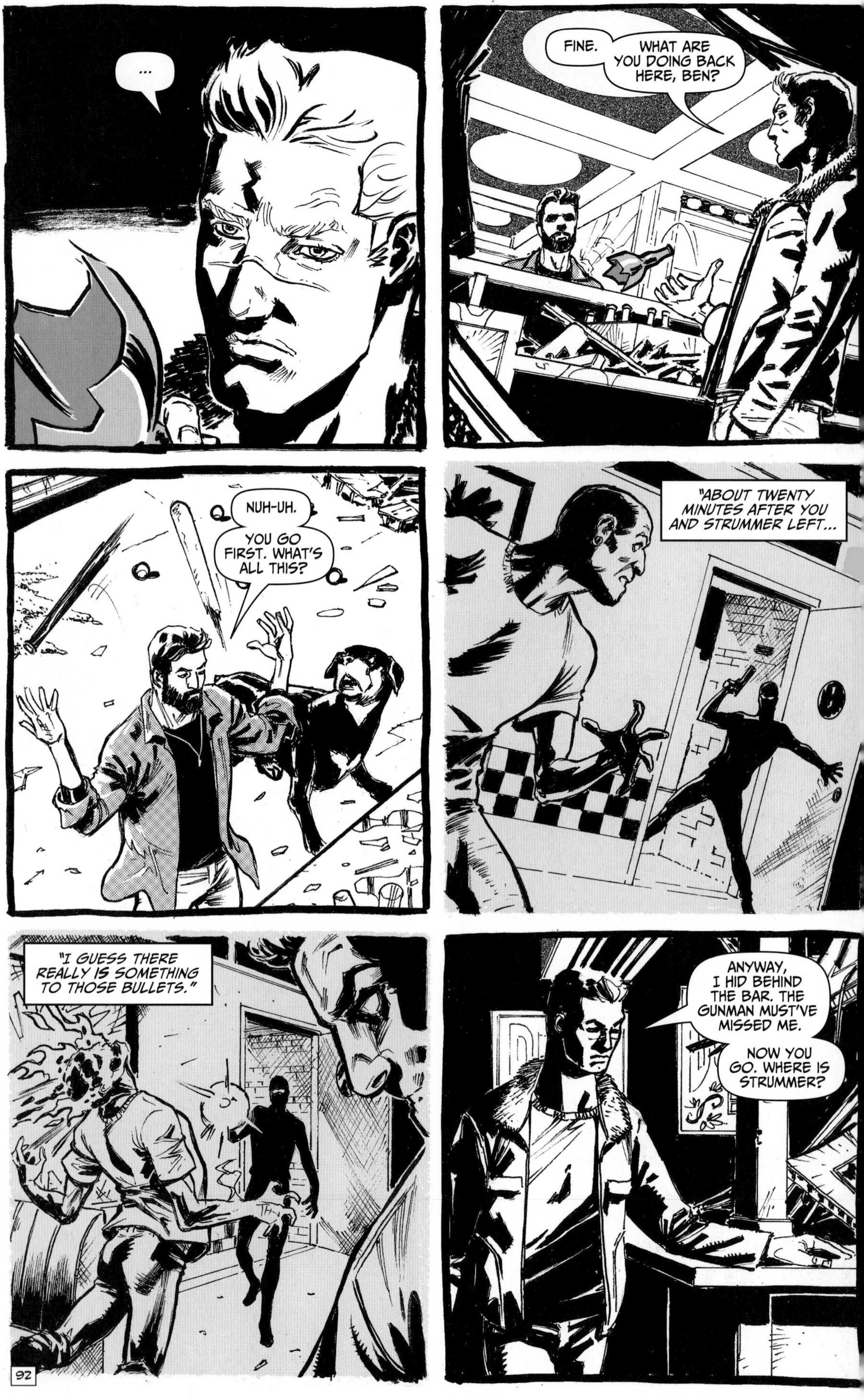
...
FINE.
WHAT ARE YOU DOING BACK HERE, BEN?
NUH-UH.
YOU GO FIRST. WHAT'S ALL THIS?
"ABOUT TWENTY MINUTES AFTER YOU AND STRUMMER LEFT...
"I GUESS THERE REALLY IS SOMETHING TO THOSE BULLETS."
ANYWAY, I HID BEHIND THE BAR. THE GUNMAN MUST'VE MISSED ME.
NOW YOU GO. WHERE IS STRUMMER?

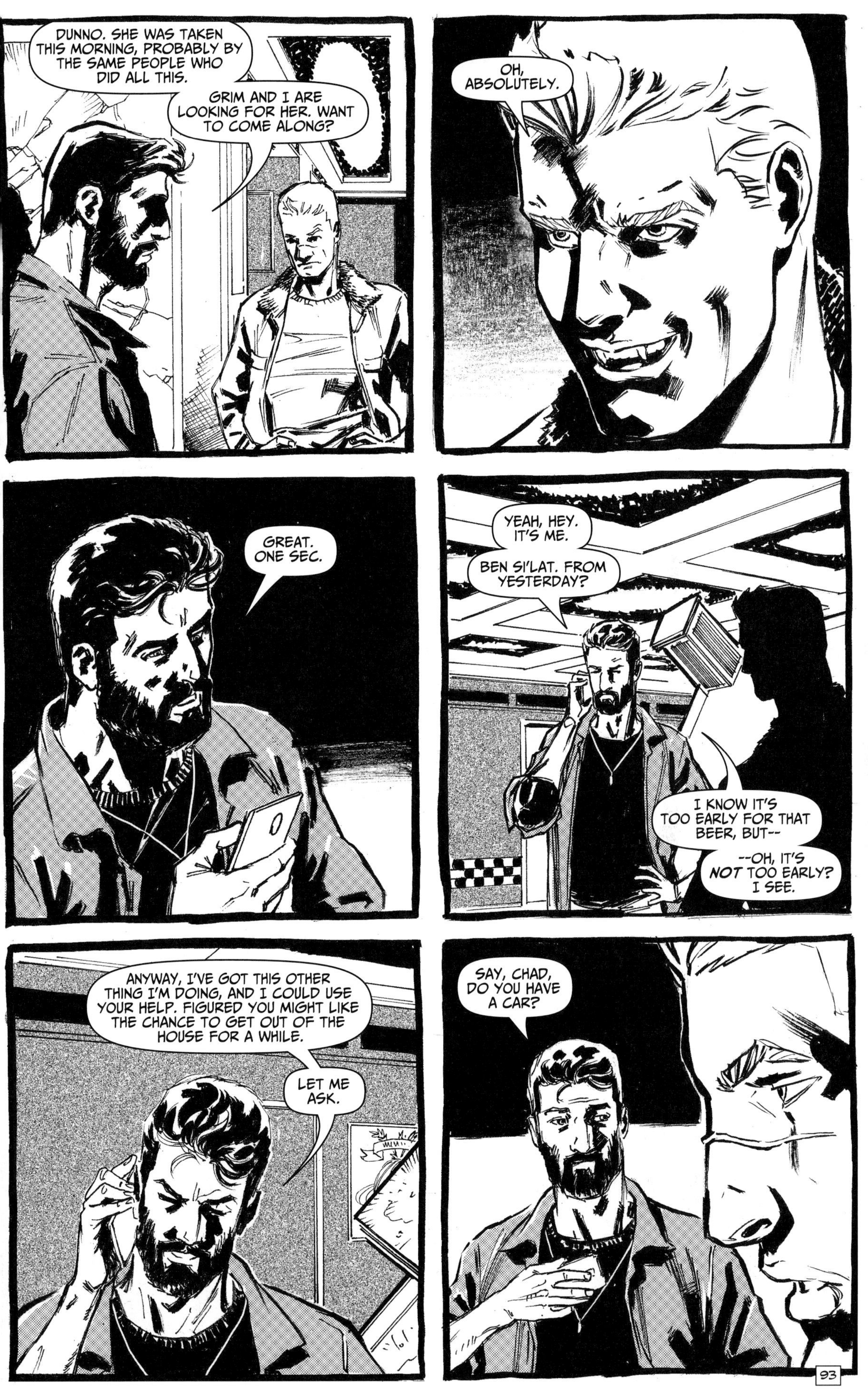
DUNNO. SHE WAS TAKEN THIS MORNING, PROBABLY BY THE SAME PEOPLE WHO DID ALL THIS.
GRIM AND I ARE LOOKING FOR HER. WANT TO COME ALONG?
OH, ABSOLUTELY.
GREAT. ONE SEC.
YEAH, HEY. IT'S ME.
BEN SI'LAT. FROM YESTERDAY?
I KNOW IT'S TOO EARLY FOR THAT BEER, BUT--
--OH, IT'S *NOT* TOO EARLY? I SEE.
ANYWAY, I'VE GOT THIS OTHER THING I'M DOING, AND I COULD USE YOUR HELP. FIGURED YOU MIGHT LIKE THE CHANCE TO GET OUT OF THE HOUSE FOR A WHILE.
LET ME ASK.
SAY, CHAD, DO YOU HAVE A CAR?

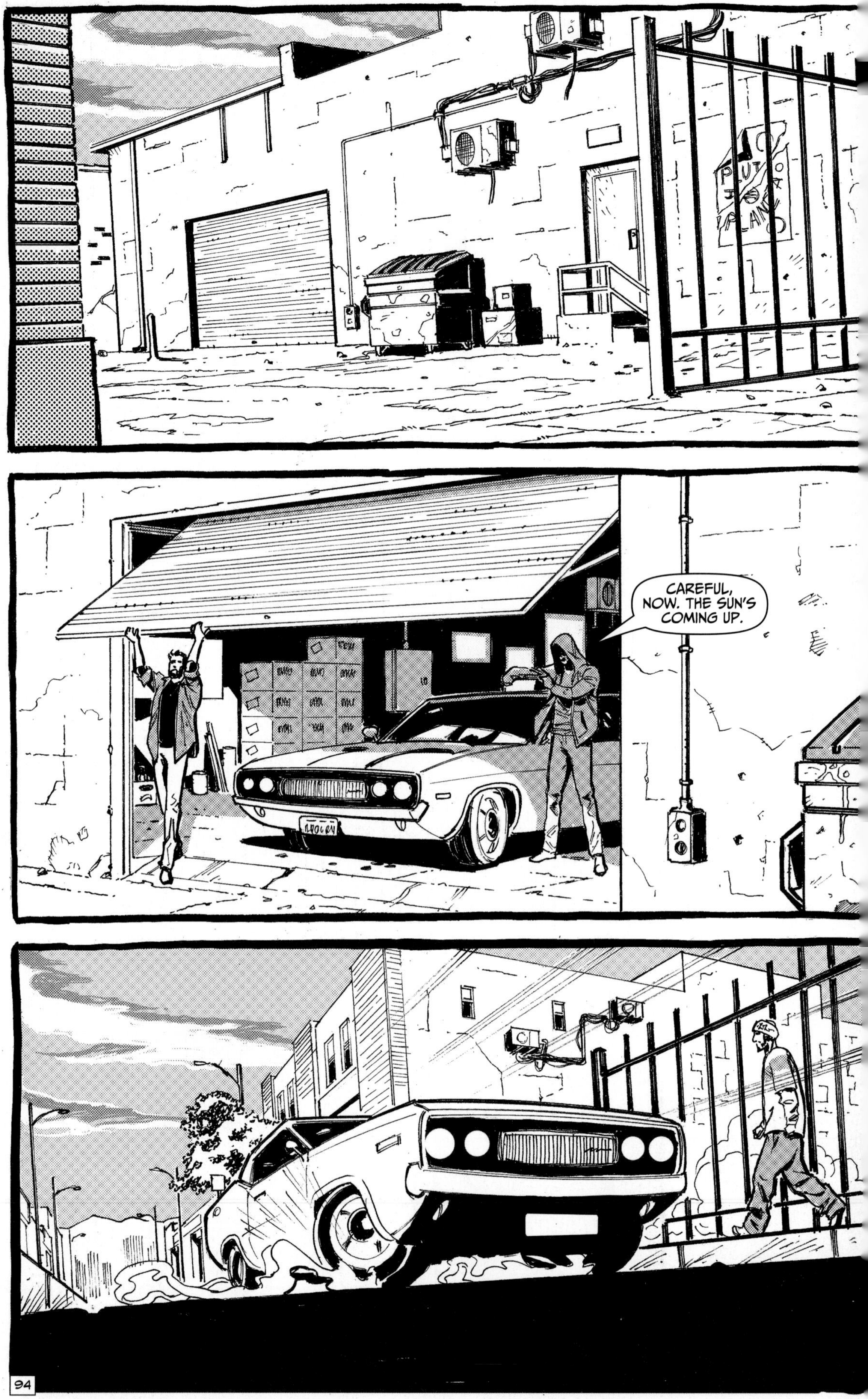
CAREFUL, NOW. THE SUN'S COMING UP.

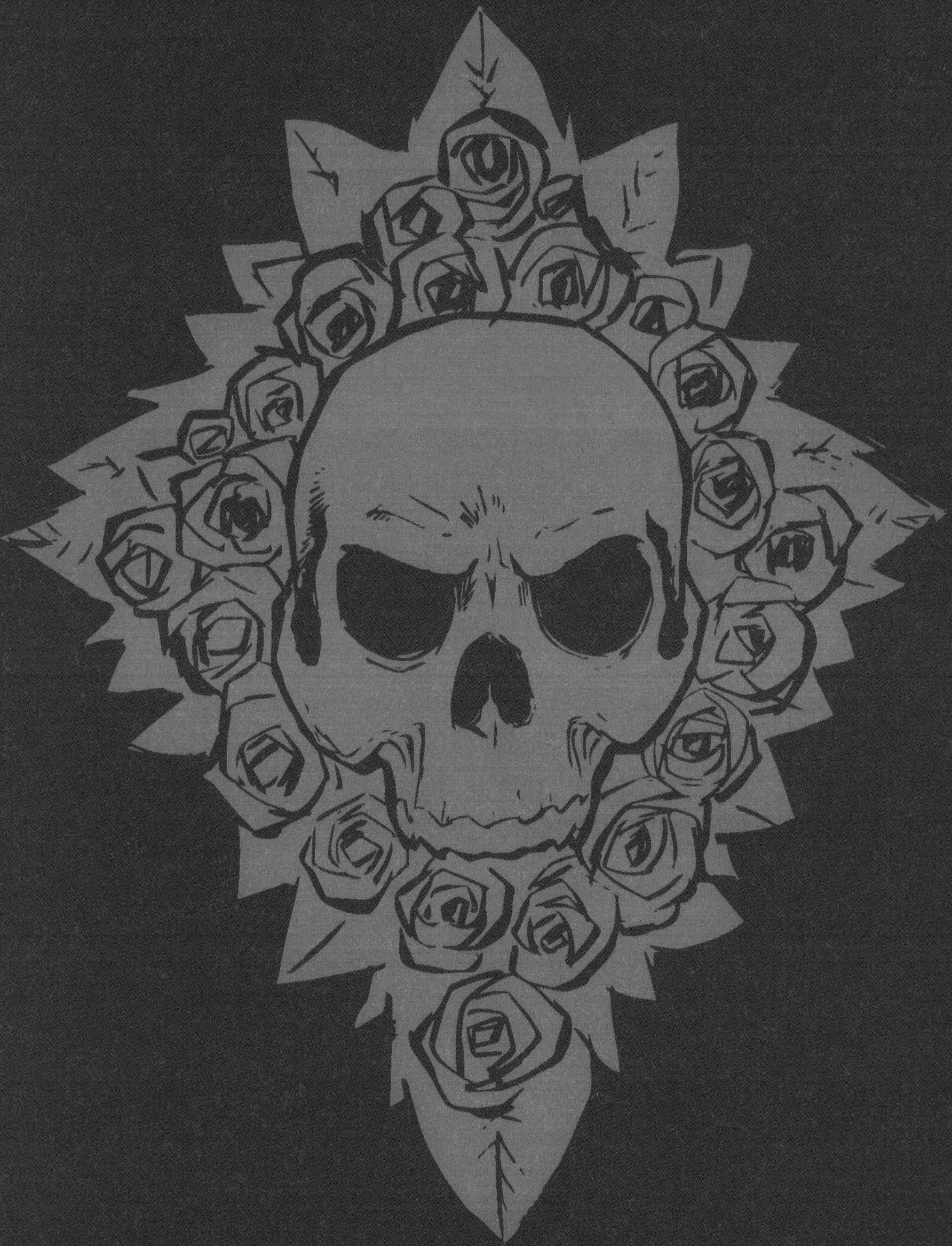

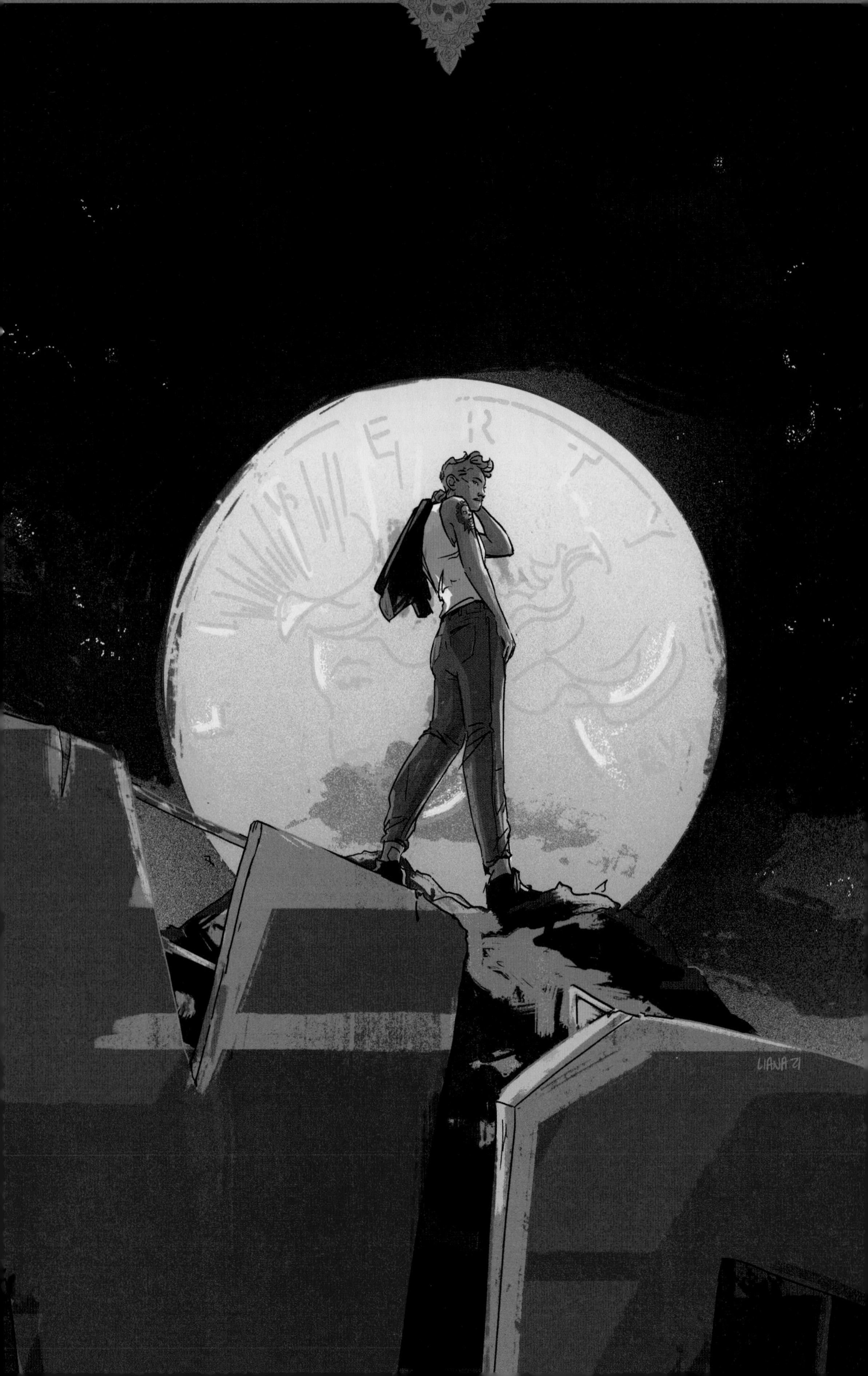
LIANA 21

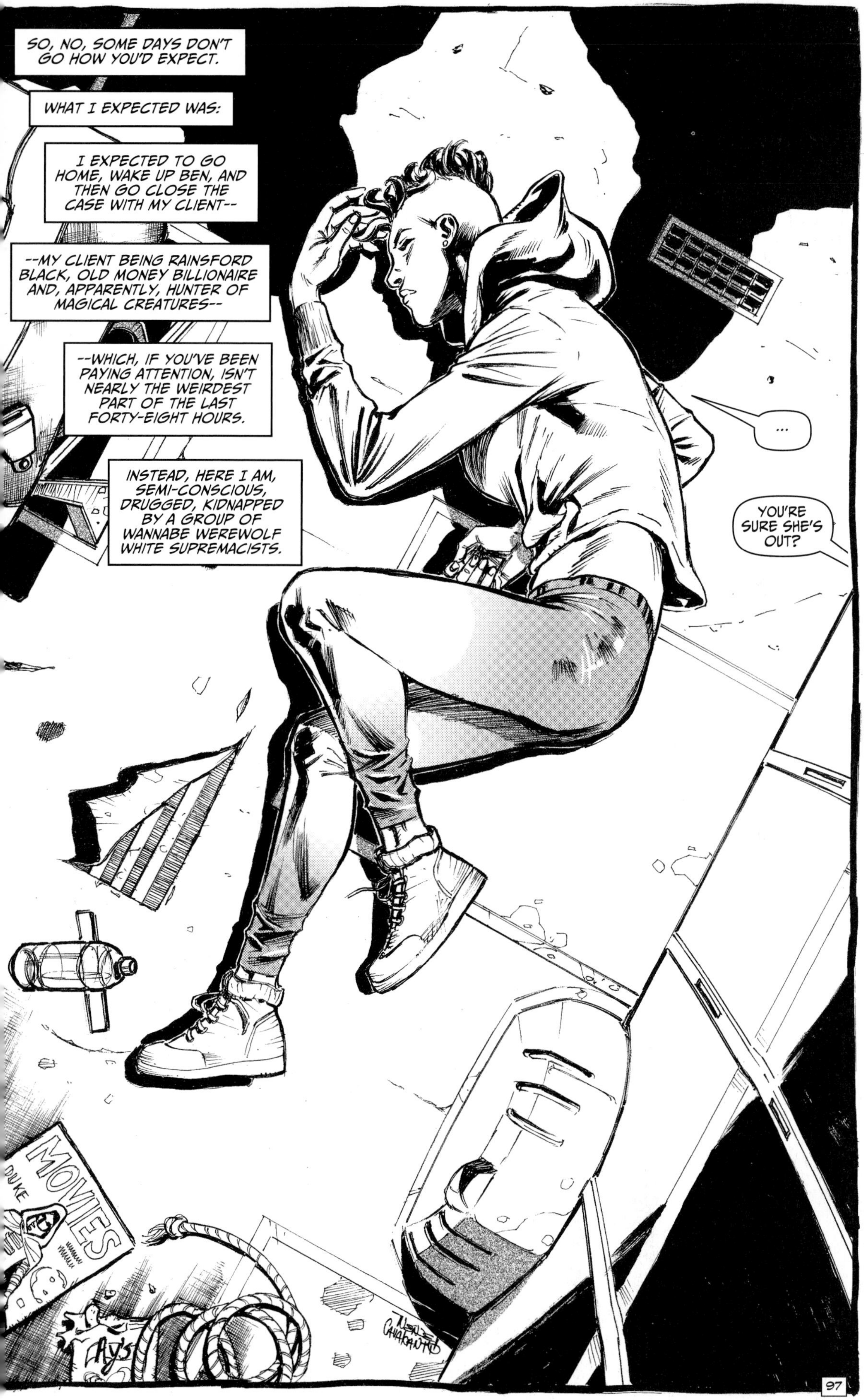
SO, NO, SOME DAYS DON'T GO HOW YOU'D EXPECT.
WHAT I EXPECTED WAS:
I EXPECTED TO GO HOME, WAKE UP BEN, AND THEN GO CLOSE THE CASE WITH MY CLIENT--
--MY CLIENT BEING RAINSFORD BLACK, OLD MONEY BILLIONAIRE AND, APPARENTLY, HUNTER OF MAGICAL CREATURES--
--WHICH, IF YOU'VE BEEN PAYING ATTENTION, ISN'T NEARLY THE WEIRDEST PART OF THE LAST FORTY-EIGHT HOURS.
INSTEAD, HERE I AM, SEMI-CONSCIOUS, DRUGGED, KIDNAPPED BY A GROUP OF WANNABE WEREWOLF WHITE SUPREMACISTS.
...
YOU'RE SURE SHE'S OUT?
MOVIES
DUKE

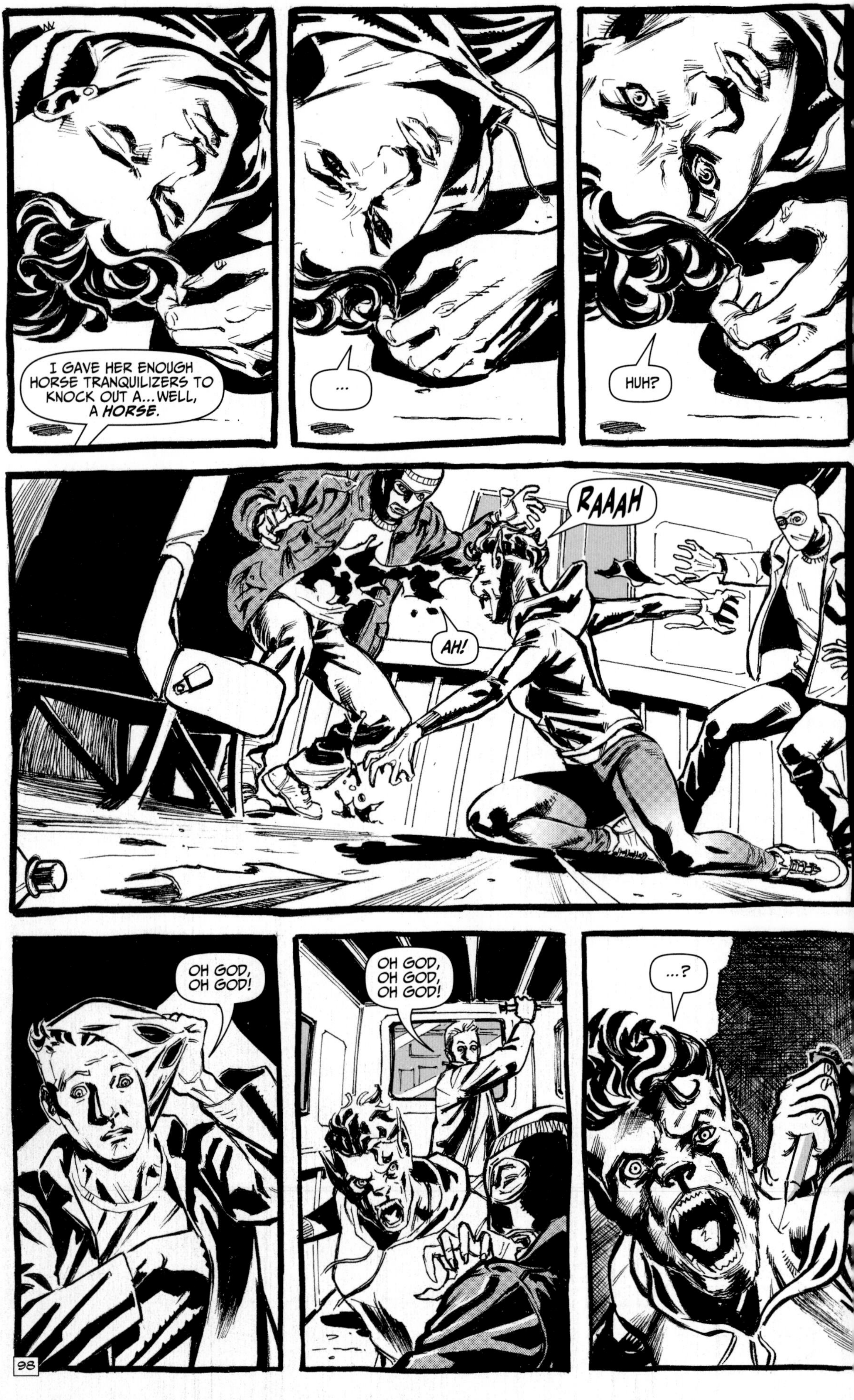

I GAVE HER ENOUGH HORSE TRANQUILIZERS TO KNOCK OUT A...WELL, A *HORSE*.
...
HUH?
RAAAH
AH!
OH GOD, OH GOD!
OH GOD, OH GOD, OH GOD!
...?

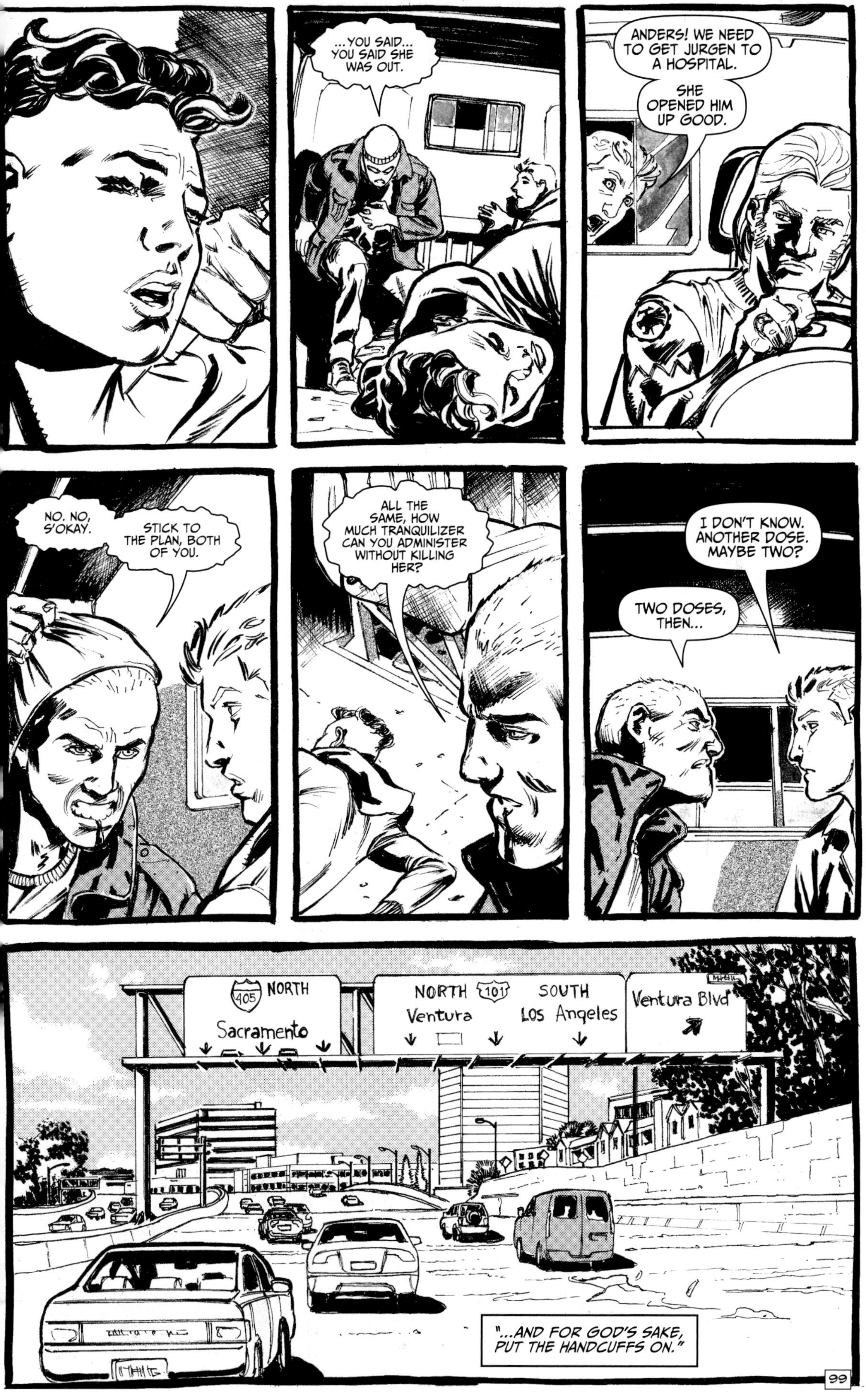

...YOU SAID... YOU SAID SHE WAS OUT.
ANDERS! WE NEED TO GET JURGEN TO A HOSPITAL.
SHE OPENED HIM UP GOOD.
NO. NO, S'OKAY.
STICK TO THE PLAN, BOTH OF YOU.
ALL THE SAME, HOW MUCH TRANQUILIZER CAN YOU ADMINISTER WITHOUT KILLING HER?
I DON'T KNOW. ANOTHER DOSE. MAYBE TWO?
TWO DOSES, THEN...
405 NORTH
Sacramento
NORTH 101 SOUTH
Ventura Los Angeles
Ventura Blvd
"...AND FOR GOD'S SAKE, PUT THE HANDCUFFS ON."

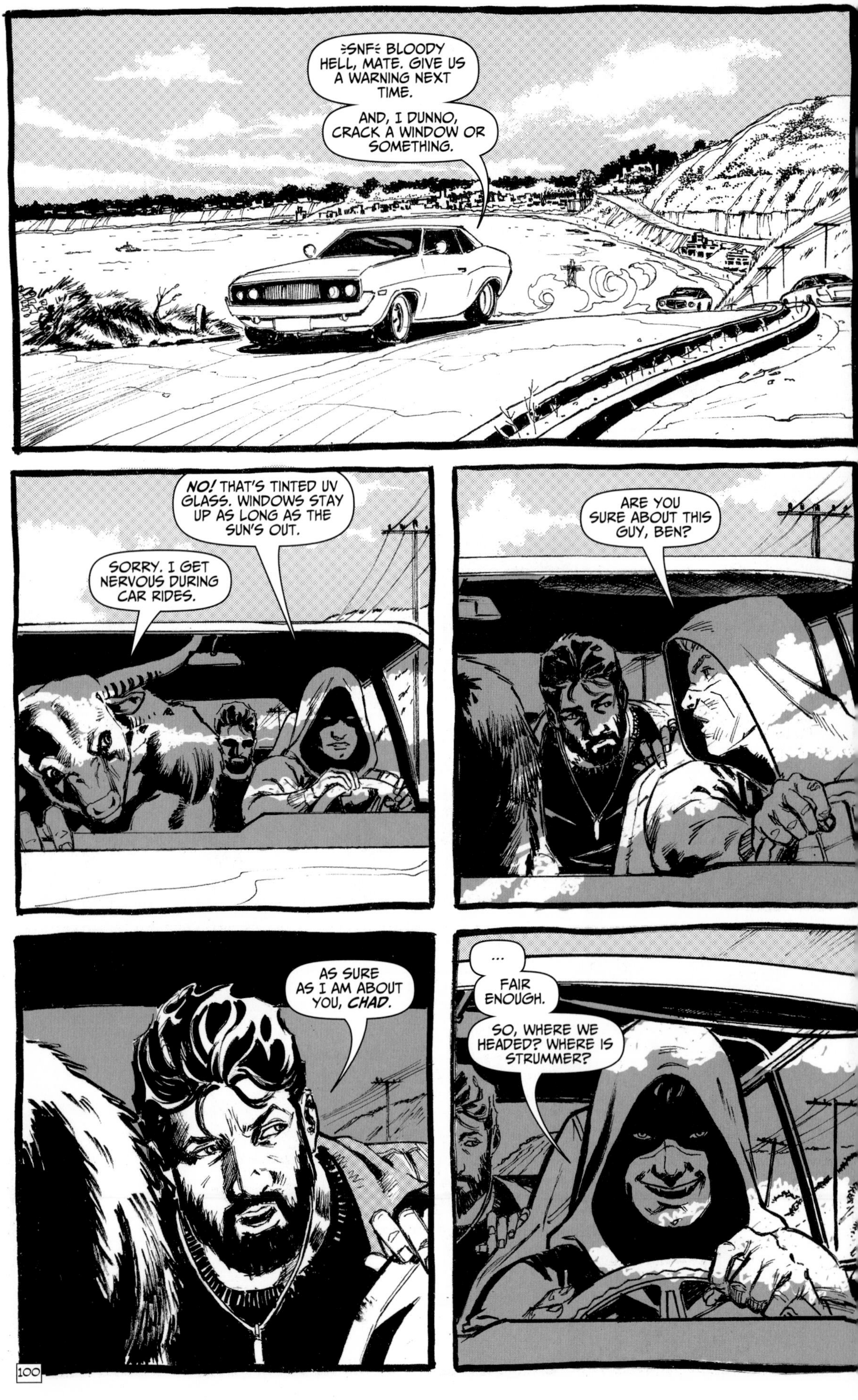

≶SNF≶ BLOODY HELL, MATE. GIVE US A WARNING NEXT TIME.
AND, I DUNNO, CRACK A WINDOW OR SOMETHING.
NO! THAT'S TINTED UV GLASS. WINDOWS STAY UP AS LONG AS THE SUN'S OUT.
SORRY. I GET NERVOUS DURING CAR RIDES.
ARE YOU SURE ABOUT THIS GUY, BEN?
AS SURE AS I AM ABOUT YOU, CHAD.
...
FAIR ENOUGH.
SO, WHERE WE HEADED? WHERE IS STRUMMER?

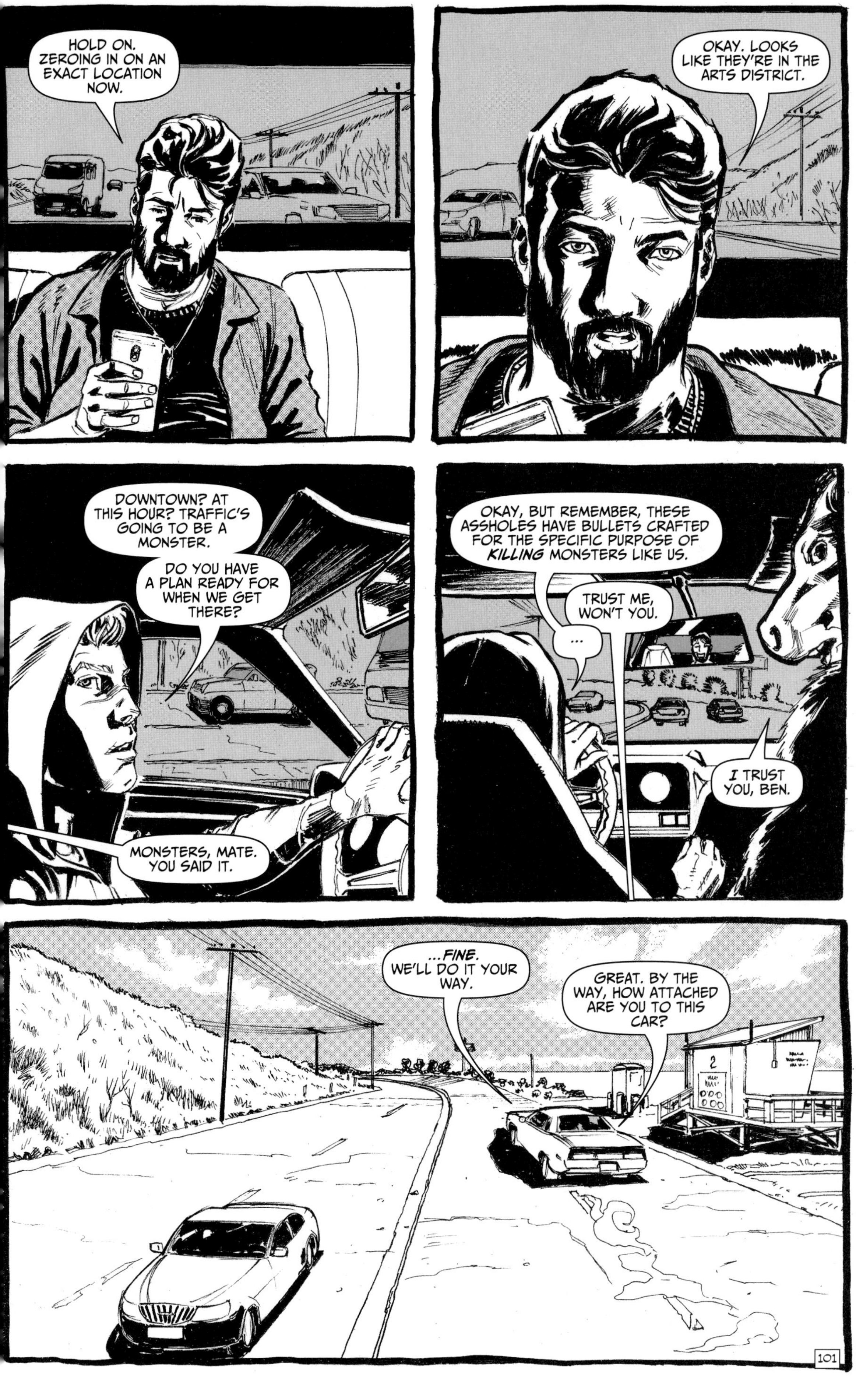
HOLD ON. ZEROING IN ON AN EXACT LOCATION NOW.
OKAY. LOOKS LIKE THEY'RE IN THE ARTS DISTRICT.
DOWNTOWN? AT THIS HOUR? TRAFFIC'S GOING TO BE A MONSTER.
DO YOU HAVE A PLAN READY FOR WHEN WE GET THERE?
MONSTERS, MATE. YOU SAID IT.
OKAY, BUT REMEMBER, THESE ASSHOLES HAVE BULLETS CRAFTED FOR THE SPECIFIC PURPOSE OF *KILLING* MONSTERS LIKE US.
TRUST ME, WON'T YOU.
...
I TRUST YOU, BEN.
...*FINE*. WE'LL DO IT YOUR WAY.
GREAT. BY THE WAY, HOW ATTACHED ARE YOU TO THIS CAR?

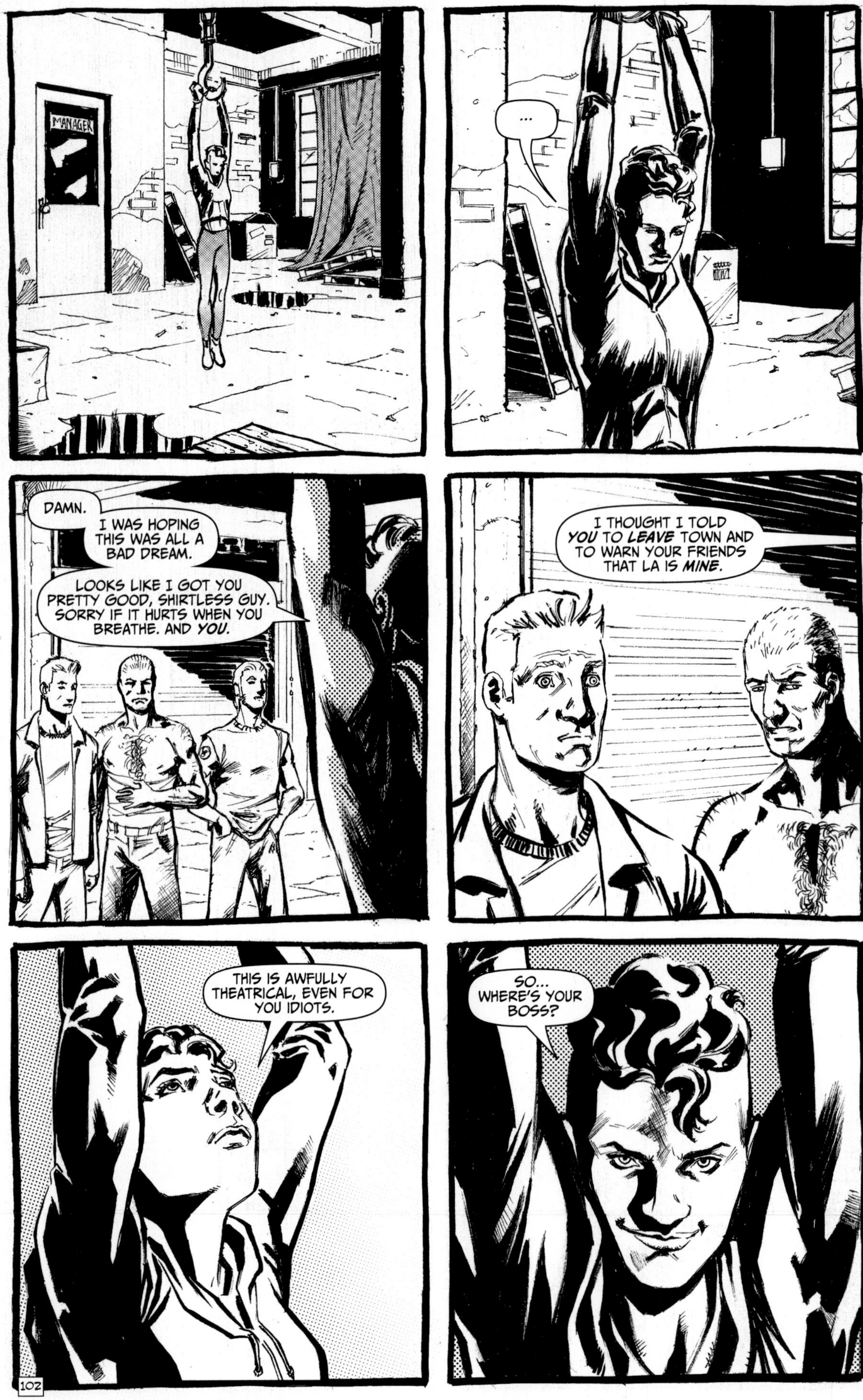
MANAGER
...
DAMN.
I WAS HOPING THIS WAS ALL A BAD DREAM.
LOOKS LIKE I GOT YOU PRETTY GOOD, SHIRTLESS GUY. SORRY IF IT HURTS WHEN YOU BREATHE. AND *YOU*.
I THOUGHT I TOLD *YOU* TO *LEAVE* TOWN AND TO WARN YOUR FRIENDS THAT LA IS *MINE*.
THIS IS AWFULLY THEATRICAL, EVEN FOR YOU IDIOTS.
SO... WHERE'S YOUR BOSS?

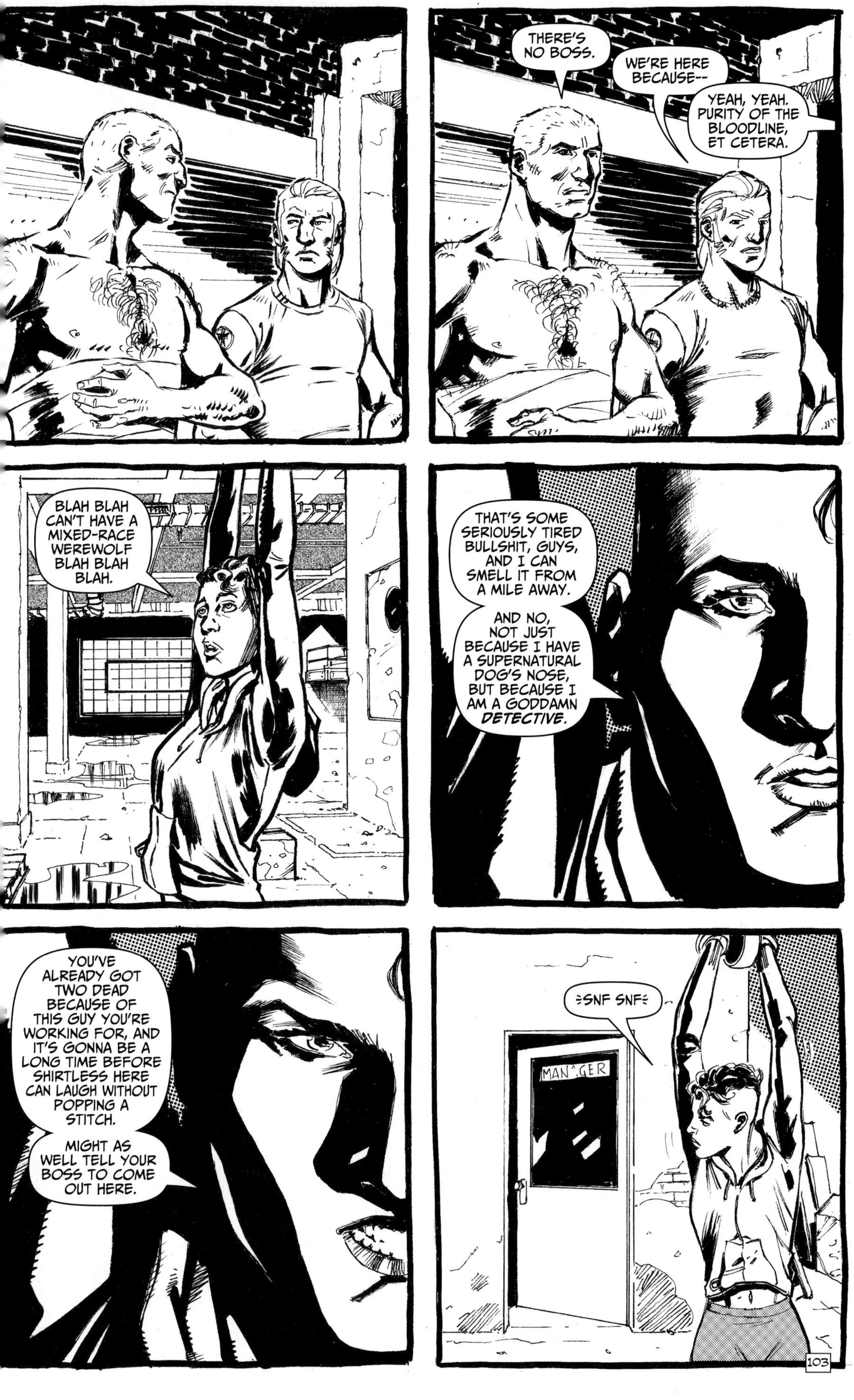
THERE'S NO BOSS.
WE'RE HERE BECAUSE--
YEAH, YEAH. PURITY OF THE BLOODLINE, ET CETERA.
BLAH BLAH CAN'T HAVE A MIXED-RACE WEREWOLF BLAH BLAH BLAH.
THAT'S SOME SERIOUSLY TIRED BULLSHIT, GUYS, AND I CAN SMELL IT FROM A MILE AWAY.
AND NO, NOT JUST BECAUSE I HAVE A SUPERNATURAL DOG'S NOSE, BUT BECAUSE I AM A GODDAMN *DETECTIVE*.
YOU'VE ALREADY GOT TWO DEAD BECAUSE OF THIS GUY YOU'RE WORKING FOR, AND IT'S GONNA BE A LONG TIME BEFORE SHIRTLESS HERE CAN LAUGH WITHOUT POPPING A STITCH.
MIGHT AS WELL TELL YOUR BOSS TO COME OUT HERE.
SNF SNF
MAN".GER

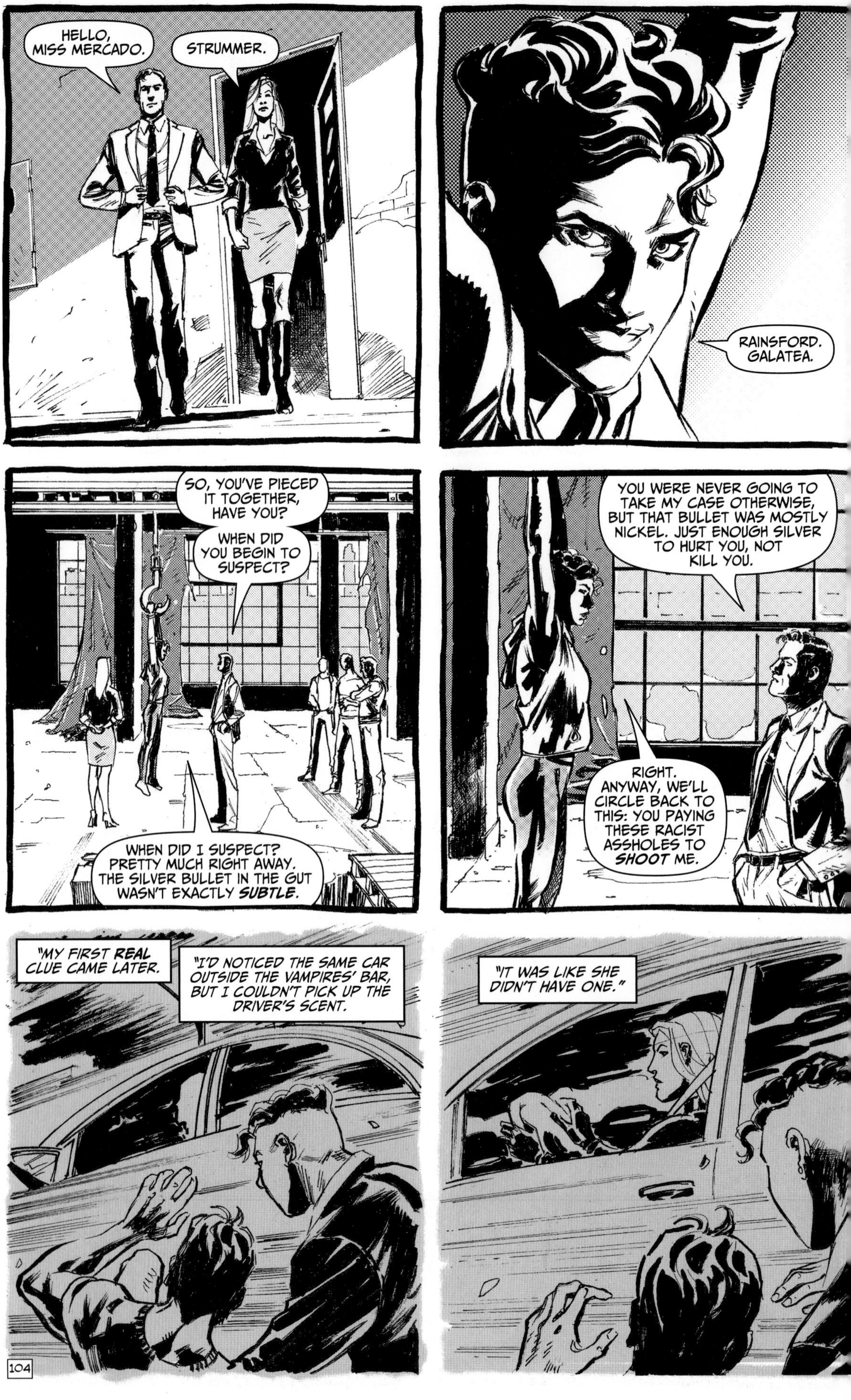
HELLO, MISS MERCADO.
STRUMMER.
RAINSFORD. GALATEA.
SO, YOU'VE PIECED IT TOGETHER, HAVE YOU?
WHEN DID YOU BEGIN TO SUSPECT?
WHEN DID I SUSPECT? PRETTY MUCH RIGHT AWAY. THE SILVER BULLET IN THE GUT WASN'T EXACTLY SUBTLE.
YOU WERE NEVER GOING TO TAKE MY CASE OTHERWISE, BUT THAT BULLET WAS MOSTLY NICKEL. JUST ENOUGH SILVER TO HURT YOU, NOT KILL YOU.
RIGHT. ANYWAY, WE'LL CIRCLE BACK TO THIS: YOU PAYING THESE RACIST ASSHOLES TO SHOOT ME.
"MY FIRST REAL CLUE CAME LATER.
"I'D NOTICED THE SAME CAR OUTSIDE THE VAMPIRES' BAR, BUT I COULDN'T PICK UP THE DRIVER'S SCENT.
"IT WAS LIKE SHE DIDN'T HAVE ONE."

LIKE SHE'D BEEN CARVED OUT OF MARBLE.

IT WAS *THIN*-- MAYBE YOU'D JUST SENT HER ALONG TO KEEP TABS--BUT IT WAS A *START*.

SINCE NO ONE SEEMED TO CARE ABOUT YOUR BULLETS, MY FIRST INSTINCT WAS, YOU WERE USING ME TO CREATE A MARKET FOR THEM.

"AND THEN I SPOKE TO THE OLD MAN ONE LAST TIME.

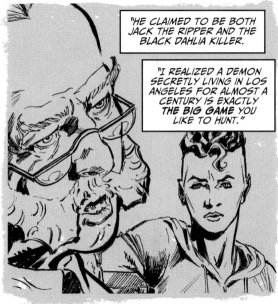

"HE CLAIMED TO BE BOTH JACK THE RIPPER AND THE BLACK DAHLIA KILLER.

"I REALIZED A DEMON SECRETLY LIVING IN LOS ANGELES FOR ALMOST A CENTURY IS EXACTLY *THE BIG GAME* YOU LIKE TO HUNT."

HE WAS JACK THE RIPPER *AND* THE BLACK DAHLIA KILLER?

YES!

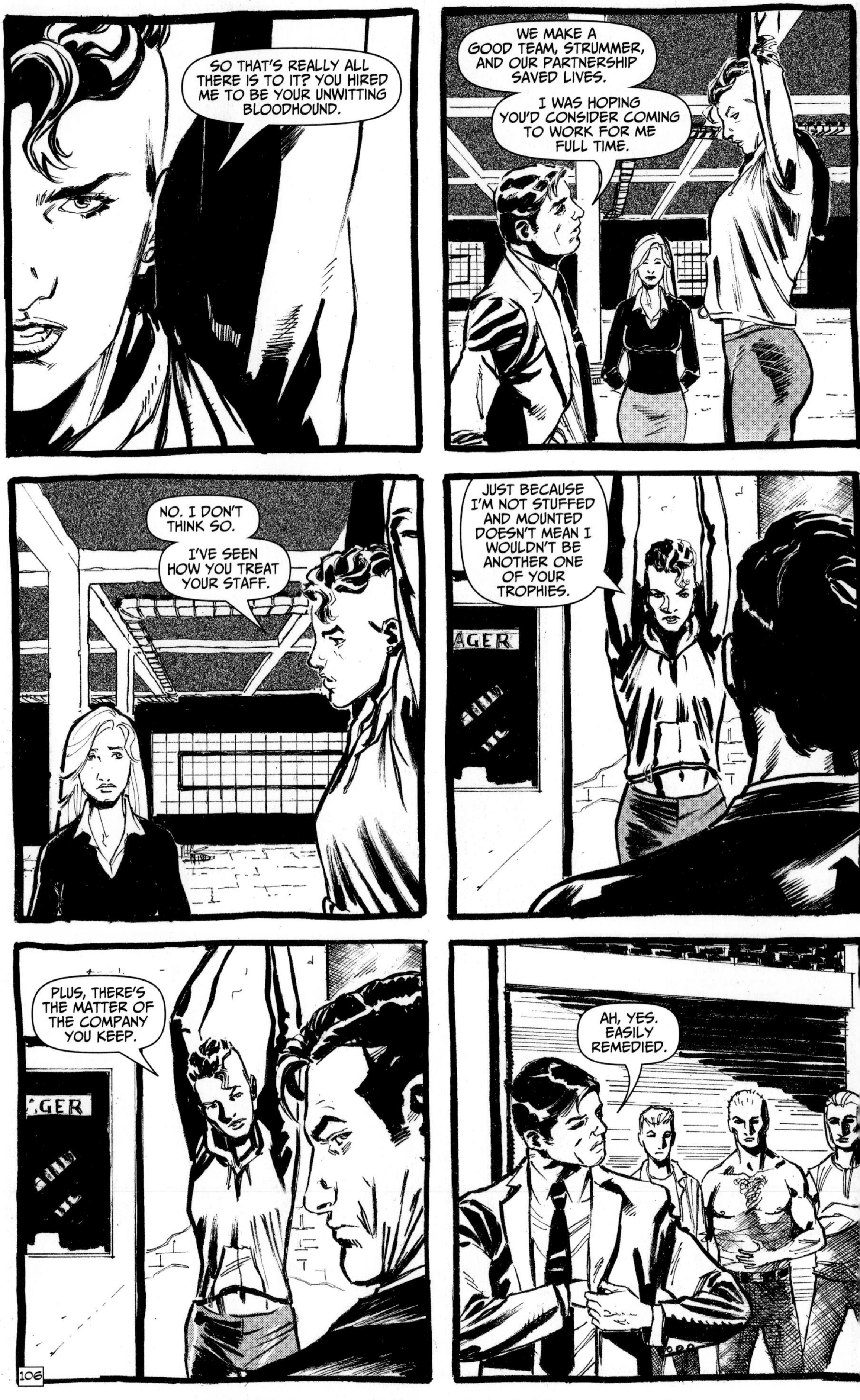
SO THAT'S REALLY ALL THERE IS TO IT? YOU HIRED ME TO BE YOUR UNWITTING BLOODHOUND.
WE MAKE A GOOD TEAM, STRUMMER, AND OUR PARTNERSHIP SAVED LIVES.
I WAS HOPING YOU'D CONSIDER COMING TO WORK FOR ME FULL TIME.
NO. I DON'T THINK SO.
I'VE SEEN HOW YOU TREAT YOUR STAFF.
JUST BECAUSE I'M NOT STUFFED AND MOUNTED DOESN'T MEAN I WOULDN'T BE ANOTHER ONE OF YOUR TROPHIES.
AGER
PLUS, THERE'S THE MATTER OF THE COMPANY YOU KEEP.
GER
AH, YES. EASILY REMEDIED.

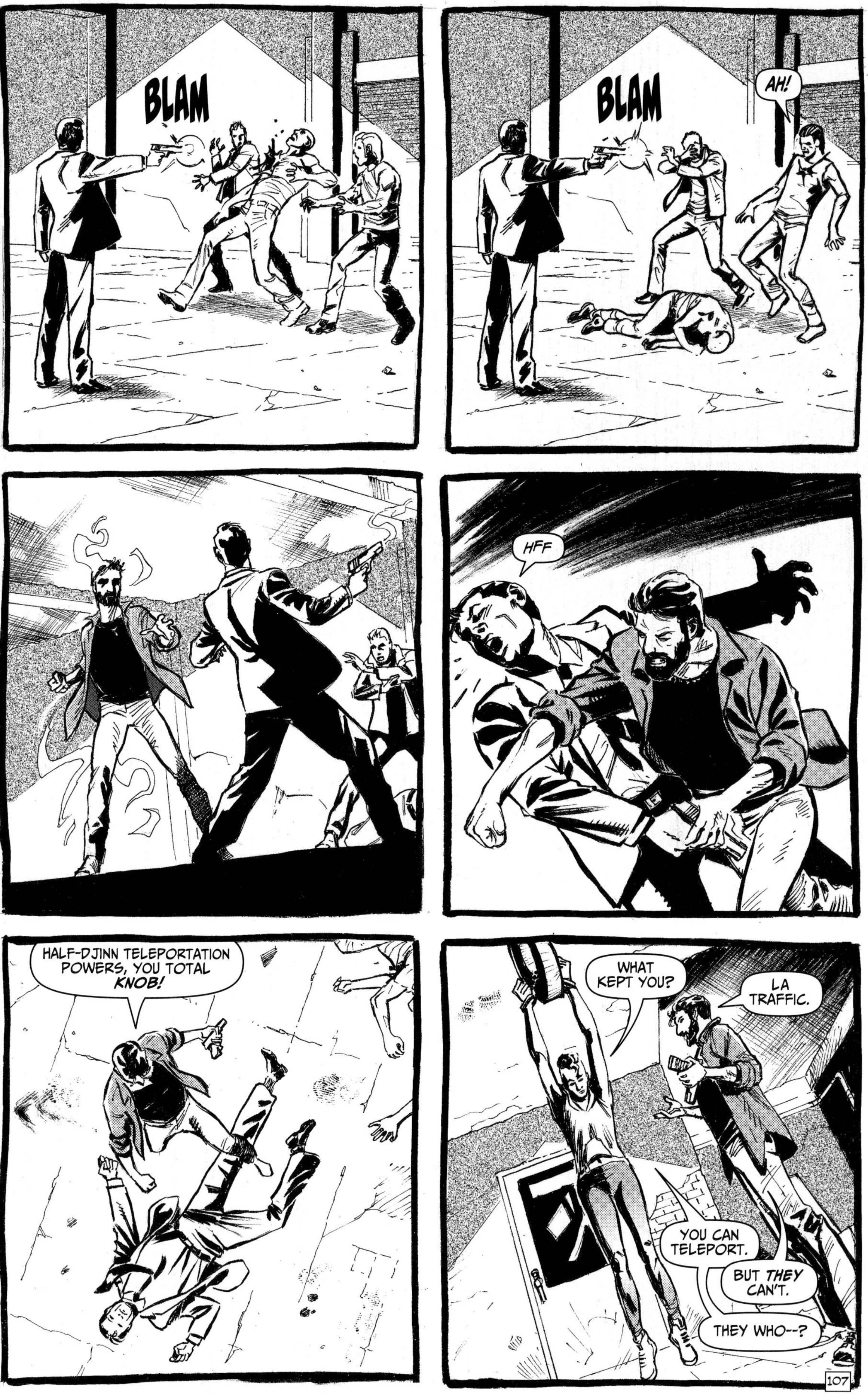
BLAM
BLAM
AH!
HFF
HALF-DJINN TELEPORTATION POWERS, YOU TOTAL KNOB!
WHAT KEPT YOU?
LA TRAFFIC.
YOU CAN TELEPORT.
BUT THEY CAN'T.
THEY WHO--?

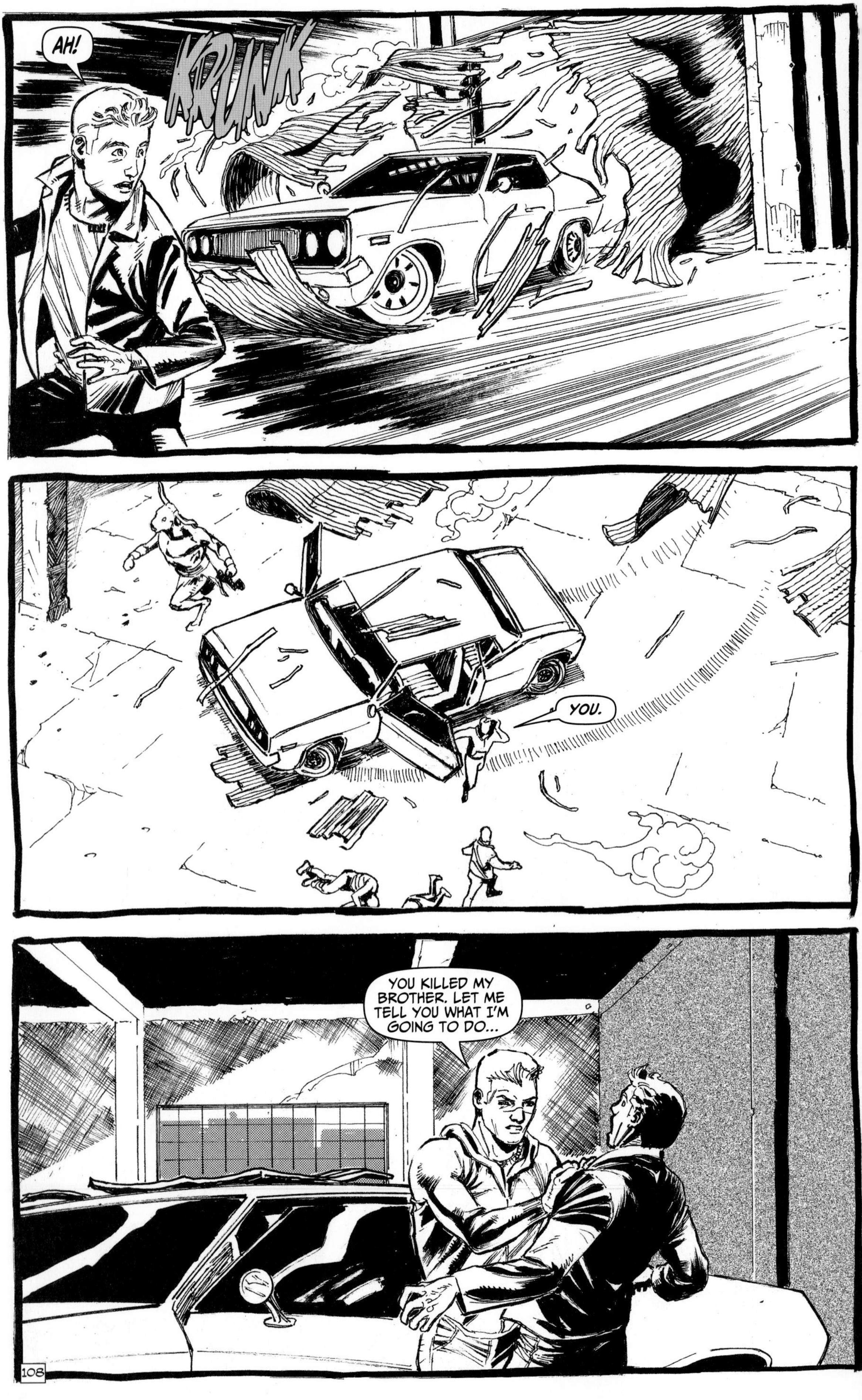
AH!
KRUNK
YOU.
YOU KILLED MY BROTHER. LET ME TELL YOU WHAT I'M GOING TO DO...

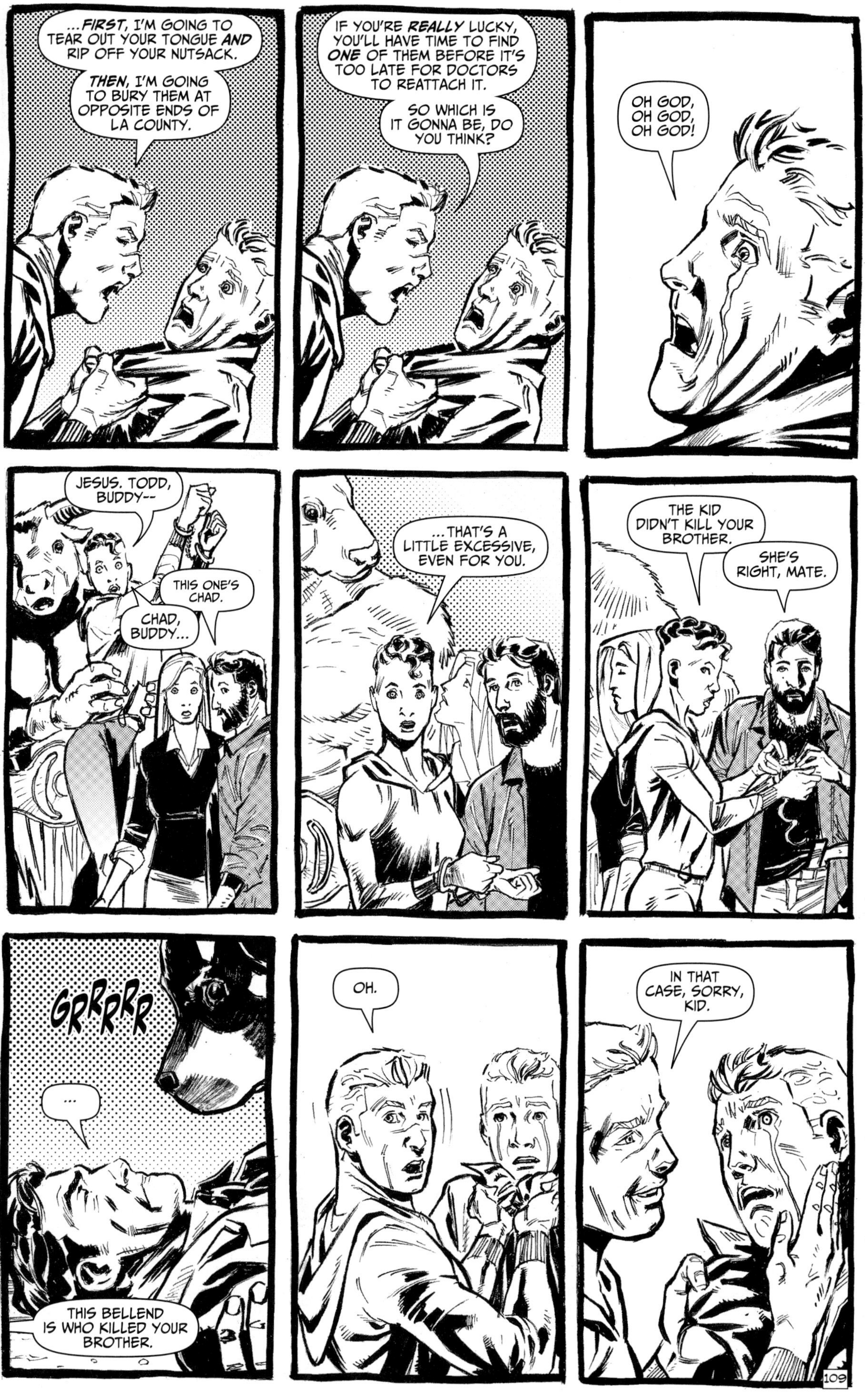
...FIRST, I'M GOING TO TEAR OUT YOUR TONGUE AND RIP OFF YOUR NUTSACK.
THEN, I'M GOING TO BURY THEM AT OPPOSITE ENDS OF LA COUNTY.
IF YOU'RE REALLY LUCKY, YOU'LL HAVE TIME TO FIND ONE OF THEM BEFORE IT'S TOO LATE FOR DOCTORS TO REATTACH IT.
SO WHICH IS IT GONNA BE, DO YOU THINK?
OH GOD, OH GOD, OH GOD!
JESUS. TODD, BUDDY--
THIS ONE'S CHAD.
CHAD, BUDDY...
...THAT'S A LITTLE EXCESSIVE, EVEN FOR YOU.
THE KID DIDN'T KILL YOUR BROTHER.
SHE'S RIGHT, MATE.
GRRRRR
...
THIS BELLEND IS WHO KILLED YOUR BROTHER.
OH.
IN THAT CASE, SORRY, KID.

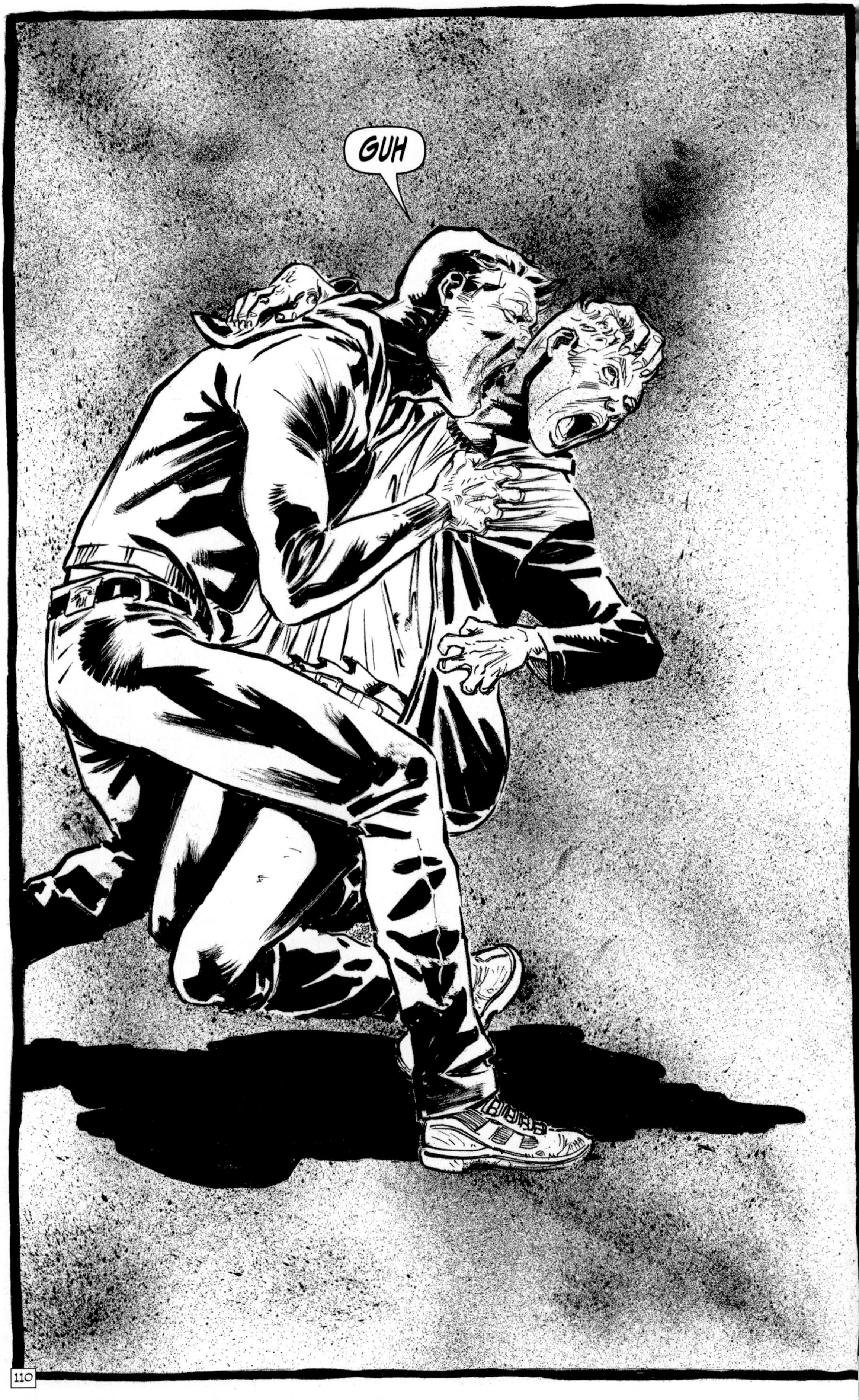
GUH

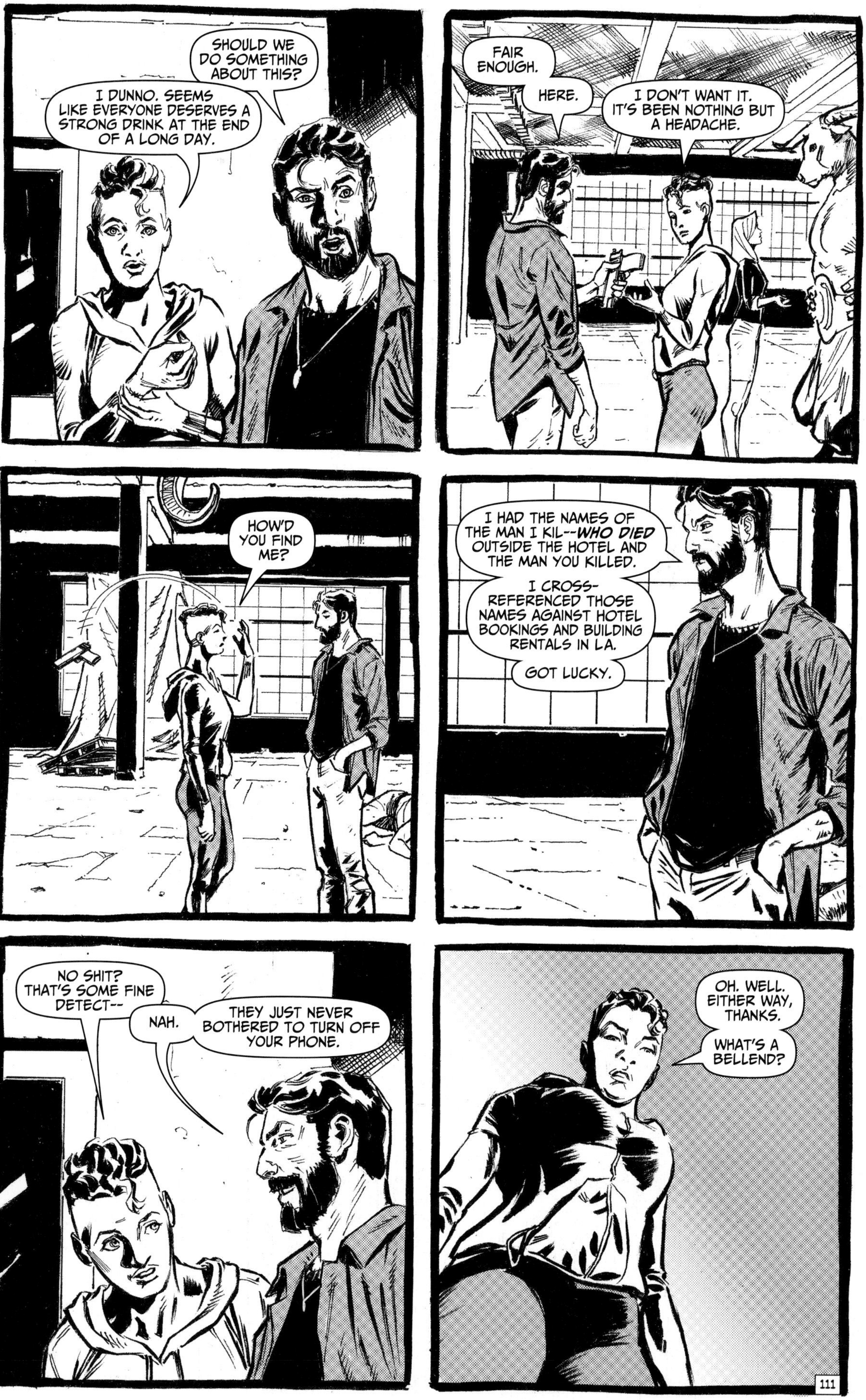
SHOULD WE DO SOMETHING ABOUT THIS?
I DUNNO. SEEMS LIKE EVERYONE DESERVES A STRONG DRINK AT THE END OF A LONG DAY.
FAIR ENOUGH.
HERE.
I DON'T WANT IT. IT'S BEEN NOTHING BUT A HEADACHE.
HOW'D YOU FIND ME?
I HAD THE NAMES OF THE MAN I KIL--*WHO DIED* OUTSIDE THE HOTEL AND THE MAN YOU KILLED.
I CROSS-REFERENCED THOSE NAMES AGAINST HOTEL BOOKINGS AND BUILDING RENTALS IN LA.
GOT LUCKY.
NO SHIT? THAT'S SOME FINE DETECT--
NAH.
THEY JUST NEVER BOTHERED TO TURN OFF YOUR PHONE.
OH. WELL. EITHER WAY, THANKS.
WHAT'S A BELLEND?

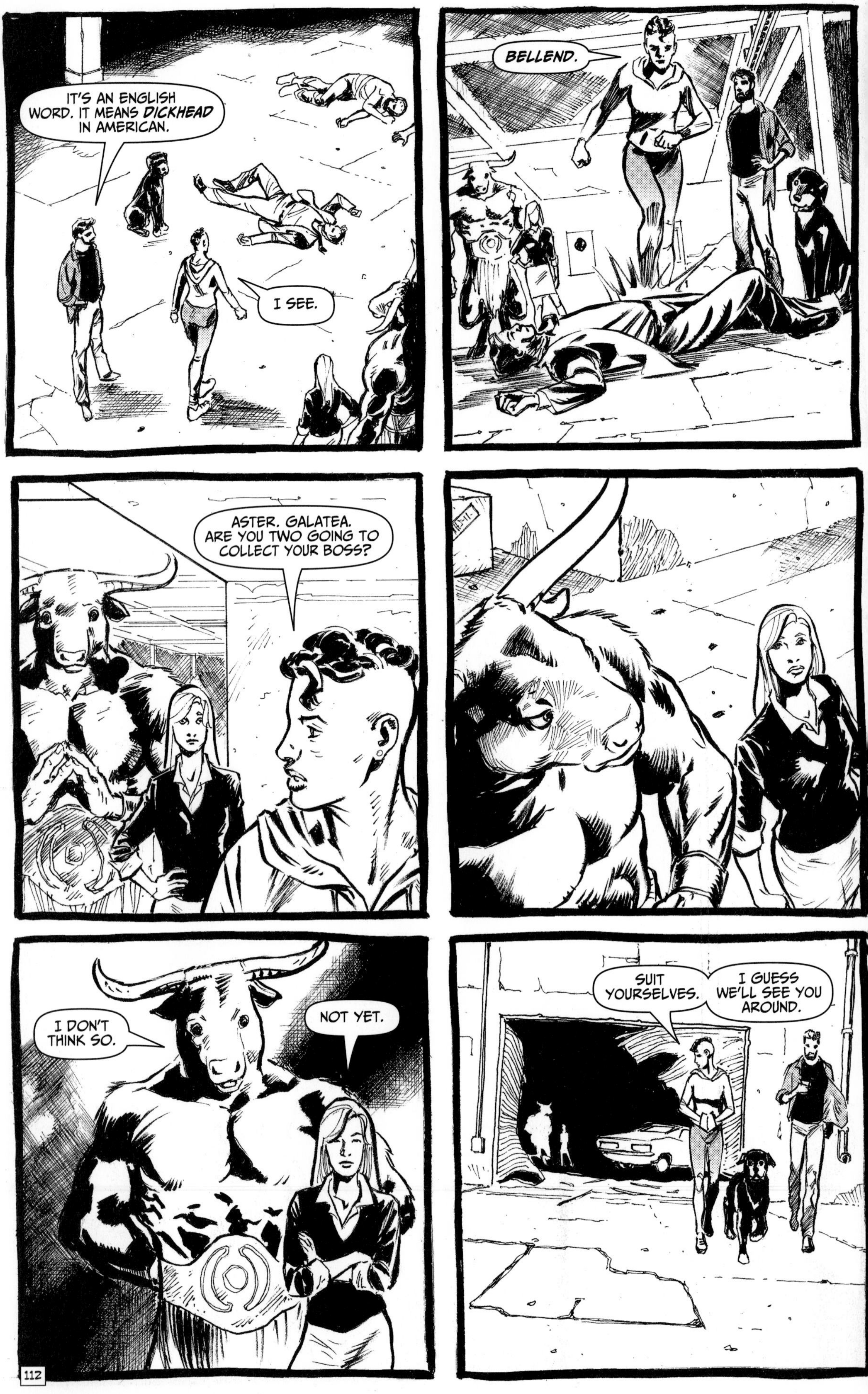
IT'S AN ENGLISH WORD. IT MEANS *DICKHEAD* IN AMERICAN.
I SEE.
BELLEND.
ASTER. GALATEA. ARE YOU TWO GOING TO COLLECT YOUR BOSS?
I DON'T THINK SO.
NOT YET.
SUIT YOURSELVES.
I GUESS WE'LL SEE YOU AROUND.

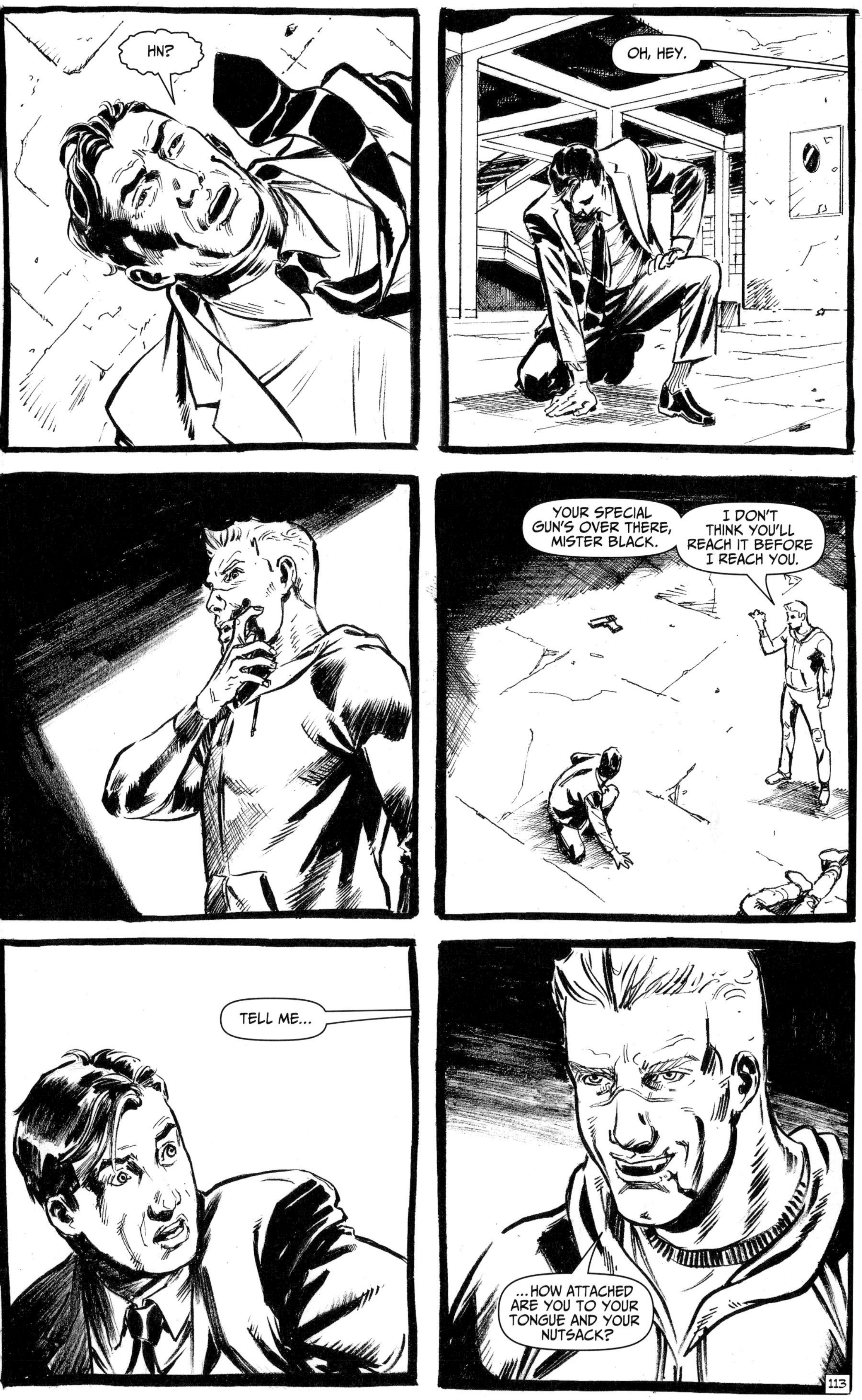
HN?
OH, HEY.
YOUR SPECIAL GUN'S OVER THERE, MISTER BLACK.
I DON'T THINK YOU'LL REACH IT BEFORE I REACH YOU.
TELL ME...
...HOW ATTACHED ARE YOU TO YOUR TONGUE AND YOUR NUTSACK?

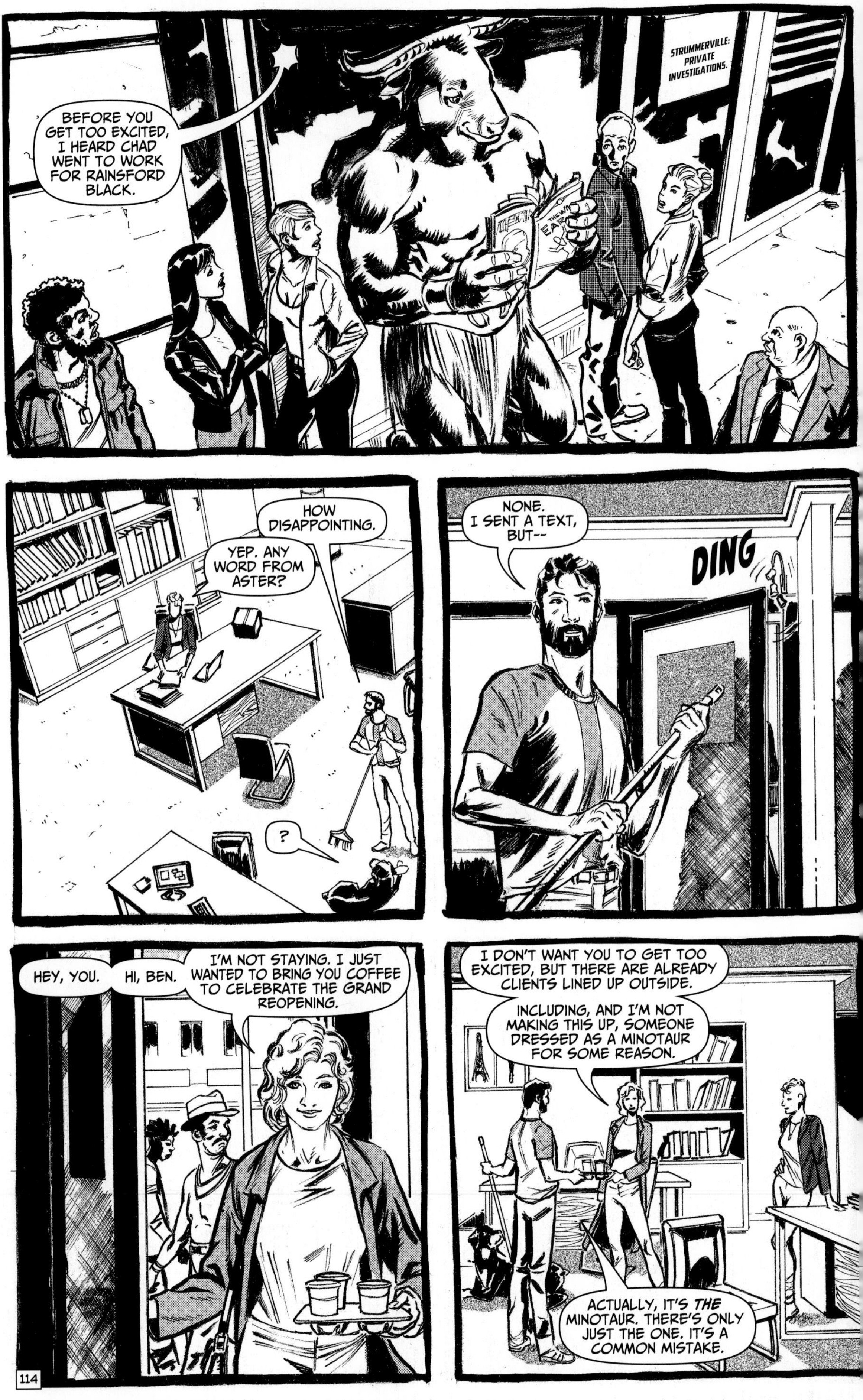

STRUMMERVILLE: PRIVATE INVESTIGATIONS.
BEFORE YOU GET TOO EXCITED, I HEARD CHAD WENT TO WORK FOR RAINSFORD BLACK.
HOW DISAPPOINTING.
YEP. ANY WORD FROM ASTER?
?
NONE. I SENT A TEXT, BUT--
DING
HEY, YOU.
HI, BEN.
I'M NOT STAYING. I JUST WANTED TO BRING YOU COFFEE TO CELEBRATE THE GRAND REOPENING.
I DON'T WANT YOU TO GET TOO EXCITED, BUT THERE ARE ALREADY CLIENTS LINED UP OUTSIDE.
INCLUDING, AND I'M NOT MAKING THIS UP, SOMEONE DRESSED AS A MINOTAUR FOR SOME REASON.
ACTUALLY, IT'S *THE* MINOTAUR. THERE'S ONLY JUST THE ONE. IT'S A COMMON MISTAKE.

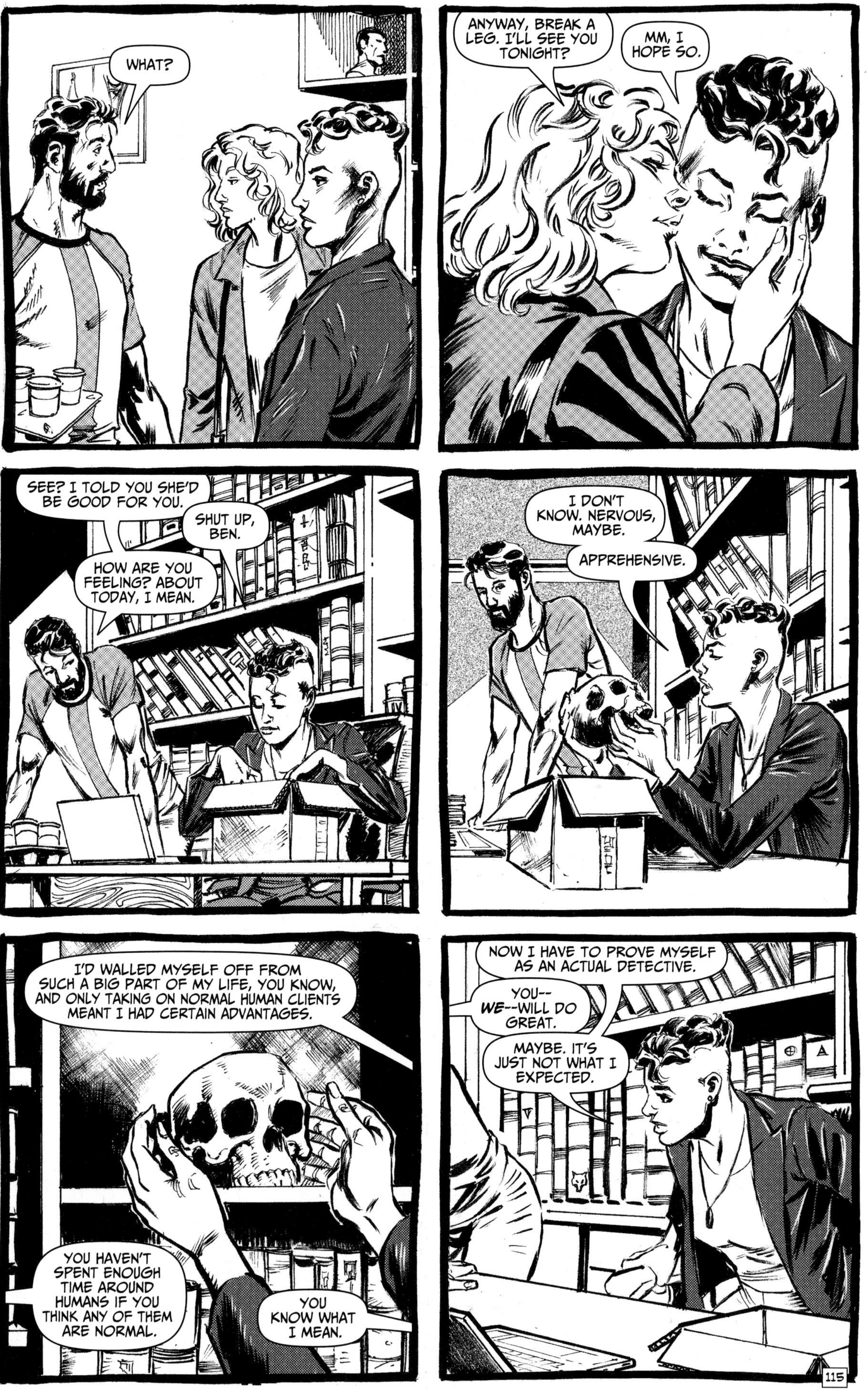
WHAT?
ANYWAY, BREAK A LEG. I'LL SEE YOU TONIGHT?
MM, I HOPE SO.
SEE? I TOLD YOU SHE'D BE GOOD FOR YOU.
SHUT UP, BEN.
HOW ARE YOU FEELING? ABOUT TODAY, I MEAN.
I DON'T KNOW. NERVOUS, MAYBE.
APPREHENSIVE.
I'D WALLED MYSELF OFF FROM SUCH A BIG PART OF MY LIFE, YOU KNOW, AND ONLY TAKING ON NORMAL HUMAN CLIENTS MEANT I HAD CERTAIN ADVANTAGES.
YOU HAVEN'T SPENT ENOUGH TIME AROUND HUMANS IF YOU THINK ANY OF THEM ARE NORMAL.
YOU KNOW WHAT I MEAN.
NOW I HAVE TO PROVE MYSELF AS AN ACTUAL DETECTIVE.
YOU-- *WE*--WILL DO GREAT.
MAYBE. IT'S JUST NOT WHAT I EXPECTED.

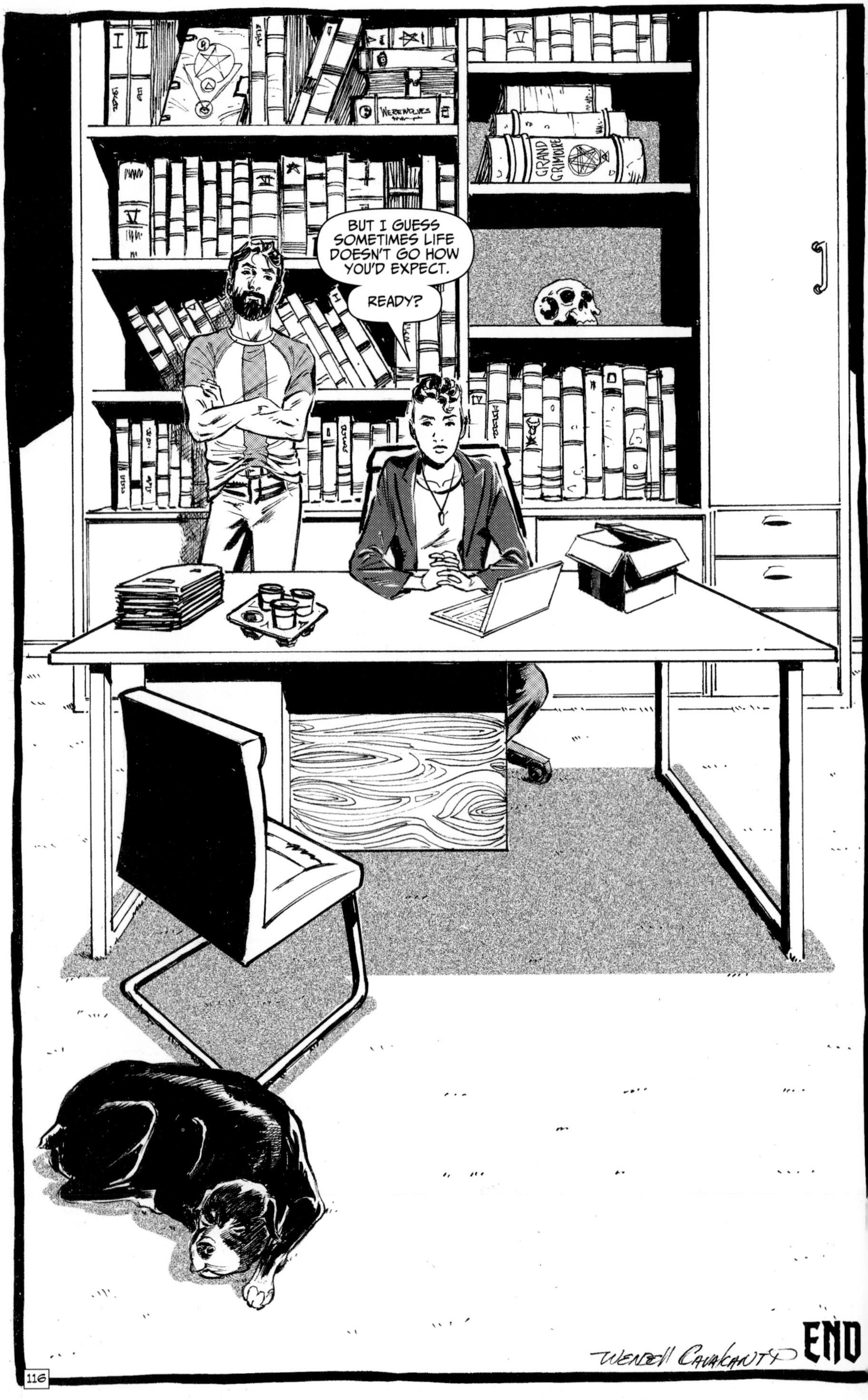
BUT I GUESS SOMETIMES LIFE DOESN'T GO HOW YOU'D EXPECT.
READY?
GRAND GRIMOIRE
WEREWOLVES
WENDELL CAVALCANTI
END

Ben Si'lat character design
by Wendell Cavalcanti

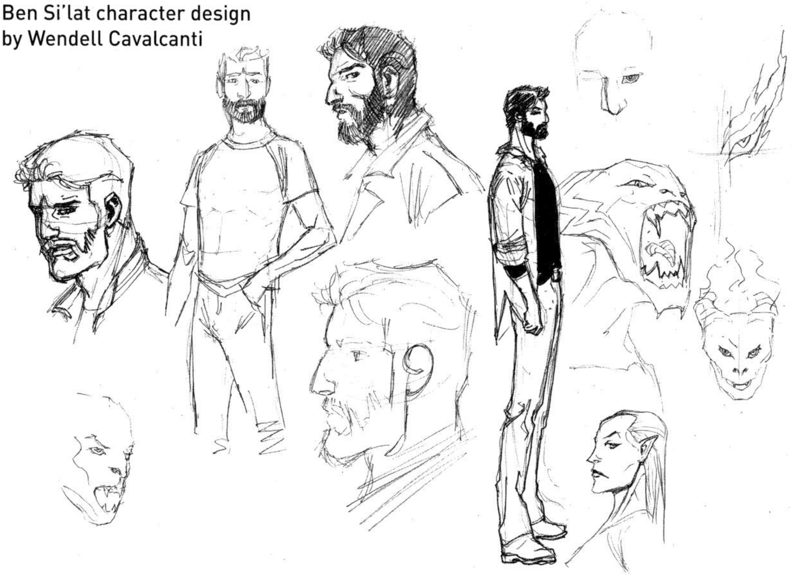

I described Ben in the script as "a handsome Brit of Middle Eastern descent (think Riz Ahmed) with tousled black hair, slim..." sometimes wearing jeans with sneakers or boots and a Harrington jacket over a fifty-dollar t-shirt. Wendell ran with my notes and gave us our perfect Ben.

— ERIC PALICKI

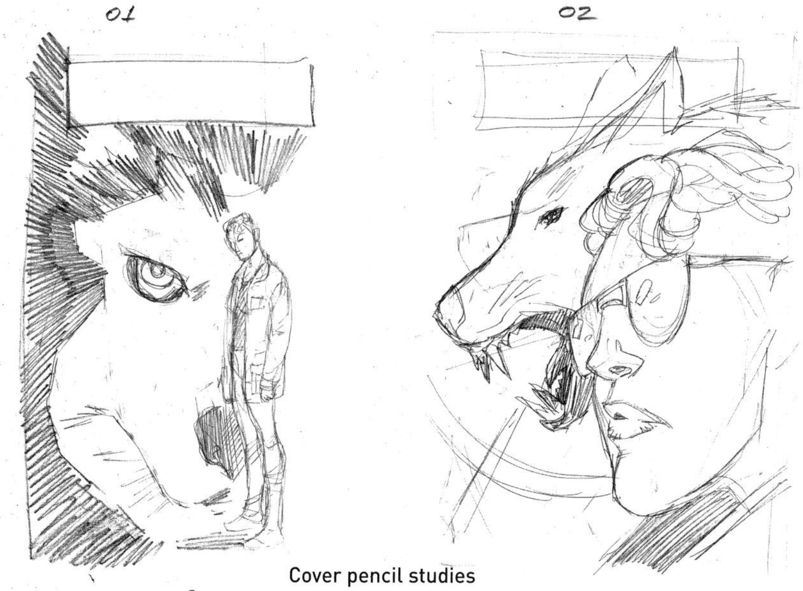
01
02

Cover pencil studies
by Liana Kangas

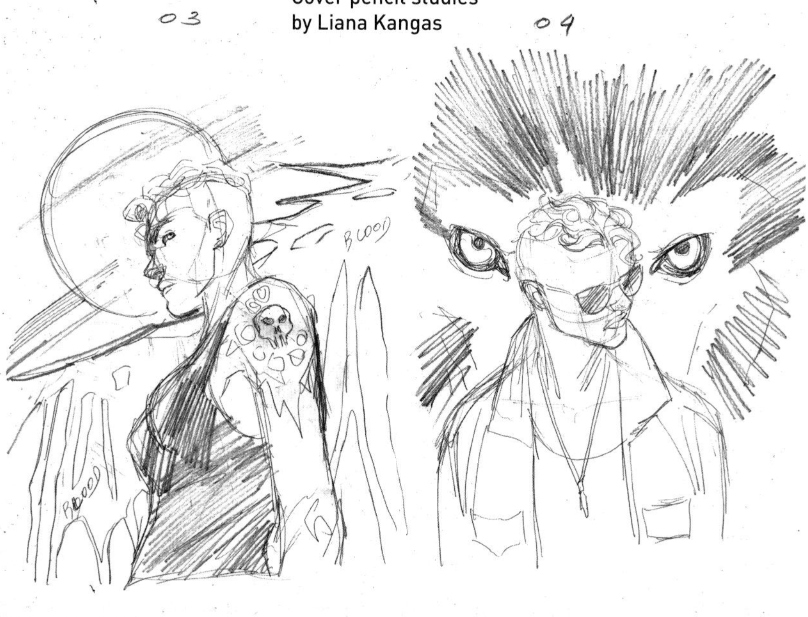
03
04

Hello there! Liana Kangas here, to dig into creating the covers for ***BLACK'S MYTH***.

Having worked with series editor Sarah Litt previously, and being a fan of Eric and Wendell's work, I was very excited—especially after getting to read so much of the book before it hit shelves.

Sarah suggested a neon pulp direction. I utilized a ton of vintage alcohol and tobacco ads and old '60s mystery novels to get inspiration for each cover and tell its story.

I asked my friend Aviva Artzy to help model with me and my partner for a lot of the cover poses. My favorite cover? Issue #3's duality of Strummer—a preview of her finally revealed as a werewolf.

The color palette came from a mixture of grindhouse and sci-fi movie posters, so I tried to finalize each cover with a load of texture to make it look gritty. I had the honor of creating the series logo as well, working alongside Sarah & AHOY's designer.

I'm really proud to have worked with this team on ***BLACK'S MYTH***!

— LIANA KANGAS

This is not the first time Wendell surprised me with promotional artwork for a project we've collaborated on together. I think Wendell and I should keep collaborating so he'll keep surprising me with promotional artwork. Colors, this time, by the excellent Daniel Junior.

— ERIC PALICKI

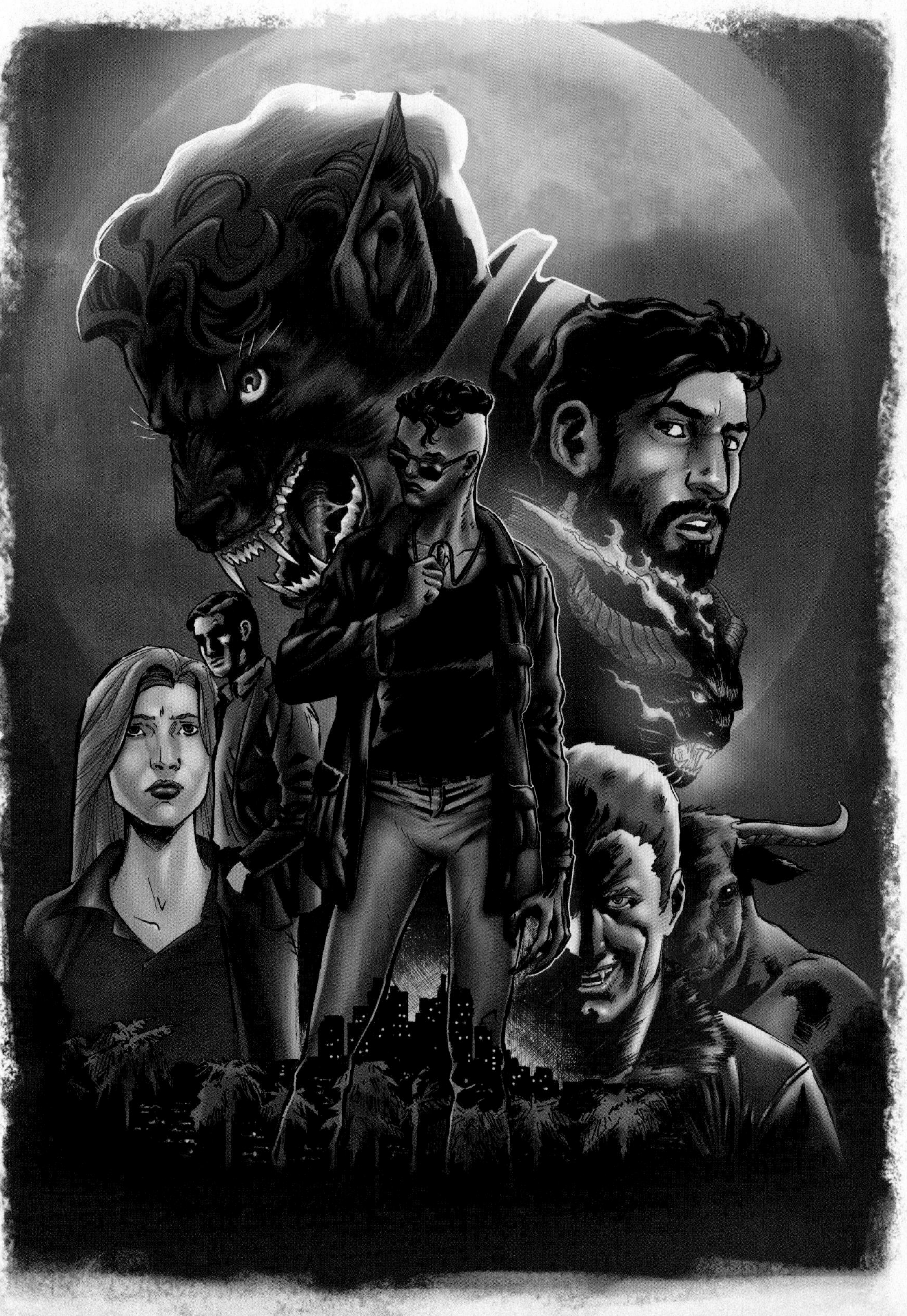

The original **BLACK'S MYTH** pitch had colors by Dee Cuniffe, but when the team saw Wendell's inks and tones, we decided that a black-and-white look would give the book a very noir feel.

— SARAH LITT

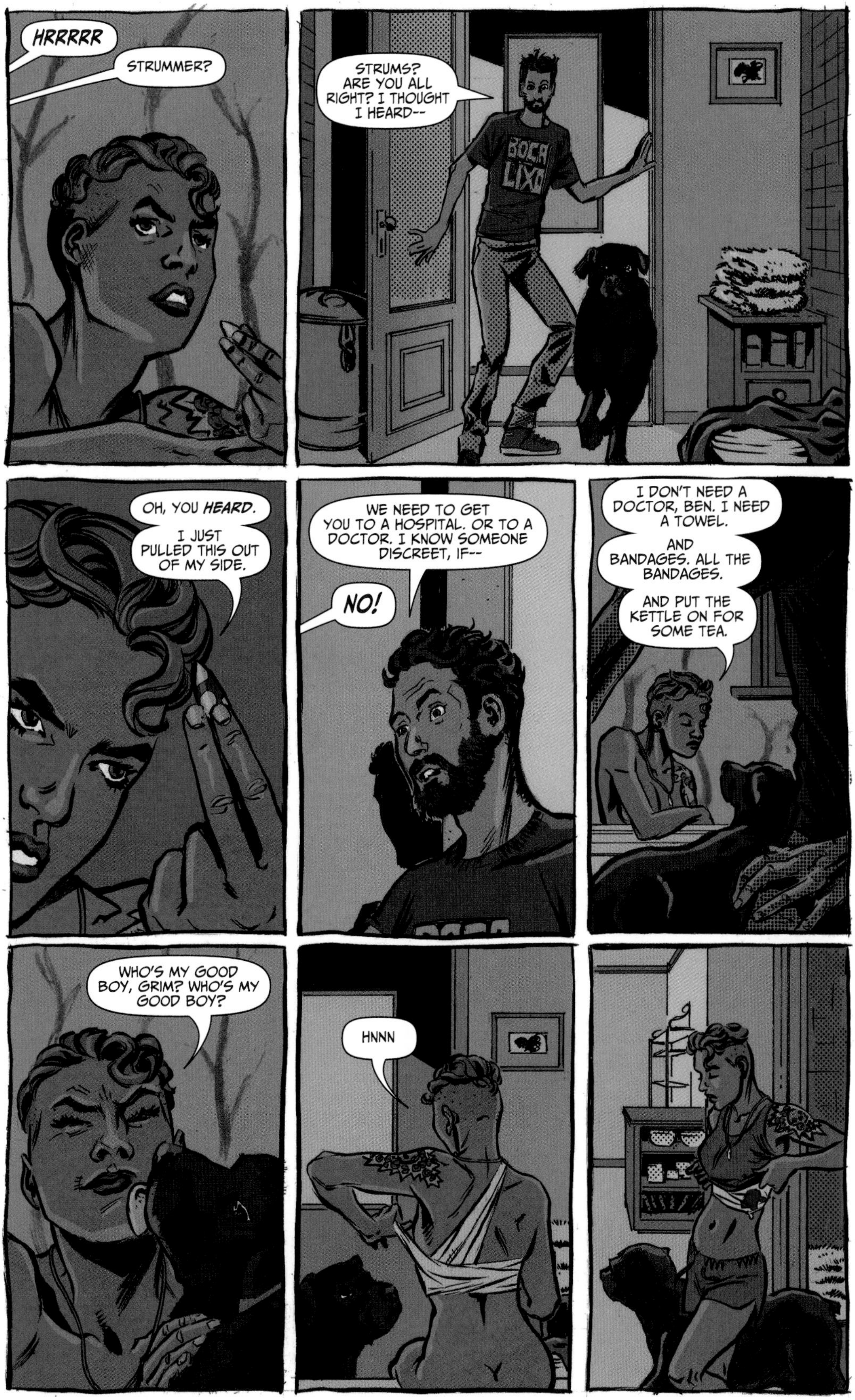
HRRRRR
STRUMMER?
STRUMS? ARE YOU ALL RIGHT? I THOUGHT I HEARD--
OH, YOU ***HEARD***.
I JUST PULLED THIS OUT OF MY SIDE.
WE NEED TO GET YOU TO A HOSPITAL. OR TO A DOCTOR. I KNOW SOMEONE DISCREET, IF--
NO!
I DON'T NEED A DOCTOR, BEN. I NEED A TOWEL.
AND BANDAGES. ALL THE BANDAGES.
AND PUT THE KETTLE ON FOR SOME TEA.
WHO'S MY GOOD BOY, GRIM? WHO'S MY GOOD BOY?
HNNN

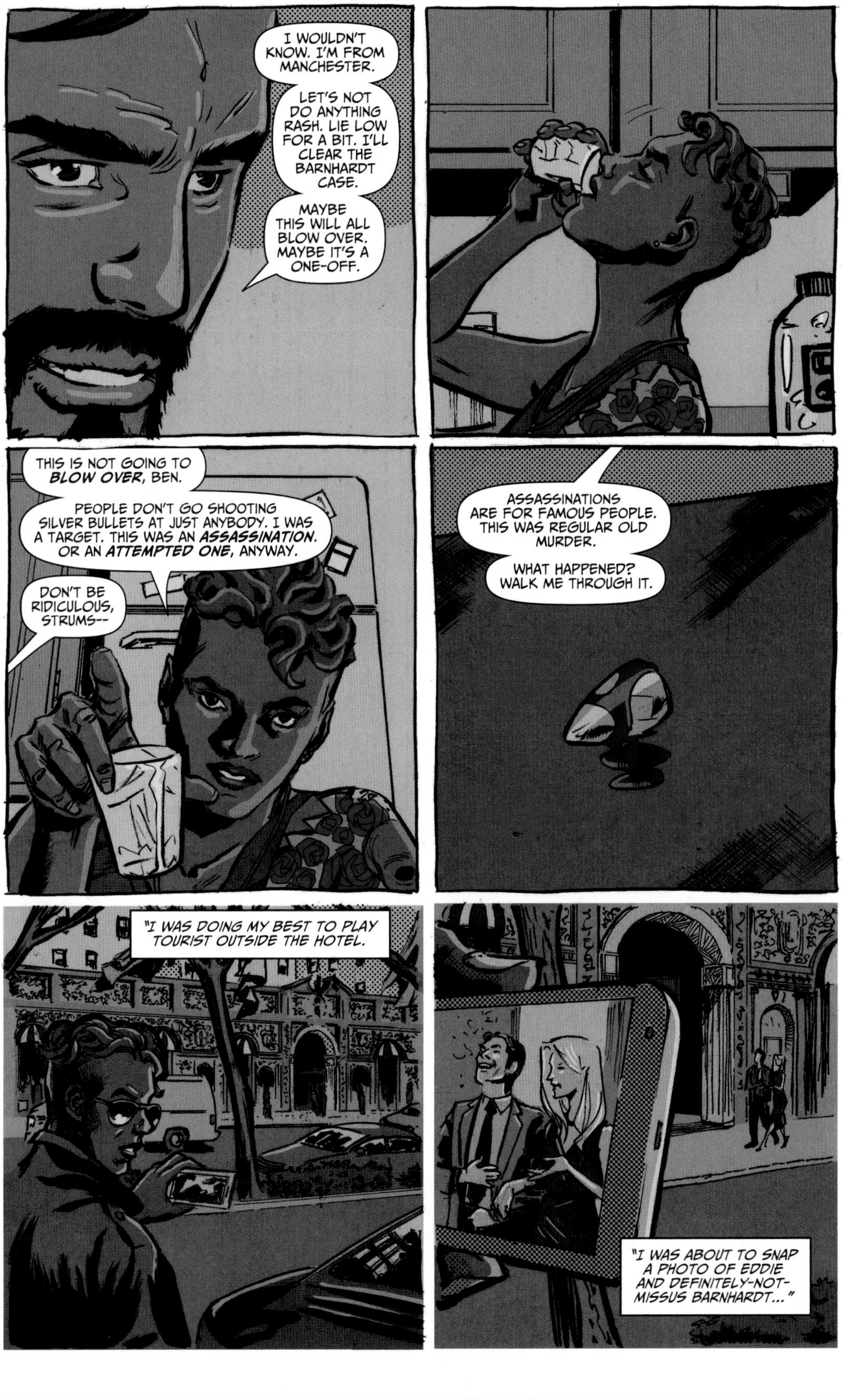
I WOULDN'T KNOW. I'M FROM MANCHESTER.
LET'S NOT DO ANYTHING RASH. LIE LOW FOR A BIT. I'LL CLEAR THE BARNHARDT CASE.
MAYBE THIS WILL ALL BLOW OVER. MAYBE IT'S A ONE-OFF.
THIS IS NOT GOING TO ***BLOW OVER***, BEN.
PEOPLE DON'T GO SHOOTING SILVER BULLETS AT JUST ANYBODY. I WAS A TARGET. THIS WAS AN ***ASSASSINATION***. OR AN ***ATTEMPTED ONE***, ANYWAY.
DON'T BE RIDICULOUS, STRUMS--
ASSASSINATIONS ARE FOR FAMOUS PEOPLE. THIS WAS REGULAR OLD MURDER.
WHAT HAPPENED? WALK ME THROUGH IT.
"I WAS DOING MY BEST TO PLAY TOURIST OUTSIDE THE HOTEL.
"I WAS ABOUT TO SNAP A PHOTO OF EDDIE AND DEFINITELY-NOT-MISSUS BARNHARDT..."

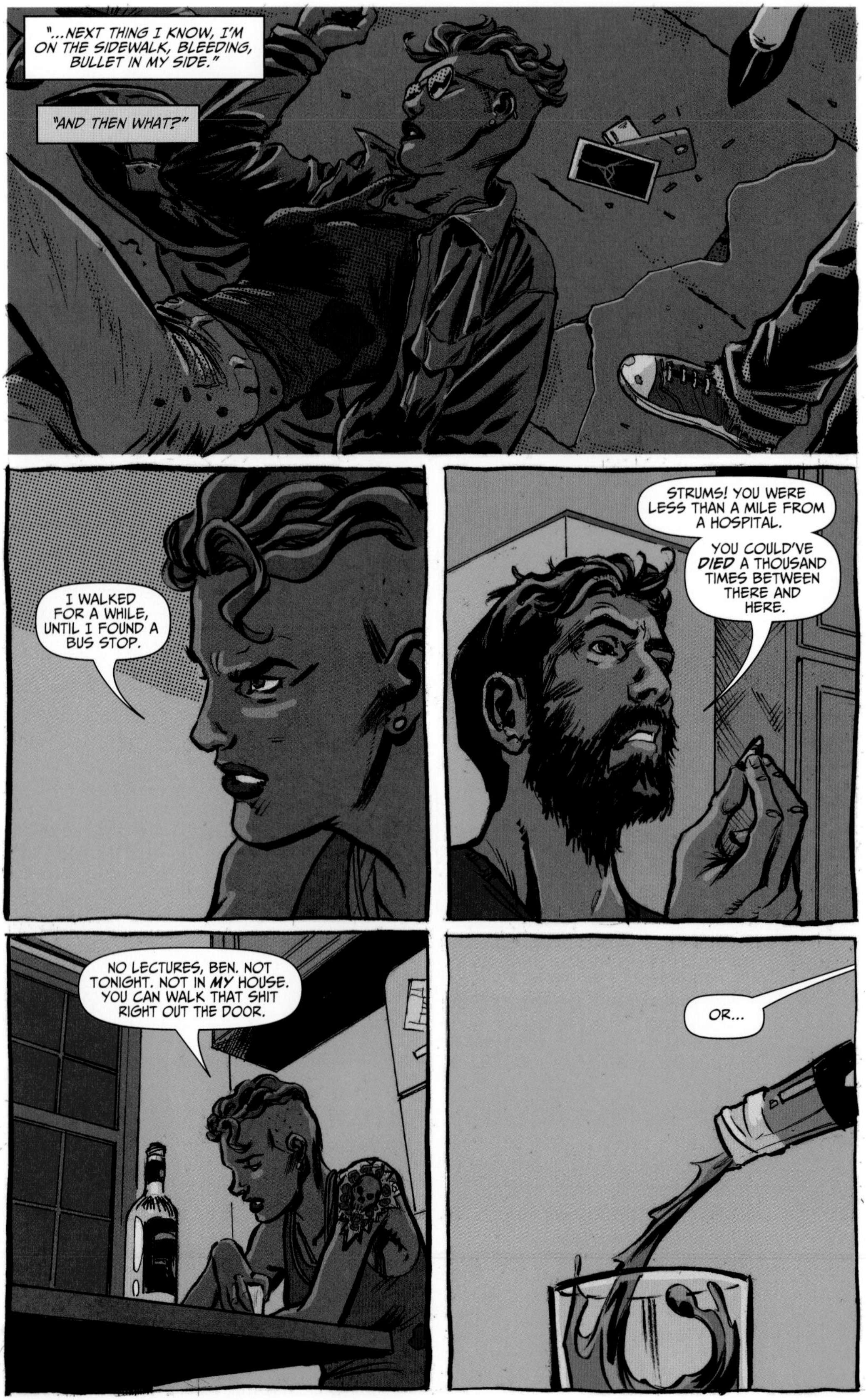
"...NEXT THING I KNOW, I'M ON THE SIDEWALK, BLEEDING, BULLET IN MY SIDE."
"AND THEN WHAT?"
I WALKED FOR A WHILE, UNTIL I FOUND A BUS STOP.
STRUMS! YOU WERE LESS THAN A MILE FROM A HOSPITAL.
YOU COULD'VE DIED A THOUSAND TIMES BETWEEN THERE AND HERE.
NO LECTURES, BEN. NOT TONIGHT. NOT IN MY HOUSE. YOU CAN WALK THAT SHIT RIGHT OUT THE DOOR.
OR...

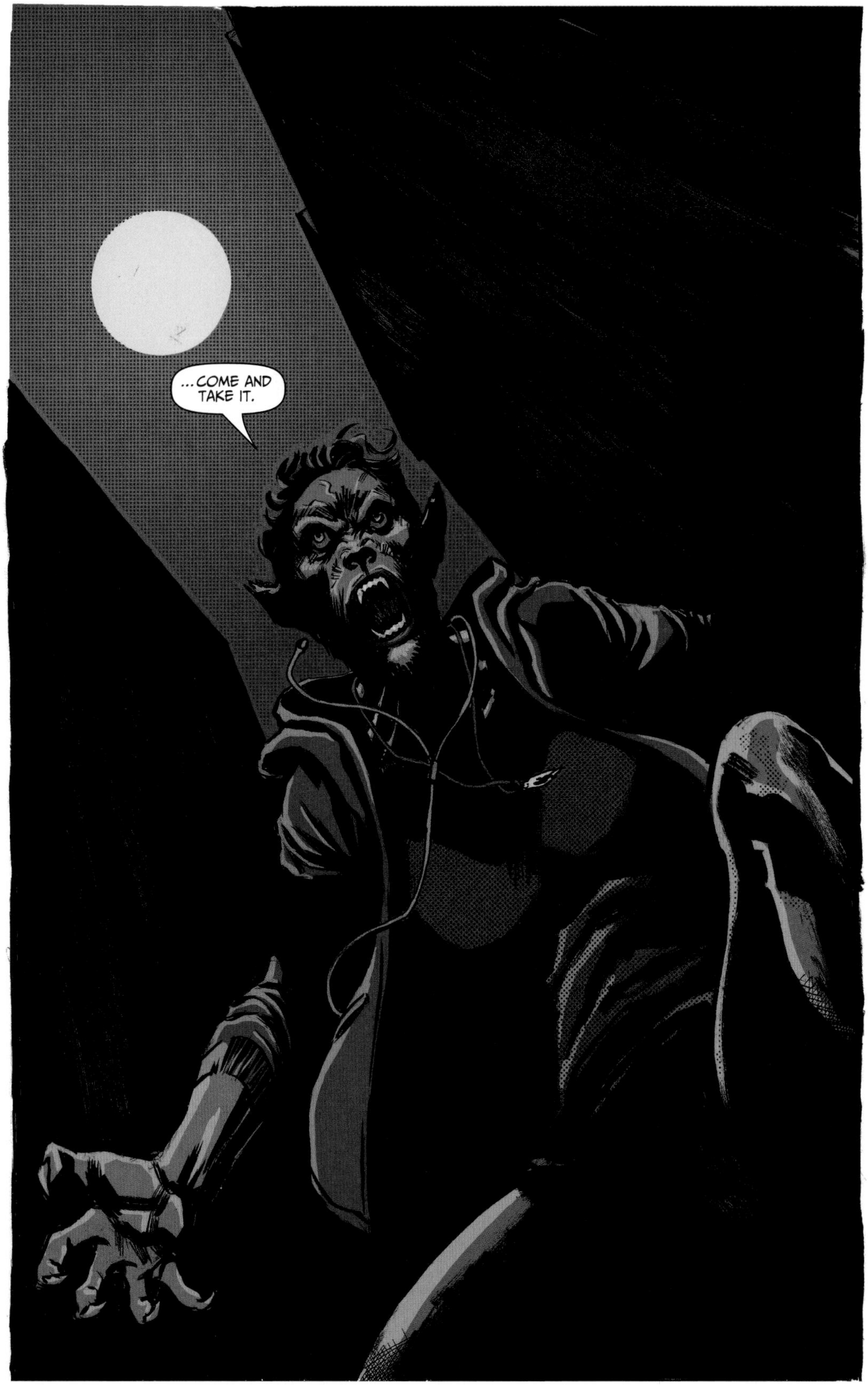
...COME AND TAKE IT.

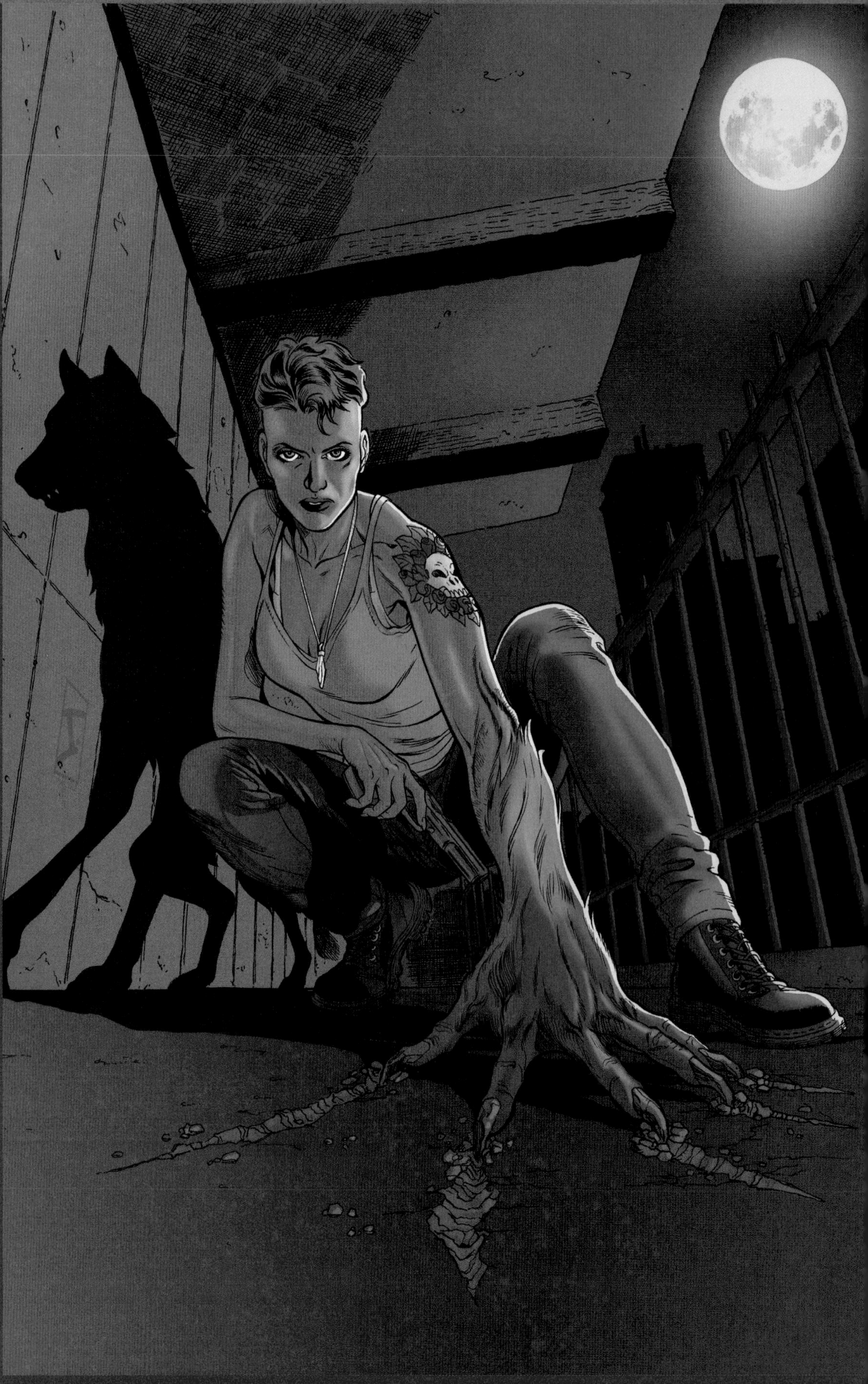

BLACK'S MYTH #2 VARIANT COVER by Steve Pugh

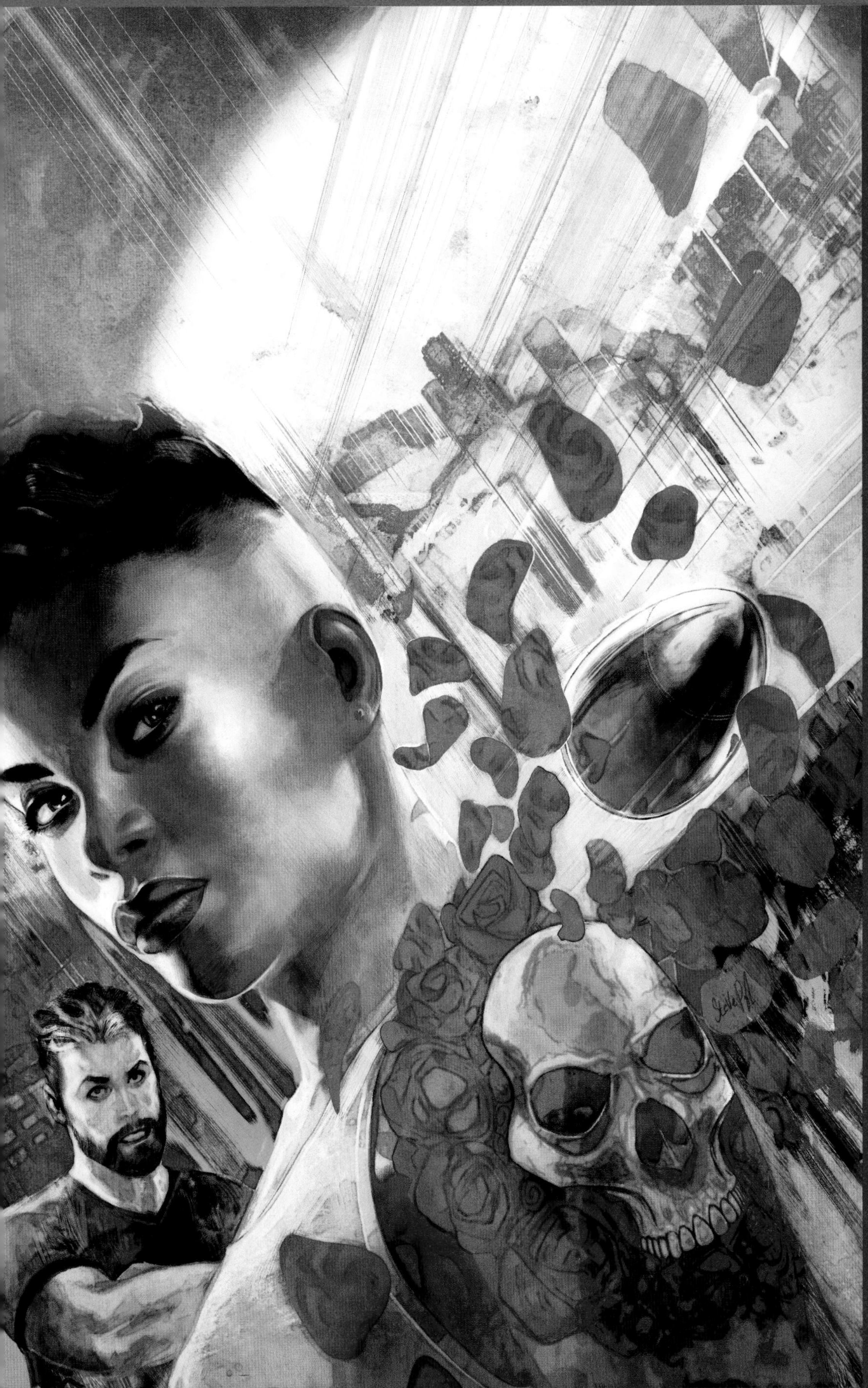

BIOGRAPHIES

ERIC PALICKI lives and writes in Seattle, Washington. His previous work includes the graphic novels *Fake Empire*, *No Angel*, and *Atlantis Wasn't Built for Tourists*, as well as contributions to the story collections *Everything is Going Wrong*, *Mine!*, and Marvel Comics' *Guardians of Infinity*. Eric's work as an editor includes the award-nominated anthologies *All We Ever Wanted*, *Maybe Someday*, and *Dead Beats*.

WENDELL CAVALCANTI lives and works in his native Brazil and has previously illustrated *BlackAcre* for Image Comics and *The Phantom* for Frew Publications. Wendell previously collaborated with Eric Palicki on *Atlantis Wasn't Built for Tourists*, published by Scout Comics.

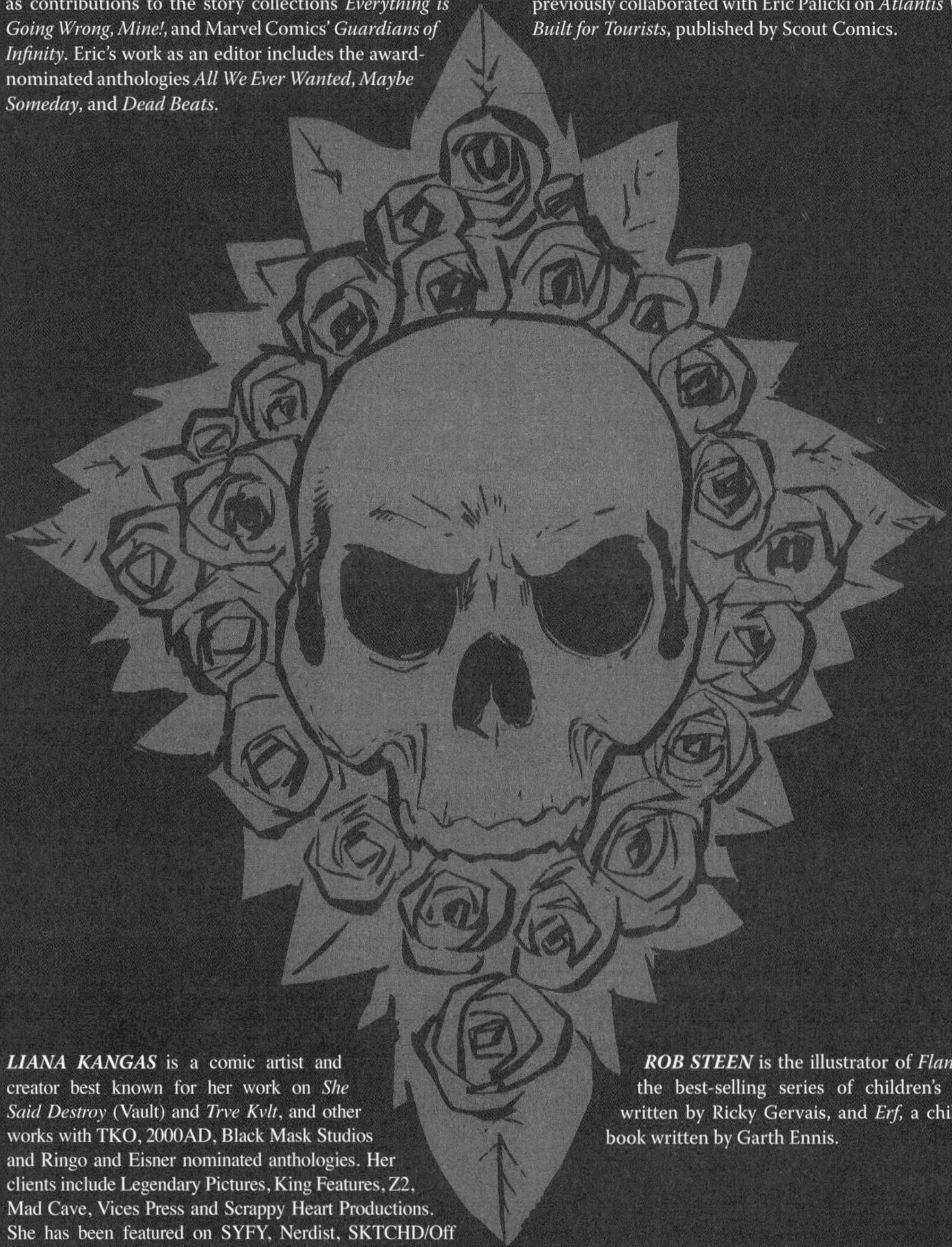

LIANA KANGAS is a comic artist and creator best known for her work on *She Said Destroy* (Vault) and *Trve Kvlt*, and other works with TKO, 2000AD, Black Mask Studios and Ringo and Eisner nominated anthologies. Her clients include Legendary Pictures, King Features, Z2, Mad Cave, Vices Press and Scrappy Heart Productions. She has been featured on SYFY, Nerdist, SKTCHD/Off Panel, Panel x Panel and more.

JAMAL IGLE is the writer/artist/creator of *Molly Danger* for Action Lab Entertainment; the co-creator of *Venture* with writer Jay Faerber; the artist of the series *Black* from Black Mask Studios; and your penciller here on *THE WRONG EARTH*. In 2011, he received a richly deserved Inkpot Award for outstanding achievement in comic art.

ROB STEEN is the illustrator of *Flanimals*, the best-selling series of children's books written by Ricky Gervais, and *Erf*, a children's book written by Garth Ennis.

STEVE PUGH is a British artist and sometimes writer, born and based in the Midlands of England. Recruited for DC's Vertigo imprint at its inception, he worked on titles including *Hellblazer*, *Animal Man*, and *Preacher: Saint of Killers*. Later, he wrote and illustrated *Hotwire* for Radical Comics and received Eisner nominations for his art on the critically acclaimed reimaginings of *The Flintstones* and *Harley Quinn: Breaking Glass*.